White Sports/
Black Sports

White Sports/ Black Sports

Racial Disparities in Athletic Programs

LORI LATRICE MARTIN

Racism in American Institutions
Brian D. Behnken, Series Editor

 PRAEGER

AN IMPRINT OF ABC-CLIO, LLC
Santa Barbara, California • Denver, Colorado • Oxford, England

Library of Congress Cataloging-in-Publication Data

Martin, Lori Latrice.
  White sports, black sports : racial disparities in athletic programs / Lori Latrice Martin.
    pages cm. — (Racism in American Institutions / Brian D. Behnken, Series Editor.)
  Includes bibliographical references and index.
  ISBN 978–1–4408–0053–5 (hard copy : acid-free paper) — ISBN 978–1–4408–0054–2 (ebook) 1. Racism in sports—United States—History. I. Title.
GV706.32.M385   2015
796.089'96073—dc23   2014038633

ISBN: 978–1–4408–0053–5
EISBN: 978–1–4408–0054–2

19 18 17 16   2 3 4 5

This book is also available on the World Wide Web as an eBook.
Visit www.abc-clio.com for details.

Praeger
An Imprint of ABC-CLIO, LLC

ABC-CLIO, LLC
130 Cremona Drive, P.O. Box 1911
Santa Barbara, California 93116-1911

This book is printed on acid-free paper ∞

Manufactured in the United States of America

To
Barbara Ann Johnson
and
Larry Darnell Matthews

Contents

Series Foreword

White Sports/Black Sports is the second book in Praeger Publisher's series Racism in American Institutions (RAI) to explore racial disparities in American sports and the second offering from Lori Latrice Martin. The RAI series was designed to examine the ways in which racism has become, and remains, a part of the fabric of many American institutions. For example, while the United States may have done away with overtly racist policies such as disfranchisement laws, racism still affects many of America's established institutions from the local voting registrar to political advertisements that marginalize communities of color. Law enforcement, like much of the American legal system, is supposed to be impartial, and yet people of color make up the majority of those incarcerated in American prisons. Recent twenty-first-century examples of racism in sports, from mascots that caricature Native American figures to sportscasters who argue that African Americans make superior athletes because of the legacy of slavery, also abound. This open-ended series of works examines the problem of racism in established American institutions. Each book in the RAI series traces the prevalence of racism within a particular institution throughout the history of the United States and explores the problem in that institution today, looking at ways in which the institution has attempted to rectify racism, but also the ways in which it has not.

In *White Sports/Black Sports*, Lori Latrice Martin shifts our focus to the myriad ways race has shaped sports as an institution. Many Americans seem to think that certain ethno-racial communities somehow naturally occupy certain sports. For example, some people believe African Americans are naturally better at basketball. Martin challenges these beliefs, demonstrating that racial socialization—the process by which members of various ethnic groups learn what is expected in U.S. society—has gone far in establishing the beliefs and opinions of Americans about race and sports. This may mean the widespread acceptance of black players in basketball, while simultaneously a widespread rejection of blacks in, say, NASCAR or professional golf. Martin demonstrates that numerous social issues outside of the sports arena have caused this socialization.

Martin, a sociologist by training, has published widely in the fields of income inequality and race studies. Her published works and academic training make her the perfect author for a book like *White Sports/Black Sports*. Despite the increasing presence of black athletes in a variety of American sports, as well as other athletes of color, racism in sports endures because it has become institutionalized over time. *White Sports/Black Sports* explains how that institutionalization happened.

Brian D. Behnken
Iowa State University
Ames, Iowa

Acknowledgments

The author wishes to acknowledge the support of the following individuals throughout the development of this project: Shanielle Mosely Thomas, Dione Cooper-Footman, Hayward Derrick Horton, Mark Naison, Teresa A. Booker, Kwando and Imani Kinshasha, Lee and Edith Burns, Walter Martin, Leroy Evans, Calvin and Ethipia McIver, Sonya Williams, Dorthea Swann, Raynette Hilton, Elizabeth Butler, Everett Newton, Raymond C. Caliman, Eugene Jones, Sr., Johnnie G. McCann, McKinley and Sue Johnson, Raymond Jetson, Mondrall Eathers, Christopher Tyson, Kenneth Fasching-Varner, Emir Sykes, Derrick Martin, Leola Graham, Vivian Grantham, Elma Warren, Raymond Graham, Sidney J. Rand, Daisy McDaniel, Doris Graham, Lee Burns, Mahima Christian, Emily and John Thornton, Constance Slaughter Harvey, Roland Mitchell, Melinda Jackson, Dari Green, Peter Massenat, Keith L. T. Wright, Cheryl Ellis, Kelly Norman Ellis, Carolyn Slaughter, Constance Harvey-Burwell, Michael Thornton, Henry Louis Taylor, Bill Batson, Frances Pratt, Joseph Adams, LaToria Burns, Alicia Crowe, Patricia Bullock, Mary White, James Herschberger, David Rudder, Geraldine Jones, Alice Crowe Bell, and Michael Wilt.

Chapter 1

Toward a Unifying Perspective of Race, Racism, and Sports

For some Americans, race is a significant determinant of one's chances in life. Given that the United States has historically been characterized as having a biracial classification system, this has meant that some actions, behaviors, and activities are either black or white. Just as some names are said to "sound white" or to "sound black," some sports are more closely associated with some racial and ethnic groups than with others.[1]

How did this happen? How did we come to associate certain sports with certain races? To what extent have those associations changed over time? What has been the role of racial socialization, historically and in contemporary times, in undermining or supporting ideas about white sports and black sports?

This book examines the social processes by which individuals learn the ways of society that pertain to those who have membership in a particular racial group. Through the process of racial socialization, blacks and whites come to learn what is expected. Through agents of racial socialization such as sports, the media, schools, peer groups, and the family, blacks and whites gain an understanding of what constitutes whiteness and blackness. Members of each group gain a key understanding about their position in society in relationship to one another. The process of racial socialization not only leads to the identification of selected sports as white sports or black sports, but failure to adhere to racial norms and racial etiquette can lead to overt manifestations of racism. The mere existence of racial norms and racial etiquette that govern expectations about behavior in itself is evidence of racism—the multidimensional system whereby a dominant group oppresses and scapegoats one or more subordinate groups. Population and structural changes in the society at large and in sports can exacerbate overt manifestations of racism, which may range from differences in the media coverage of black and white athletes engaged in deviant acts to the institutionalization of seemingly race-neutral laws that target black players. Central to the discussion, examination, and exploration of racial socialization and the identification of sports by race is an analysis of other key theories and theoretical perspectives, including: critical race theory, colorism, the population and structural change thesis, and the critical demography paradigm. The analysis enhances the understanding of the canyon between American idealism and realism in sports and in the society as a whole.

American Sports and Intergroup Relations

The association of certain sports with certain racial groups has its origins in early American history, when Americans forcefully separated individuals by race in a number of areas of public and private life. The nation has, at one point or another, supported the forced separation of people by race in houses of worship, cemeteries, schools, and neighborhoods; on buses and railcars; in the labor market; and even in the world of sports. While the history of segregation in some areas of society is well known, the history of segregation in other areas—particularly segregation in sports—is arguably less understood.[2]

Most Americans are probably familiar with the name Jackie Robinson and his role in the integration of modern Major League Baseball in 1947. Fewer people know about the history of segregation in professional football and the role of Charles Follis in bringing it to an end.[3] In his book *Outside the Lines*, Charles K. Ross tells this less well known story, documenting the history of blacks in professional football from 1904 to 1962. Specifically, the author reveals that a small number of black players were in the National Football League in 1933 and were then locked out for a time. Black players were reintegrated in 1946, but change was not fully realized until the early 1960s, when white owners sought ways to fight off the momentum of a competing league. The exclusion of blacks from competing in the National Football League led some Americans to associate the sport with whites. Although black players succeeded on the fields at historically black colleges and universities, very few played on teams at predominantly white colleges and universities. For white America, football was a white sport. For blacks, football was yet another sport where blacks where kept from competing against their white counterparts because of policies and attitudes about whiteness and blackness.

Baseball and football were not alone in the segregation of players by race. Tennis was segregated because of race and in part because it was "a class-oriented activity, most of the game was played in private country clubs with restricted membership."[4] Like most sports, tennis integrated after the Second World War. The defining moment occurred in 1940 when Wilson Sporting Goods Company sponsored an interracial exhibition between the champion of the American Tennis Association (ATA), a black organization, and a former U.S. National champion. Significantly, this match between Jimmy McDaniel and Don Budge was played in Harlem, New York.[5]

An exhibition match in which Alice Marble and Mary Hartwig played in a mixed-doubles match with ATA players Boy Ryland and Reginald Weir was also instrumental in desegregating the game. Marble, who became aware of ATA player Althea Gibson, wrote a letter that led to the inclusion of Gibson in the U.S. National tournament in Queens, New York, in the summer of 1950. Gibson became the first black person to play in the U.S. National tournament, reaching the finals just six years after her debut. She won the tournament the next year.[6]

Segregation in sports was evidenced not only in professional sports but at the college level as well. Barriers remained even after the walls of segregation were cracking. In basketball, limitations were placed upon the number of black players allowed on any one team at a given time. For a time, it was rare to see a starting five comprised entirely of people of color. An example of this can be seen in the men's basketball team at Loyola University in Chicago, where the university's Digital Special Collection includes artifacts connected to the integration of college basketball. The members and management of Loyola's 1963 basketball team are described as "pioneers in the integration of college basketball by having four black players in the starting line-up at a time when most coaches only allowed one or two players on a team."[7]

Efforts to assimilate athletes, particularly in sports where racial and ethnic minority groups are more numerous, are well documented. The response to the famed Fab Five at the University of Michigan and the implementation of a dress code in the National Basketball Association (NBA) are two good examples.

The Fab Five—Juwan Howard, Jimmy King, Ray Jackson, Chris Webber, and Jalen Rose—were described as "the greatest class ever recruited," according to sportswriter Thomas Neumann. And yet, Neumann describes the freshmen in this way:

In their heyday, the Fab Five were widely portrayed as the root of all evil in college sports. They wore baggy shorts and black socks. They blasted hip-hop music in the locker room. They talked trash. A lot.

Those types of uniforms and behavior might be commonplace today, but 20 years ago it was revolutionary, polarizing and heavily influential to a generation of young athletes. Although the Fab Five never got into serious trouble off the court, the players symbolized to many people a clear shift in the sports world and youth culture. Fans of all races and demographics spent millions of dollars on Michigan jerseys, shorts and the like, trying to capture a tiny slice of the group's mystique. By the end of their second year together, the Fab Five were routinely battered in the national media for the way they carried themselves. Articles and television reports painted them as brash villains or worse—as thugs.[8]

Clearly, this group of talented young men, several of whom would go on to have stellar professional basketball careers, did not conform to the established norms set forth by members of the dominant group, and many of those members, both affiliated and unaffiliated with the University of Michigan, made their disapproval known.

Jalen Rose responded this way when asked whether reactions to the team were race based:

People *do* view you based on your appearance and judge you based on that. If we're five black guys at the University of Michigan, and it's like, "You have the nerve to jump up in Christian Laettner's face and talk trash? He's God to us. You have black shoes, black socks, bald heads, long shorts?" Like, that's too much at one time. . . . It wasn't just the media; there were people who really had a sincere hatred because not only did they not like us, but they didn't want their kids to be like us.[9]

When David Stern, commissioner of the NBA, instituted a dress code in 2005, many saw the move as an effort to appease members of the dominant racial group. John Eligon, writing for the *New York Times*, describes the business casual dress code as "the NBA's latest push to look a little less gangsta and little more genteel." Stern claimed, according to Eligon, that "the reputation of our players was not as good as our players are, and we could do small things to improve that."[10]

The code called for players to wear either collared shirts or turtlenecks at team or league functions, along with slacks, khakis, or dress jeans. Moreover, the dress codes required players to wear dress shoes or boots with socks. Eligon observed that some teams, such as the New York Knicks, already had dress codes in place, but the league had in all of its history not instituted such a policy.

Sociologist David J. Leonard links the NBA dress code to what scholars call "the new racism," and he does so while reflecting on the reactions to the killing of Trayvon Martin. Martin, a barely 17-year-old boy, was killed by volunteer neighborhood watchman George Zimmerman in Sanford, Florida. Leonard examines such critical questions as "How is a black body, inherently criminal and suspect when read within a hoodie; what are the dialectics between the hoodie and the black body within these processes of criminalization?"[11]

The questions surrounding the death of Trayvon Martin are in keeping with Leonard's work on black athletes. He adds, "As a scholar of race and sport, these questions have guided my work: how do representations of black athletes, particularly those in the NBA, buttress larger ideological, political, and criminalizing processes? How does the ubiquitous references to NBA players as 'thugs' and 'gangstas' as 'criminals' and 'punks' normalize blackness as questionable, undesirable, and inherently suspect?"[12]

Eligon suggests that the move toward a league-wide dress code had less to do with the clothes worn by the players and more to do with public reaction to a number of high-profile scandals. He cites the 2003 rape charges against Kobe Bryant and the 2004 fight between the Indiana Pacers and Detroit Pistons, in which Indiana's Metta World Peace, then known as Ron Artest, climbed into the stands and made physical contact with a fan.

David J. Leonard notes that shortly after that fight, Stern and others in the league were concerned by the behavior of the 2004 Olympic basketball team, which was made up largely of players from the NBA. Described as "a significant embarrassment for the NBA in the wake of its efforts to conceal blackness from the league," the incident involved a dinner that was held to honor the team. Some members of the team showed up at the restaurant "in sweat suits, oversized jeans and shirts, large platinum chains, and of course, diamond earrings." The dress code was therefore created, in Leonard's words, to "lighten, if not whiten, these players in the national (white) imagination. It sought to re-create the illusion of racial transcendence among its African American players."[13]

A historical event leading up to the introduction of the dress code was the retirement of the greatest man to ever play the game, Michael Jordan, in 1993—the first of his three retirements. Jordan had such a tremendous impact on the league and the game, including economically, that when he walked away from the game, many fans walked away too. Rick Weinberg, writing in 1993, described the impact of Jordan's 1993 announcement this way: "Sadness and gloom filled the room as a city, a nation, and a league mourns. The impact of the NBA, television, attendance, competition, revenue, merchandise sales (other than MJ's jersey of course) is staggering. The man who generates billions for others is not going to cost them millions. There is no aspect of the league that Jordan's presence doesn't touch."[14] During the 1991–92 season alone, economists estimate that Jordan generated over $52 million for the league. The loss of Michael Jordan and the search for the next "Great *Black* Hope" provide an excellent example of how, in the words of Kathleen S. Yep, "liberal multiculturalism involves racial triangulation and the simultaneous processes of hyper-racialization and de-racialization."[15] Yep highlights the issue of multiculturalism, or pluralism, which we understand as "a state in which people of all races and ethnicities are distinct but have equal social standing."[16]

Sports and the Myth of Postracial Space

Basketball represents, as Yep puts it, "a post-racial space where all talented players, regardless of their race, can thrive if they work hard." Yep goes on to demonstrate that this could not be further from the truth. It was not the case in the 1930s on the barnstorming basketball circuit, and it is not the case in contemporary times. Yep compares whites with three racial minority groups and examines the hero, threat, and novelty narratives created to market basketball teams in the late 1930s and "sheds light on the simultaneity of hyper-racialization and de-racialization in sports discourse."[17]

White players, as shown in the marketing of barnstorming baseball team the House of David Bearded Aces, were depicted as heroes. "Against the trope of heroic whiteness, the marketing cast African American masculinity as a threatening outsider to white America, and the Chinese American and Native American teams as the novelties." While marketing techniques highlighted the assumed threat of blackness, the antics of the talented black players "modulated these racialized fears."[18]

Yep highlights the role of the media in communicating race-based messages, but there are other ways in which such messages are transmitted. Our understanding of what is expected of us, whether in the world of sports or in some other social world environment, brings us to a concept in sociology called *racial socialization*. Much has been written about racial socialization, which Shirley A. Hill defines as "parents' efforts to teach their children about race, how to cope with racism and rejection, and how to challenge the dominant culture's negative depictions of African Americans."[19] To that end, sociologists and other scholars have linked racial socialization with a host of outcomes, including academic success, and with a host of racial and ethnic minority groups. Racial socialization has been used to understand the effects of racial discrimination on black youth and by the children of immigrants from diverse populations.[20]

Racial Socialization and the Designation of Sports as White versus Black

Although racial socialization is often understood as occurring in the relationship of parent and child, I argue that racial socialization involves much more. Racial socialization is based upon the understanding of group difference. In American society, individuals are grouped according to their race. Racial groups are ranked. Racial groups with the greatest access to wealth, status, and power are at the highest levels of the hierarchical racial structure. Individuals with less access to wealth, status, and power are at relatively lower levels of the hierarchical system. Racial groups come to be placed at various levels based upon a host of factors, including the ability of one group to use a range of tactics and resources to place other groups in subordinate positions.

In the case of the United States, the involuntary migration of people of African ancestry and the continued unequal treatment of their descendants created and segmented the nation's racial stratification system. In an effort to perpetuate the myth of white superiority and black inferiority, a web of processes has developed to communicate what is expected of whites and blacks to maintain the racial status quo. This process of communicating, perpetuating, and transforming ideas about what constitutes blackness and what constitutes whiteness is not static, but variable and forever changing. One constant is that the role of race is not tangential, it is *foundational*, so even when efforts to define blackness and whiteness appear to be fading they are merely being reinvented, repackaged, and reproduced in an effort to yield the desired outcome: an ongoing racialized social system where whites are dominant and blacks and other racial minority groups are subordinate.

Much of the research on racial socialization focuses on the family. Little attention, if any, is devoted to institutions such as sports as agents of racial socialization. To be clear, there is an abundance of research on race and sports, but relatively few studies that specifically tackle racial socialization as the set of processes by which members of the dominant racial group and members of a racial minority group come to "know" their place in the social structure and within the institutions. This is a significant gap, particularly at a time when much of American society is celebrating the "death of racism" and the ushering in of a "postracial era." Through sports, messages are communicated as to what is acceptable participation and behavior for groups within various racial and ethnic groups. Sports are, arguably, one of the best places to convey such messages, because most players and spectators are focused on the performance of the individual or team and are not keenly aware of the context within which the game is taking place. Spectators, in particular, are so caught up in the excitement and demonstration of talent and abilities that seem almost supernatural that it is hard for them to fathom that the players are in any way oppressed—especially when the annual salaries of some players far exceed what some American workers will earn over the course of a lifetime.

The significance and influence of sports in our lives cannot be underestimated. Even people who claim to detest the violence associated with some sports, or who express boredom at the idea of watching a game, line up with the rest of us in the days leading up to Super Bowl Sunday, buying food, drinks, televisions, and so on—even if they claim they are interested only in the commercials. Parents with little interest in sports can be found at the local Catholic church, regardless of their religious affiliation, signing their children up to play on the Catholic Youth Organization (CYO) team. They peddle raffle tickets to support the Pop Warner cheerleading squad or junior midgets going to a championship tournament. Their taxes go to building the stadium for the professional team or for the construction of a new athletic complex in the community, which is said to generate jobs and revenue for their local towns. The children they have loved and nurtured can often recite the stats for their favorite team or player more easily than they can name each of the 50 United States. Sports are an important agent of socialization, particularly racial socialization.

So, what is the core theoretical and methodological issue surrounding racial socialization and sports? The issue is that the literature on race and sports tends to ignore socialization, and the literature on socialization tends to ignore issues of race and sports. Jay Coakley correctly observes that over the last half century, the literature on socialization has focused primarily on three areas: "the process of becoming involved and staying involved in sports; the process of changing or ending sport participation; and the impact of being involved in sports." Matters of race are not viewed as central to these processes. "The meanings given to sport experiences vary from one person to another because social relationships are influenced by social definitions, which may or may not, include race."[21] This understanding of socialization and the prevailing understanding of racial socialization in particular are based upon the microlevel interactionist perspective, which focuses on face-to-face interactions and small-group relationships, and has replaced models based on structural theories, which, according to Coakley, dominated the literature prior to the 1980s.

There is a need for scholars interested in studying race and sports to revisit the overreliance on socialization from a microlevel perspective. Instead, scholars must explore the methodological and theoretical implications of understanding the multilevel and multidimensional nature of racial socialization in sports. This will allow scholars to adequately account for the centrality of race in our society and the centrality of race in sports.

Understanding racial socialization as I have defined it here—the process by which blacks and whites learn what is expected of them to maintain the racial status quo and the myth of white supremacy and black inferiority—means that we need to look at race and sports through nontraditional lenses. We must look to other paradigms that might help us account for changes in what constitutes blackness or whiteness, and might help us understand why members of the dominant group respond to certain actions by white and black players in different ways. Consequently, we must look beyond generalized theories about socialization and perspectives such as critical race theory and colorism and incorporate other frameworks, including the population and structural change thesis and the critical demography paradigm. The latter provide a framework for assessing change over time and identifying seemingly race-neutral tactics that have meaningful consequences for individuals according to race. Scholars Lori Latrice Martin and Hayward Derrick Horton lay out the argument in a book chapter entitled "Racism Front and Center," in which they offer the following analysis.[22]

In the modern era, certain sports have come to be associated with certain racial and ethnic groups. Some maintain the belief that biology equals destiny. Phenotype, bone density, muscle dexterity, and so on are thought to determine one's athletic destination, with race serving as one of the main filters. One would think that such claims, which have been disproven time and time again, would fade into the deep recesses of our collective consciousness; sadly, they have not. Often cloaked in new raiment, the idea that blacks and whites are predisposed to participation and success in different sports remains with us still. While there are a host of theories, perspectives, and paradigms in the social sciences, particularly in sociology, arguing for the continuing significance of race in our society, few have found their way into scholarly discussions about sports. Considering that these race-based theories have been used to explain various phenomena, they have been limited in important ways, including the failure to place racism front and center. What is needed is an overarching, unifying framework that will aid in our understanding of not just the continuing significance of race in sports but also the significance of *racism* in sports. The multilevel and multidimensional roles of race and racism in determining athletic participation and destinations can best be understood within this suggested framework.

Understanding why racial groups are drawn to particular sports using a critical lens and a keen understanding of the structure and composition of populations, Martin and Horton's work draws from the strengths of critical race theory, the colorism perspective, the population structural change thesis, and the critical demography paradigm; namely, the centrality of race, while also addressing the observed weaknesses. Although critical race theory and colorism place the focus squarely on race and skin complexion, neither places racism at the forefront. Moreover, neither critical race theory nor colorism substantively take into consideration the impact of population size on intergroup relations. Further, to date neither the population structural change thesis nor the critical demography paradigm has been used to understand the unlevel playing field that characterizes American sports.

Critical Race Theory

Although it has its origins among legal scholars, critical race theory is used to examine the linkages between race and education, the family, immigration, public health, and sports. Critical race theory, like other social theories, theses, and perspectives, has supporters and critics. To fully understand the ongoing debates surrounding critical race theory, it is important to examine more closely its origins, development, and use over time.

Derrick Bell is among the scholars credited with institutionalizing the interest in systematically studying the lived reality of race. The purpose of introducing critical race theory was to draw attention to society as it is and society as it ought to be. Bell felt it was necessary to address the gap between the real and the imagined, and to do so in a way that was simultaneously a radical critique *of* the law and a radical emancipation *by* the law.

Critical race theory was developed to address the aforementioned tension head-on.[23]

Many legal scholars quickly gravitated to critical race theory, due in large part to the key principles outlined. First, critical race theory holds that society is organized around race. Second, people of color receive unequal treatment when compared with members of the dominant racial group. The unequal treatment experienced by people of color not only occurs on a personal level but is also, more importantly, institutionalized. Moreover, critical race theory explains how individuals within a given social system participate in the perpetuation of racialized social systems through social practices. Lastly, critical race theory enhances our understanding of racial and ethnic identities as variable, social constructions that change across place and time.[24]

Critical race theory was intended to assist legal scholars in explaining various phenomena, *and* it was intended to be inclusive and transformative. Critical race theory was to bring to the center, from the margins, scholars of color, whom Derrick Bell argued were often silenced, discredited, or altogether ignored. Bell writes, "We seek to empower and include traditionally excluded views and see all-inclusiveness as the ideal because of our belief and collective wisdom."[25]

As important as the work of Bell and others is and has been, they were not the first to address such concerns about the law or society in general, but their desire to "fight the silence about the intersection of race, racism, and the law"[26] ushered in a wave of scholarly research that moved concepts such as intersectionality, antiessentialism, normality of race, social construction, and differential racialization toward the forefront of progressive thinking and scholarship. Through the use of personal narratives, among other techniques, critical race theorists also raised awareness about bias, conscious, and unconscious in America's social institutions, including in the criminal justice system.

In the end, critical race theory was to be the driving force behind efforts to bring about a more just society in which people of color would be regarded in the same manner as members of the dominant group and not perpetually regarded as "others," which had historically been the case.

Scholars see merit in applying critical race theory to the sports world because, as Kevin Hylton says, "racial thinking in sports is perpetuated by four weak theoretical propositions,"[27] elucidated by Brett St. Louis:

1. Sports are based on theoretical principals of equality.
2. The results of sport competition are unequal.

3. This inequality of results has a racial bias.
4. Therefore, given the equality of access and opportunity, the explanation of the unequal results lies in racial physicality.[28]

Critical race theory has the power to address the identified weak propositions with its emphasis on race and racism. It also has the power to challenge the notion of color-blindness. Critical race theory has many other positive attributes, including the commitment to social justice, and its ability to transcend disciplinary boundaries.

Moreover, critical race theory has the potential to enhance our understanding of the processes involved in the formation of power and ideologies by race. Critical race theory has the power to inform the process of theorizing in leisure studies and "generate a useful theoretical vocabulary for the practice of progressive racial politics in sport."[29]

Despite the contributions of critical race theory to legal studies, and beyond, there are identified weaknesses. Scholars call into question whether critical race theory is, or is not, a theory. Critical race theory "lacks the articulation of a set of precisely stated and logically related propositions that explain a relationship between concepts, to the formation of a structured conceptual scheme that provides a general interpretation or critique of social reality."[30] Critical race theory, at best, say some scholars, is an intellectual movement.

Additionally, the use of narratives or storytelling, while a central feature in the application of critical race theory, is problematic, particularly for social scientists with a quantitative orientation. The narratives, while informative and illustrative of important concepts and themes, fail to meet the robust standards expected by many in the social sciences. One cannot, in good faith, generalize the findings to a known population.

Colorism

Still others argue critical race theory does not devote adequate attention to *colorism*, defined as "the discriminatory treatment of individuals falling within the same 'racial' group on the basis of skin color. It operates both intraracially and interracially." Colorism "is historically contingent on supremacist assumptions. In the United States color preferences are typically measured against putative European (i.e., White) standards."[31]

Critical race theory has been used, almost exclusively until recently, to understand the black/white dichotomy that has dominated American history since the foundation of the nation. The problem, as identified by scholars, is that although blacks may be disadvantaged relative to whites, blacks may not be equally disadvantaged. There is a substantial body of literature that points to the advantages afforded light-skinned individuals relative to darker-skinned individuals of African background.[32]

Colorism affects socialization practices within racial groups. Moreover, colorism holds that "a person's skin will take on more importance in determining how she is treated by others than her ancestry." Colorism is the result, by some, of a shift in the demographic composition of the nation, as well as a change in racial ideologies. It is an indication that racism is not dead; rather, discussions surrounding racism are muted. Dr. Angela Harris views colorism as the next stage in the continuum of racialized social systems in America. Harris further argues that colorism and racism are related, yet distinct.[33]

There is much to disagree with in the assertions made by Harris about colorism. First, the implication is that colorism is a relatively new phenomenon. We know that skin tone was used in antebellum America as a mechanism for creating discord and disharmony among enslaved and free black people. Colorism can best be understood, as Cedric Herring conceptualizes it, as a manifestation of racism, not a replacement of it. Moreover, Angela Harris represents scholars who understand colorism to be an intragroup phenomenon. Some even refer to colorism as intragroup discrimination as it is devoid of any relationship to the larger set of processes by which racial groups are systematically oppressed and scapegoated by the dominant group. Herring correctly defines colorism as intra- and interracial. Claims such as those levied by Harris seek to equate tensions *within* racial groups with racism *between* whites and racial minority groups.[34]

Colorism, despite differing views on what it is and is not, is an underutilized perspective in the social sciences. It is particularly underutilized in the analysis of race and sports. John Robst and colleagues conducted one of the few studies linking colorism and sports.[35] The researchers examined the effects of skin tone on wages of free agents in the National Basketball Association. They employed computer software to objectively determine the skin tone of the subjects. The researchers argue this methodological approach represents a departure from other studies on colorism that rely on the judgment of interviewers in determining where a respondent falls on the skin tone spectrum.[36]

Robst et al. did not find evidence of a statistically significant relationship between skin tone and wages. Their study, however, is not without limitations.

The researchers acknowledge the relatively small sample size as potentially problematic. Other recent studies have reported declines in the significance of skin tone as a predictor on a host of outcomes.[37]

Another issue is the use of existing photographs. Secondary analysis, including content analysis, may suffer from the fact that researchers have a lack of control over the data because they were initially collected by someone other than the researcher or research team. In this case, since the researchers did not take the photographs themselves, they have no way of knowing the extent to which the photographs actually represent the complexion of the subjects under study. Moreover, the assignment of photographs as lighter or darker, even if the system is based on red and green, instead of black or white, is still somewhat subjective, if not outright arbitrary.

The lack of understanding of the relationship between colorism and racism and the potential for bias in classifying subjects based upon a sociopolitical construct may point to the need to revisit the perspective by developing more testable propositions with which to examine this form of intragroup and intergroup discrimination, particularly as it relates to the world of sports.

Population and Structural Change Thesis

Missing from discussions about race and sports is an adequate treatment of the effects of population and structural change on various outcomes, including on the types of sports blacks and whites are drawn to and the association of specific sports with either blacks or whites. On the one hand, it is apparent that certain racial groups are overrepresented in some sports and underrepresented in others. Beyond exploring events that led to the integration of previously segregated sports, very little scholarly attention has been devoted to understanding the impact of population and structural changes, both inside and outside of the world of sports, on players, spectators, owners, and the like. Population changes might include an increase in the black population in a particular area or region, or the flight of whites from the central city to suburban areas within a metropolitan region. Structural changes might include changes in the economy that increase or decrease employment rates. Structural changes might also include alterations in investments in public education, low- or no-cost sports programs, or even the placement of open spaces and recreational facilities in various communities.

It is difficult to tackle any subject matter involving race without accounting for population and structural changes. The few studies that give these matters due treatment are far too often descriptive in nature and seldom use proven demographic techniques and frameworks for understanding the complex linkages between race and sports. Studies that help us understand the role of population and structural changes are valuable tools that should be widely used in sports studies, particularly if we wish to substantively address issues related to race.

Changes in both the minority population and the social structure, according to Horton and Allen, "interact to exacerbate racial inequality in society."[38] Looking at the effects of place and family structure on black family poverty, Horton and Allen argued that the existence of and the persistence of race as a predictor of black family poverty support the population and structural change thesis. Likewise, the existence and persistence of race as a predictor of a host of sport outcomes provides support for the population and structural change thesis, which has yet to be adequately explored in sports and leisure studies. The significance of this is quite clear.

Beyond the social realities of the sports world, population changes and changes to the social structure matter. As the size and composition of America changes—economically, politically, and culturally, not just in athletics—the effects of race in virtually all areas of society become even more salient and manifestations of racism become more overt. For example, as predictions that American racial and ethnic minorities will one day become the numerical majority occur at the same time as an economic downturn or a change in the political winds, efforts to reestablish the myth of group superiority become more dominant. This can be seen in many areas of social life, not just in sports.

As the racial and ethnic minority population has increased, efforts to exert more control and authority over matters of criminal justice and education have increased. This is due in part to unfounded fears on the part of some members of the dominant racial group, especially those in the lower and working classes, that their historic position in society is being threatened. Draconian policies that have led to the overrepresentation of people of color in American prisons and in failing schools are just two examples. In the world of sports, population and structural changes have led to the institutionalization of white middle-class standards in the adoption of dress codes, in the stacking of players in positions by color, and by the existence of glass ceilings and glass walls when it comes to ownership and employment in decision-making positions. It has also led to the adoption of color-blind language, a topic addressed later in this chapter.

Although the population and structural change thesis can inform research on race and sports, it too has some limitations. The population and structural change thesis does not fully account for variations within racial groups. Again, blacks may not be equally disadvantaged. Skin tone, ethnicity, and social class position are all factors that have been shown to have significant effects on a host of sociological outcomes. Much like critical race theory and the colorism perspective, the population and structural thesis aids in our understanding of race and sports, but is limited in the ways outlined.

Critical Demography

The critical demography paradigm addresses some of the shortcomings associated with critical race theory, colorism, and the population and structural change thesis in a manner that has yet to be explored. Established in 1999, the critical demography paradigm offered a critique of conventional demography. The founder of the critical demography paradigm, Dr. Hayward Derrick Horton, observed that demographers were very reluctant to use racism as a concept of analysis, particularly demographers conducting research on race. Racism, after all, is a primary component of the social structure and it is central to understanding population growth and development.

The main strength of the critical demography paradigm is its ability to show how the social structure differentiates dominant and subordinate populations. To that end, the nature of power is an important part of the paradigm. Unlike in the case of critical race theory and colorism, *race* is not central; rather, *racism* is central to any analysis involving minority and majority group relations.[39]

Much of the work conducted by American demographers, argues Horton, is descriptive, but the critical demography paradigm calls for scholarly works that are both explanatory and predictive. Critical demography also calls for analyses that are driven by theory, not data, and analyses that challenge the status quo. Furthermore, critical demography, unlike conventional demography, is reflexive and not assumptive.

Scholars who are working in the area of sports and leisure studies should take note of an article in the journal *Perspectives* that includes a discussion among conventional demographers about the civil rights movement. It is observed that this period of social change and upheaval was treated by demographers as a historical event with little, if any, attention devoted to the demographic implications. The role of the civil rights movement in growing the black middle class was not anticipated and studied substantively by conventional demographers, but could arguably have been predicted using a framework akin to the one developed by Horton.

The piece by Dr. Horton extols the use of the population and structural change thesis to aid in our understanding of the connection between changes in the size and composition of peoples and changes in the social structure and the effects of race on sociological outcomes. In the world of sports and beyond, we have seen that as the composition of players and spectators changes, policy changes also. As the number of black players, particularly from economically disadvantaged backgrounds, increased, the number of white fans decreased, and policy changes such as the dress code were established. Recruitment efforts also changed. Greater efforts to obtain international players in the National Basketball Association, particularly players from Europe, are evidenced by recent draft outcomes, and some contend it may be due, at least in part, to efforts to find the next Great White Hope for professional basketball.

The percentage of white players in the NBA, for example, decreased from the 1989–90 season to the 2012–13 season, while the percentage of black players held relatively steady. The percentage of international players, many of them from European countries, increased during this same period. During the 2003–4 season, nearly 76 percent of the NBA was black. Just over 22 percent of players were white and almost 17 percent were international. By the 2012–13 season, the percentage of black players remained at about 76 percent while white players fell to 19 percent and foreign players increased to almost 19 percent.[40]

The most important contribution of the critical demography paradigm to the sociology of sports in general, and the sociology of race and sports in particular, is the centrality of racism, not merely race, and the call for the operationalization of this oft-used concept.

A Critical Demography of Athletic Destinations

Martin and Horton pulled together the elements that critical race theory, colorism, the population structural change thesis, and critical demography offer studies about racism and sports, and introduced a framework that contributes to the understanding of why people of selected racial groups end up participating in certain sports and how certain sports come to be

associated with blacks and other sports with whites. Population and structural changes are important contributing factors that are often neglected.
When these changes occur, and particularly when the minority population
in a sport and/or in society increases and these increases are accompanied
by structural changes (e.g., economic recession, change in political leadership at the federal level), overt manifestations of racism increase.

A critical demography approach to understanding the choices blacks
and whites make concerning sports, and the choices that are made *for*
blacks and whites concerning sports participation, makes it clear that not
only is *race* important, as seen in critical race theory, but *racism* is at the
core of all analyses. Using the newly introduced critical demography of athletic destinations approach, it can be shown that colorism is not understood as the latest iteration of racism; instead, colorism is itself a
manifestation of racism. Population changes matter—whether inside or
outside of sports—as do changes in the social structure, such as increases
in unemployment, political mistrust, or unrest. Critical demography, with
its ability to account for power, is an important paradigm that can and
should inform debates about the intersections between racism and sports,
including as they relate to sports participation. The quantitative representation of certain racial groups in particular sports can be understood, more
than many other variables in the study of sports, as a manifestation of racism in sports.

A critical demography of sports participation by race incorporates the
following principles:

1. Racism is a central feature of American social systems.
2. Racism is institutional.
3. Institutions, and the groups and individuals that make them up, reproduce
   these systems through social practices and policies.
4. Members of the dominant group receive unmerited privileges, while members of subordinate racial minority groups receive unequal treatment.
5. Racism remains part of the our social system, changing in form, but not function.

Racism is a central feature of sports in America. From the very first time
both blacks and whites put on the gloves or picked up a ball, participants were
largely separated by race. Racism is merely reflected in the behaviors and attitudes of ignorant players, coaches, owners, and fans, but it is institutionalized.
Policies have long been in place that privilege some racial groups and disadvantage others. Social practices and policies are reproduced in sports,

although given changes in the society at large, the manifestations of the practices and policies may be harder to detect over time.

Using the critical demography of sports participation by race perspective, we can see how racism was central in determining when, where, and how people of various races participated in and consumed sports. We can see how federal officials and wealthy team owners were able to exert their will over the society at large, but particularly over the black population, despite opposition. This is the essence of power.

Conclusion

We must take into account the impact of changes in the size and composition of populations and other changes in society, such as economic downturns, that may further impact people's perceptions about race, especially perceptions about white superiority and black inferiority and threats to the racialized social system that is the foundation of American society and American sports. The literature on race and sports tends to ignore the sociological process of racial socialization—revisited here—and the literature on socialization and racial socialization in particular tends to ignore the centrality of race in sports, particularly in the American context.

The framework for understanding how some sports come to be associated with whites, and other sports come to be associated with blacks, involves redefining racial socialization as a process where the ways of society are communicated to blacks and whites in distinct ways such that each group is aware of its position in society relative to the other. Within this framework, failure to adhere to the expectations set forth for blacks and whites as they relate to sports participation have in the past led to overt manifestations of racism. In the so-called postracial era, manifestations are more covert and often appear in seemingly race-neutral institutional practices and personal actions. These manifestations of overt and covert racism may be exacerbated by changes inside and outside of the sport, by the size and composition of groups, and by the economy. The next chapter presents a closer examination of the impact of population characteristics, specifically neighborhood conditions. Neighborhood conditions are closely tied to sports participation as well as to perceptions about sports as an escalator toward upward social mobility or a treadmill (to use Harry Edwards's analogy). They also provide further evidence of the gap between American idealism and realism where issues of fairness, equality, and justice are concerned, in sports and beyond.

Chapter 2

Race, Place, and Sports

Racial socialization—the process by which blacks and whites learn their prescribed roles in society—occurs in direct connection with where we live. Racial residential segregation identifies neighborhoods by race. Neighborhoods that are predominantly white tend to have more homeowners than renters, higher housing values, and greater access to resources and quality schools with quality sports programs and facilities. Neighborhoods that are predominantly black tend to have more renters than homeowners, lower housing values, and less access to resources and quality schools with quality programs and facilities. Underresourced neighborhoods are also often plagued by a host of social problems that cause residents to explore ways to experience upward social mobility. Due to the history and legacy of racial discrimination in education, housing, and the criminal justice system, some blacks see sports as one of the few avenues for upward social mobility.

Messages about expected behavior, including expected behavior in sports for blacks and whites, are communicated in the interactions of people at the neighborhood level. Pushback for violations of racial norms and etiquette often begin here, as does the association of race with place and sports. Neighborhood schools—which are often segregated by race—become known for many things, including their athletic programs. Good or even great basketball teams at a predominantly black high school may reinforce the idea that basketball is a black sport. Good or even great lacrosse teams at a high school—usually on the other side of town—may reinforce the idea that lacrosse is largely a white sport. Covert and overt manifestations of racism may increase or decrease with changes in the neighborhood composition and overall economic well-being. A large influx or exodus to or from a particular group may negatively impact intergroup relations and contribute to calls for changes in racial norms as they relate to sports participation. Rapid social change can lead to further conflicts as members of the dominant group seek to maintain the racial social order.

The neighborhood is an important unit of inquiry as evidenced by the neighborhood characteristics in which blacks and whites have historically lived and continue to live, along with the effect of these characteristics on sports participation and the association of selected sports as black or white. In this chapter, we explore in detail the significance of race, place, and sports. We examine the role of neighborhoods in communicating what society deems appropriate behaviors for individuals by race, especially where sports participation is concerned. We will also explore the impact of neighborhood population and economic changes on blacks' and whites' sports participation. Three case studies will highlight the tendency of young male athletes to use sports as a means for improving their overall socioeconomic status. We will also look at the over- and underrepresentation of blacks in sports, and offer a contemporary analysis and critique of what Harry Edwards described as the triumph and tragedy hidden below the veil of sports. At the neighborhood level, the inconsistencies between what we claim to value and how we behave are observable and measurable.

Residential Segregation: Causes and Consequences

While America is one of the most diverse nations in the world, it also is one of the most segregated. The segregation of neighborhoods can be directly linked to the segregation of schools and the segregation of sports, especially amateur sports. Just how our neighborhoods came to be segregated is a not so quietly kept secret, and is essential to understanding the segregation of sports and variations in sports participation by race.

Neighborhoods were not always as segregated as they are in contemporary times. Residential segregation is defined as "the separation of racial groups in urban space" and is measured most often by using the Index of Dissimilarity. The index measures the extent to which a neighborhood, for example, looks demographically like the larger surrounding geographical area, such as a city or metropolitan area.[1]

Contemporary residential segregation is the result of a host of factors, including discrimination, suburbanization, income, and attitudes. The significance of racial economic inequality at the neighborhood level and beyond cannot be overstated. Unemployment rates for blacks were higher than for whites before one of the most devastating economic periods in our country since the Great Depression—the Great Recession, which began in 2007. In the 1970s, unemployment rates for blacks were about twice as high as the unemployment rates for whites. During that decade black unemployment reached nearly 15 percent. The highest point for whites during the same time period was less than 9 percent. A decade later, according to the Bureau of Labor Statistics (BLS), about one-fifth of blacks was unemployed. For whites, never more than 10 percent of the population was unemployed in the 1980s. Black unemployment was over 14 percent at its highest point in the 1990s, compared to about 7 percent for whites. In the years leading up to the Great Recession, blacks continued to be unemployed at substantially higher levels than whites. Evidence of the racial divide was also present after the Great Recession ended. While the unemployment rate for the country peaked around 10 percent in 2009, black unemployment exceeded 16 percent, and about half of black youth were unemployed in 2010. Black male unemployment in 2010 was 19 percent and black female employment was 13 percent. Data from the BLS also show that unemployment rates were even higher for college-educated blacks than for college-educated whites following the Great Recession. Blacks with some college, but no college degree, were unemployed at a rate of 12.4 percent. The rate for comparable whites was much lower, at 7.6 percent. The unemployment rate for blacks with at least a four-year degree was 7.9 percent, compared to 4.3 percent for similar whites.

The overrepresentation of blacks in certain industries may help explain why blacks were especially impacted by the recession, according to a forthcoming study conducted by Martin, Horton, and Booker. The study shows that about 64 percent of black male workers and almost 76 percent of black women were employed in either public administration; education and health services; wholesale and retail trade; manufacturing; or professional and business services before the Great Recession. Blacks were unemployed at higher rates than whites and were overrepresented in certain sectors. Racial discrimination and prejudice contributed to the observed racial differences.

The participation of blacks in the labor force was not the only risk factor for blacks in the years leading up to the Great Recession. Martin and colleagues found that the targeting of blacks by financial lending institutions was another contributing factor. Evidence shows that blacks were 30 percent more likely to receive high-interest-rate loans than whites. This was the case for black and white borrowers with identical qualifications. The findings were consistent across the income spectrum. The U.S. Department of Housing and Urban Development (HUD) also found that blacks were more likely than whites to receive subprime loans. The overrepresentation of blacks receiving subprime loans could be described as an epidemic since blacks across the country were impacted in locations ranging from Los Angeles to New York. In the case of New York City, subprime financing accounted for a quarter of loans in more than 50 percent of census tracts. Additionally, black neighborhoods were home to nearly half of all the subprime lending in the entire city.[2]

The issue of racial economic inequality and racial differences in neighborhood quality is arguably harder to discern today. Specifically, housing discrimination was easy to spot in the past, but in recent times it is oftentimes harder to identify as such. The institutionalization of redlining, which leads to residential segregation, is one clear example of overt race-based housing discrimination. Present-day efforts to discriminate against blacks are subtler, more covert, and take place at virtually every phase of the real estate process.[3]

Suburbanization is said to be a cause of residential segregation because access to the suburbs, following World War II, remained relatively closed. More recently, it has been shown that blacks who do live in the suburbs are more segregated from whites than other nonwhite groups, and they tend to live in areas of the suburbs that are less desirable. Additionally, blacks living in the suburbs tend to be poorer than other residents. Income disparities are thus another cause of residential segregation. Housing costs are often greater in the suburbs than in the cities, which may also cause residential segregation. However, blacks of all income levels are more highly segregated from whites than other nonwhite groups. Additionally, research shows whites prefer neighborhoods with relatively few blacks, while blacks prefer more racially mixed living environments.[4]

"Housing segregation and discrimination," says Nancy A. Denton, "define and determine much of what happens in neighborhood housing markets as well as what happens to neighborhood residents." Poor tax bases may mean limited access to school-sponsored sports programs. Neighborhoods are significant because they "determine school quality, job opportunities, safety, exposure to crime and asset accumulation, among a host of other things."[5] Neighborhood location also determines access to school-sponsored sports and to public recreational programs and facilities, to name a few public assets. Participation in youth sports is often connected to where a child lives or attends school. Blacks and other children of color are unfortunately overrepresented in underresourced communities and schools. Black children, therefore, may have ample access to sports and leisure activities such as basketball and track and field, which have lower costs for participation, while white children living in communities with adequate and abundant resources have a broader range of options.

Racial differences in access to sports programs and other leisure activities are evidenced in a number of areas including in racial health disparities. Individuals living in segregated neighborhoods "have higher mortality risks and poorer health services."[6] With regard to economic and social advancement, the desire to experience intergenerational and intragenerational upward mobility burns within all Americans, regardless of race. However, many blacks trapped in underresourced neighborhoods see few legitimate avenues for achieving the proverbial American Dream. For many, sports are viewed as one of very few legitimate means of upward social mobility.[7] Rags-to-riches stories involving mostly black athletes are a form of inspiration to many black youth who share such athletes' social background as well as their hope to escape it.

Race, Sports, and Upward Social Mobility

One need only look at the news reports, biographies, and autobiographies of some of the nation's most talented athletes to understand the details of players' desires to make it big and improve the socioeconomic position of themselves and their families. The media love to tell stories about the promise a particular neighborhood legend did or did not realize. One example is that of a former top college basketball player, Mark Lyons of the University of Arizona. Lyons, born and raised in the Hamilton Hill section of Schenectady, New York, is a phenomenal athlete. He attended one of the nation's top prep schools and was a standout at Xavier University in Ohio before joining the squad in Arizona.[8] The news reports highlighted all of the obstacles Lyons faced growing up in a crime-ridden section of New York's capital region. Lyons's father died in a crash, reportedly running from police, when Lyons was just 15 months old. When Lyons was 10 years old, his aunt was brutally killed by a boyfriend in Lyons's home. Lyons expressed a desire to "go pro" and make enough money to get his mother and the family out of their Hamilton Hill neighborhood.

Lyons's story is not unique, particularly among young black males with aspirations of playing sports professionally. The film *Hoop Dreams* follows two talented players in the Chicago area in the 1990s. Basketball prodigies Arthur Agee and William Gates grew up in economically disadvantaged neighborhoods where drugs, poverty, and violence were all too common.[9] Agee was obsessed with Isiah Thomas and had hoped to use basketball to help his family—who were struggling to keep their lights on and food on the table—achieve a better life. Agee and Gates had to travel hours to and from their underresourced neighborhood to an affluent school to receive the type of professional coaching and develop the social capital required to make it to the next level. Conversely, the high schools that most black youth attended were not only underresourced, but athletic competitions were seen as places of potential violence. A win or a loss could result in a violent episode. The lack of academic rigor at these schools also meant that the student-athletes were ill-prepared for success in high school or college. In fact, when Agee and Gates got to the elite school, they were reading several grade levels lower than they should have been.

The life of Bronx legend Allen Christopher Jones is another good example of the fixation on stories of talented young black males seeking to use sports as a vehicle to leave underresourced and sometimes violent and drug-ridden neighborhoods. Jones recently published a memoir in which he highlights how basketball helped him leave a neighborhood that was rapidly changing. *The Rat That Got Away*, however, is much more than a memoir.[10] Sure, within its pages one can read about a youngster's transition from boyhood to manhood. One can also read about a sojourn from the hallways of Paterson Houses in the Bronx to legendary outdoor basketball courts to the floors of financial institutions in Europe. Equally significant are the author's reflections about a host of issues of interest to scholars and laypersons alike. These issues include neighborhood change; the influence of various agents of socialization such as family, peers, and religion; the impact of social movements on local communities; variations in the quality of education by race and place; culture shock; the challenges facing student athletes; delinquency; and even identity formation.

As Allen Jones begins his tale, we find the Paterson Houses as a place friendly to families. It began as a multiracial, multiethnic, mixed socioeconomic community with dual-headed households employed in an array of occupations. As time passes, the Paterson Houses becomes a very different place. The change from a stable to a distressed community is attributed to a number of factors, including white flight, the exodus of middle-class blacks, drug use, and drug abuse.

Jones comes of age during some of the most tumultuous times in modern American history, the 1960s and 1970s. Jones and his peers lived through the civil rights movement, the black power movement, the antiwar movement, neighborhood blight, and drug epidemics. He, like many others, did not come out unscathed.

As the nation struggled, Allen struggled. His struggles were both internal and external, both personal and communal. Although raised in the

Catholic faith, Jones would soon stray from the church's teachings. He found the sparkle and shine associated with those involved in the underground economy (hustlers, drug dealers, drug users, prostitutes, and so on) more attractive. The former church boy exchanged his devotion to the church for "street credibility," which ultimately led to petty theft, a heroin addiction, and a stay in one of New York City's most notorious penal institutions.

Fortunately, basketball was Allen's saving grace. Basketball opened doors of opportunity Allen eventually walked through to become a professional player and a success in the financial industry.

While his nation, his neighborhood, and Jones himself experienced a lot of changes, his one constant was his love for basketball. Jones was a gifted athlete, and like many young people today he had dreams of becoming a professional athlete. Unlike many of them, however, basketball was not his immediate ticket *out* of a distressed community; rather, basketball in some ways kept him connected to it. Allen gained street credibility for his athletic abilities, his association with criminal elements in the community, and his own reputation for engaging in illegal activities ranging from drug use and drug abuse to robberies.

Having gained street credibility, a great commodity in the Paterson Houses and other distressed communities, Allen Jones was treated with the utmost respect by individuals—the hustlers and dealers—who were contributing to the decline of the quality of life in the community. At the same time, the star treatment he received left him ill-prepared for the "real world," for the world outside the Paterson Houses.

Because of the special treatment that Allen Jones received as an elite basketball player, he bought into the notion that as long as he excelled in athletics, little else would be expected of him. This clearly conflicted with the expectations that his parents had for him and the expectations he once had for himself. This cost Allen tremendously. Allen was under the mistaken belief, like far too many student-athletes, that they will just get a pass through life. That teachers and professors will promote student-athletes regardless of their academic performance. Needless to say, Allen Jones did not receive the quality of education that would facilitate admission into the type of college that is part of the professional athletics pipeline. This was partly Allen's fault, as well as a failure on the part of the educational system. Allen, like some other student-athletes, forgot that he was a student first and an athlete second.

Once Jones realized the importance of excelling on and off the court, his eyes widened and his universe expanded. This is evidenced by the culture shock he experienced. Allen Jones did not need to go to Europe to experience culture shock; like many students of color on predominantly white college campuses today, he experienced culture shock without ever leaving the United States.

Jones's basketball talent enabled him to attend a junior college hundreds of miles from where he grew up. He was surprised by the disparities in wealth he witnessed and how badly prepared he was for academic success. The difference in the levels of wealth between the faculty and students at the college and the people living in and around Paterson Houses was very apparent. Moreover, Allen Jones was shocked at the audacity shown by some white students in their drug use, as compared to the secrecy, paranoia, and covert use he had witnessed in the more distressed community in which he had grown up. Allen was becoming acutely aware of the benefits associated with what some scholars call white privilege.

Allen Jones, like many young people living in distressed communities that are often also racially and ethnically homogeneous, faced the challenge of trying to maintain credibility with those involved in illicit activities, while at the same time reaching for higher goals. Jones's book offers some insight into the struggle that young people face and some explanation as to why some succumb to the pressures while others do not.

For one, it is evident that the amount of pressure placed on young people in distressed communities may vary by gender. Young males may be more likely to give in to such pressures than young females, which is not to say that young females are immune. Strong family values and the presence of positive adult role models are important too, as is the accumulation not only of monetary capital but of social capital. Much of Allen's ultimate success came from the strong foundation laid by his parents and from the social capital and social networks he developed and nurtured owing in large part to his status as an elite athlete.

The Rat That Got Away serves, in many ways, as a model for helping a subset of young people who all too often find themselves in the same situation as Allen, torn between the glitter and glamour of illicit activities and legitimate pathways to wealth, status, and power.

Unlike in the case of Allen Jones, not everyone gets away or wants to get away. A 1990 story in the *New York Times* about Joe Hammond of Harlem is an example of one who did not get away. Hammond—known in the neighborhood as the Destroyer when he played as a young man—at the age of 40 was peddling greeting cards to get enough money to eat. It was a far cry from the days when he sold drugs and had hundreds of thousands of dollars stashed in his apartment. Jones never played high school or college basketball, but he was recruited by the Los Angeles Lakers and the American Basketball Association's New York Nets. A high school dropout, Hammond shined in the city's summer leagues and was offered a $50,000 contract. However, the $50,000 contract paled in comparison to the money Hammond was making "dealing drugs and shooting dice," according to the article.

Hammond also owned "a night club, two fancy cars, three apartments, and a house," so the appeal of playing alongside Lakers greats like Wilt Chamberlain was not enough to pull him away from the magnetic appeal of the streets. Hammond's success as a street hustler was short-lived. It landed him in prison and cost him his worldly possessions.

The article describes a game where Hammond played against basketball great Julius Erving, also known as Dr. J. Hammond scored 50 points to Erving's 39. Hammond claimed that he wanted the Lakers to pay him what they were paying players like Erving, but the Lakers refused. In the article Hammond states, "I told the Lakers that I deserved what those guys were making because I was better than most of them, but they refused to pay me. Then I asked them for a no-cut, guaranteed contract, and they refused me again. They couldn't understand how this poor boy from the slums could be playing hardball with them. And of course, I couldn't tell them."[11]

How might Hammond's life have been different had he accepted the offer from the Lakers? How might his life have been different if the Lakers acquiesced and paid him what top players in the league were earning at the time? We can never know, but we do know that he did not get away.

The idea that sports are a vehicle for anyone, but especially black males in disadvantaged neighborhoods, is a narrative that is all too common in our society. The persistence of this narrative is fodder for scholars and laypersons who believe that we are living in a postracial society. It is instrumental in perpetuating the myth that all of the material spoils that we associate with success in American society are accessible to anyone, if they would only work hard and live up to their full potential. The narrative, which can be heard virtually everywhere we look, is an important tool in the racial socialization of black and white athletes, such that black athletes come to see sports as one of few legitimate avenues for advancement in a society with a history of undervaluing and vilifying blacks in general, and black males in particular.

The long history of overemphasizing the physicality of the black male in sports and beyond helps to explain how black athletes are affected by messages communicated through the process of racial socialization in sports. Jay Coakley addresses this controversial issue, arguing that the association of the black male with physicality leads young black males to see their bodies as superior when it comes to physical abilities, which "inspires some young people to believe it is their biological and cultural destiny to play certain sports and play them better than others." Coakley adds, "When these stereotypes are combined with restricted opportunities in mainstream occupations and heavily sponsored opportunities to develop skills in certain sports, many blacks are motivated to play those sports. Over time they come to believe that it is their destiny to excel in those sports, especially relative to whites." Segregation in American neighborhoods only worsens the situation such that "there is a tendency for black males to be 'tagged' in a way that subverts their success in claiming identities that don't fit expectations based on racial ideology."[12]

Black Athletes by the Numbers

The overrepresentation of blacks in a relatively small number of sports supports the aforementioned claim that blacks perceive limited options for upward social mobility apart from sports, and especially the sports that are most accessible to minority youth in underresourced neighborhoods. One need only look to data provided by the Institute for Diversity and Ethics in Sports to see how concentrated black athletes are, for example, in basketball.[13] During the 1995–96 NBA seasons, 80 percent of the players were black and 20 percent were white. By the 1999–2000 seasons, 78 percent of players were black and 22 percent were white. For the 2011–12 seasons, 78 percent of players were black and 18 percent were white. The overrepresentation of black players is evident over time, as is the underrepresentation of blacks among owners and front-office staff. The figures are not much different in the Women's National Basketball Association (WNBA). In 1999, 64 percent of players were black and 32 percent were white. By 2005, 63 percent were black and 34 percent white. By 2012, about 75 percent of players in the WNBA were black compared to only 16 percent white.[14]

Similar patterns were observed for the National Football League (NFL). In 1996, 1999, and 2012 about 67 percent were black and about 31 percent white.

The percentage of black players in Major League Baseball (MLB) has declined over time. In 1996, 17 percent of players were black and 62 percent were white. By 1999, black players made up only 13 percent of players and the number of white players decreased by 2 percent. In 2005, less than 10 percent of MLB players were black and 60 percent were white, and these numbers were matched by the 2012 season. In Major League Soccer (MLS), the percentage of black players has increased between 1999 and 2012, while the percentage of white players has decreased. In 1999, 16 percent of MLS players were black, compared to 65 percent white. For the latest year that data are available, about a quarter of MLS players were black and less than half, or 49 percent, were white.[15]

The institute also maintains racial data on college sports. Looking only at Division I, the data show an increase in the percentage of black basketball players and decreases, although relatively small, in football and baseball. During the 2009–10 academic year, 61 percent of basketball players were black and 30 percent were white. For the 2004–5 academic year and the 1999–2000 academic year, there was a higher percentage of white players than black players. In the earliest year, 35 percent of Division I basketball players were black and 55 percent were white. Five years later, the percentage of black players dropped to 32 percent and the percentage of white players increased to 58 percent. For women, the trends are similar. Between 2004 and 2010, the percentage of black athletes surpassed that of white athletes. By 2010, 51 percent of women players were black and 40 percent were white. Five years earlier, 45 percent of players were white and 44 percent were black. In 2000, 54 percent were white and 36 percent were black.

At the Division I level, black football players represented half of all players in 2000, 45 percent in 2005, and 46 percent in 2010. Blacks were clearly underrepresented among Division I baseball players. In 2000 and in 2005, 7 percent of players were black and about 84 percent were white. By 2010, 83 percent of players were white and only 6 percent were black.[16]

Few scholars have written about the association of sports participation with the potential for upward mobility so eloquently as Dr. Harry Edwards. Writing in the late 1960s, Dr. Edwards set forth the argument that "to no small degree, blacks' highly visible accomplishments as athletes in four or five sports have served to veil the more unsavory realities of their sports involvement and to obscure the fact that virtually all other American sports remain largely segregated and lily white." This enduring finding about race and sports shows that American sports are "more a treadmill than the fabled escalator providing escape from the deprivations afflicting the black community. And because of its interdependence with other institutional structures and social processes in America, sports constitute not only a treadmill for the overwhelming majority of aspiring black athletes, but also a cruel and wickedly subtle trap, ensnaring the whole of black culture and society." Edwards added that the idea that sports provides an avenue toward upward social mobility for blacks "amounts not to mere naïveté, but to inhuman mockery."

Edwards adds that the "singular visibility of black athlete role models" is directly responsible for the fact that "high numbers of black youth are channeled into athletic career aspirations." Consequently, high numbers of black youth are not focusing their attention on other careers such as in science, technology, engineering, and math, nor are black youth being encouraged to pursue such careers by institutions of racial socialization such as the media and schools.

Edwards revealed how unlikely it was for black youth in high school to gain the ultimate prize—a college scholarship. Only a select few elite athletes make it to the college level, and the number of whites receiving athletic scholarships far outweighed the number of black athletes receiving athletic scholarships. In the mid-1970s, "whites were still receiving slightly more than 94 percent of all collegiate athletic support." Stacking and poor graduation rates are some of the problems facing black college athletes. A group of black athletes at California State University at Los Angeles even filed a lawsuit against the operation of the athletic program at the university. "But, if an athletic scholarship and a 'free education' do little to either promote black socioeconomic mobility or to substantiate the validity of other dominant group myths concerning the Afro-American experience in sport, the realities confronting blacks in the professional ranks are shattering."

Edwards goes on to show that black participation in sports at the collegiate level was limited to a few sports and that this was the case at the professional level too. While many high-profile professional athletes are black, most black professional athletes in Edwards's era earned less than whites with similar skill sets. Additionally, black athletes in Edwards's era are in positions where the likelihood of injury is greater than in the positions where whites are commonly found. Edwards also showed that up until the late 1970s, an athlete did not typically reap the "post-career pension benefits" and "seldom gets the secondary benefits of a sports career; for example advertising contracts, coaching, managing, sports media, or front-office jobs after retirement from active participation." As of the late 1970s, black athletes were also less likely to gain entry into the Hall of Fame when compared with white professional players with similar athletic abilities.[17]

Unfortunately, much of what Edwards observed in the late 1970s is still occurring today. The Institute on Diversity and Ethics found in 2012 that "the percentage of white male student-athletes, in all of Division I athletics, stands at 61.2 percent, a decrease of 1.7 percent from 2011. Of all Division I male athletes, 22 percent are African American, which was a 0.8 percent increase from 2011."

Almost 70 percent of male student-athletes at the Division I, II, and III levels combined were white. The percentage of white female student-athletes at the Division I, II, and III levels combined was over 76. Black males accounted for 16 percent of athletes in the combined levels and black females accounted for less than 9 percent of athletes in the combined levels.

Moreover, whites held most of the coaching positions at each of the divisional levels in 2012. Over 86 percent of coaches in Division 1 were white, 88 percent in Division II, and nearly 92 percent in Division III. Blacks "held 8.3 percent, 5.2 percent and 4.2 percent of the men's head coating positions in Divisions I, II, and III, respectively," and similar patterns were found where women's head coaching positions were concerned.[18] The representation of blacks among athletic directors, college associates, and assistant athletic directors is more dismal.

Despite the relatively low likelihood of black youth making it to the pros and escaping disadvantaged neighborhoods, black youth are inundated with images of exemplary talented black athletes who, we are told, come from similar backgrounds. At the same time, very few counternarratives are offered. As a result, not only are ideas about black dominance in sports and little else reinforced, but high numbers of black youth come to see athletics as one of the few legitimate avenues toward upward social mobility. Continued problems such as crime and underresourced schools serve the purpose of reinforcing the belief that blacks have limited occupational choices. The fact that most aspiring athletes will not have a rags-to-riches experience means they will have to face an already unfavorable labor market, for which far too many are ill-prepared and that already prefers white males with a criminal record to black males with no criminal record. Not only is there a school-to-prison pipeline, there appears also to be a sports-to-prison pipeline—the epiphany some black athletes experience about their likelihood of not only making a living as an athlete but building wealth may lead some to activities or relationships that result in greater contact with law enforcement and a greater risk of becoming part of the epidemic that is black mass incarceration.

Conclusion

Racial differences in sports participation are evidenced at all levels, including youth sports and at the professional and collegiate level. It is not a coincidence that blacks and whites are over- and underrepresented in certain sports. On the contrary, messages about what is expected of whites and blacks, even in the world of sports, are communicated in many ways. Expectations about how well racial groups should perform in certain environments and against certain opponents are an important part of those messages. Stories about black athletes struggling to escape poor neighborhoods using their athletic abilities are commonplace in the media and provide inspiration for young black people seeking to do the same.

In this chapter, the connections between residential segregation, racial socialization, and sports were reviewed. It was made clear that certain qualities are attributed to certain neighborhoods and the inhabitants that are based upon race. It was also shown how such racial ideologies might be internalized and, along with limited legitimate opportunity structures, impact the racial disparities in sports participation professionally and at other levels. Racial disparities in neighborhood quality and in decision-making positions—both on and off the field—highlight the ongoing struggles blacks face in the country in achieving fairness, justice, and full participation in all areas of society. In the next chapter, one of the most influential, efficient, and effective agents of racial socialization is discussed: the mass media.

Chapter 3

A Perfect Combination: The Mass Media and Representations of Race in Sports

The media is an important part of our society, and its role in teaching us the ways of society based upon the racial groups to which we belong should not be underestimated. In this chapter, we explore the role of the media in perpetuating racial and ethnic stereotypes, which contributes to the identification of certain sports with certain racial and ethnic groups. The exploration begins with a discussion of what is included in conventional and contemporary definitions of media, and the symbiotic relationship between sports and the media. Special attention is devoted to the evolution of mass media in the United States, with specific attention on the historic black press. Similarities and differences in the treatment of sports in the mainstream and in the black press are noted. Additionally, we will consider commonly held stereotypes about racial and ethnic minority groups, especially blacks and in the world of sports, and the role these stereotypes play in the process of racial socialization and determination of athletic destinations in the sports industrial complex. Race-based stereotypes contribute to decisions about sports participation by race, and their influence is often more prevalent during and after periods of population and structural change, such as changes in the economy. It is hard for average Americans to tolerate the salaries that some high-profile professional athletes make when the nation is experiencing an economic downturn, but this is especially difficult for individuals with membership in the dominant group who may turn to scapegoating people of color as the source of their economic woes. Some media outlets—as agents of racial socialization—may seek to capitalize on such sentiments with the goal of diverting attention away from members of the elite within the dominant racial group and toward people of color.

Sports and the Media Prior to the 1900s

The *Oxford English Dictionary Online* defines the mass media as "the main means of mass communication, such as television, radio, and newspapers considered collectively."[1] Robert McChesney, University of Illinois at Urbana-Champaign professor of communications, has written extensively about the media, including as it relates to sports. McChesney provides the following history of sports coverage in the United States.

McChesney observes that the mass media and sport are interdependent social institutions, both of which are driven by capitalism and the pursuit of profit. Media devote attention to sports and thereby generate revenue through circulation and advertising. McChesney notes that if sport, as institution, was well matched with capitalism as it evolved in the nineteenth century, it was even a better match for corporate-centered capitalism of the twentieth century.

To further illustrate the symbiotic relationship between sports and the media, McChesney provides a history of the media dating back to the late 1770s. Early on, most newspapers and magazines were written for wealthy audiences. Wealthy audiences comprised a relatively small segment of the overall population. By 1830 there was an increase in magazine and newspaper publishing, but such ventures were not yet profitable. Publishers, says McChesney, also served as editors, managers, and authors. Sports during this time period were not looked upon very favorably. The image of the athlete as a hero did not emerge until much later. So-called respectable sports like horse racing received a lot of attention. Sports associated with lower social classes, such as boxing, received considerably less coverage.[2]

At the same time, slavery continued to be a major social, economic, and political force in the nation. The newspapers that catered to wealthy whites and deemed selected sports undesirable also included advertisements for the sale of human beings or postings about runaway slaves. Mainstream newspapers were also places where proponents of slavery and abolitionism were given platforms.

With societal changes came changes in sports and the media. Industrialization in the Northeast, the movement of people from farms to central cities, the expansion of public education, and an overall increase in sports activity contributed to a growth in media coverage. *Spirit of the Times*, an early sports magazine started by William Porter, saw a sharp increase in circulation numbers and a change as to how certain sports were perceived. The magazine began devoting more space to boxing and to sports like cricket, which McChesney says some had hoped would become a national pastime in the 1850s. Porter was not successful in this regard, but he did help establish rules and terminology for baseball.

The 1830s and 1840s gave rise to the birth of modern newspapers. Advertising played a big role, although professional journalism did not exist at the time. Thanks to a decrease in the costs of printing and greater interest in the topic, a sports press developed and its target was working-class and middle-class Americans. These papers did not fully embrace sports coverage at the time, still believing it was not newsworthy.[3]

While there is some dispute about the origins of baseball, there is evidence to suggest that the game was played throughout the country prior to the outbreak of the Civil War. The first professional baseball league was established in 1869. As the popularity of sports like baseball increased over time, media coverage increased. McChesney notes that not only were baseball statistics published, but also articles extolling the health benefits of physical activity were featured with greater regularity. This period is transformational, as the media's attitudes toward sports changed from one that viewed most sports as vulgar to one that viewed sports as virtuous. McChesney says that the "press worked to legitimize sports as a cultural institution."[4]

During the last two decades of the nineteenth century, industrialization, urbanization, and immigration transformed the society at large in fundamental ways. More and more people were interested in sports, and media coverage of sports expanded in terms of quantity and content. There was not only more sports coverage, but also more sports received attention, including golf and bicycling. Boxing was not looked upon as negatively as it had been previously, and became more organized, but society was still very much separated on the basis of race.

Newspapers took over as the primary place for Americans to get their information and read sports news, overtaking magazines. Magazine circulation continued to increase during the 1880s and 1890s, but newspaper circulation increased at a much faster rate. Both a decrease in printing costs, due to technological advances, and the need for businesses to reach customers contributed to the differential between newspapers and magazines. The telegraph also improved the ability to share news, including sports stories, more quickly.

The first sports sections and sports departments were created by major publishing outlets, and the field of sports journalism was born during this period. These developments in the media helped transform the average American's relationship to sports. One no longer had to be physically present during an event to experience it.[5]

Sports and the Media after the 1900s

By the turn of the twentieth century, most major papers covered major sporting events. We can thank members of the military for helping to popularize sports. Like veterans of the Civil War, veterans of World War I helped increase interest in sports. The 1920s, described by some as the Golden Age of Sports, were characterized by several trends. For one, newspapers featured stories that would attract readers, as distinct from "hard news" stories. Feature stories provided readers with an escape or distraction from their everyday lives, and sports fit nicely into this trend. At this point in the history of media and sports, about a quarter of all newspapers were sold because of their sports section. Newspapers presented their product in a more uniform way, which helped to cut down on costs. Sports stories, being politically neutral, also helped newspapers deflect attention from reports of divisive politics that might offend some readers. Sports were a unifying force.

In the 1920s, we start to see the emergence of certain athletes as heroes. Radio helped the emergence of sports stars as heroes as well as increasing the popularity of sports like college football. Some thought radio would hurt attendance at sporting events, but in fact attendance increased. The advent of television helped to further cement the relationship between media and sports and America's love affair with athletic competition, although there were some casualties. In some situations, athletes became what law professor Denise Morgan calls a reluctant hero. Jack Johnson, the first black heavyweight boxing champion of the world, is a great example.[6]

While the mainstream press largely vilified Jack Johnson, many in the black community reluctantly came to his defense, even when they had reservations about some of his choices. To understand why that was the case, it is important to note that through the various phases of the development of the mass media and sports, blacks were largely excluded or not adequately represented. Black newspapers and magazines, like other historically black social institutions, then and now, were intended to fill a void created by a racialized social structure that often devalued and dehumanized people of color. The inability to see blacks as equals was evidenced in the newspaper coverage of blacks relative to whites, inside and outside the world of sports. Black newspapers and magazines, for example, were created early on to address critical issues like abolitionism, assimilation, and emigration, and to promote black intellectual thought. Examples include *Freedom's Journal*, the *Liberian Herald*, the *Rights of All*, and the *Mystery*, and the *Mirror of the Times*.[7]

The Black Press and the Curious Case of Black Boxers

The first black daily newspaper in the United States was not published until many years after mainstream papers were first published. Groups like the Associated Correspondents of Race Newspapers would not be formed until 1890. The association was made up of 40 black reporters from 10 different black newspapers across the nation. Based in Washington, DC, the aim of the association was to promote the best interest of the race through the press. From the time that the association was established up until the Golden Age of Sports, the *Memphis Free Speech*, the *Woman's Era, Boston Guardian, Chicago Defender, Pittsburgh Courier, Amsterdam News*, and *Crisis* were among the black newspapers and magazines in print. A. Philip Randolph published the *Messenger* at this time and Marcus Garvey published *Negro World*.

By 1919, Claude Barnett founded the Associated Negro Press. Records from the association reveal that press releases typically covered "civil rights activities, court decisions, legislation, United Nations news, music reviews, reports on black colleges and churches, and several obituaries" as well as articles on Adam Clayton Powell, John F. Kennedy, and Harry Truman.[8]

Sports were not often the primary subject matter in the black press. Lynching and women's rights were far more pressing issues. Many in the black press felt compelled to defend Jack Johnson, which contributed to his status as a hero, at least among many blacks.[9]

Jack Johnson was regarded as one of the greatest of his day. Blacks have long boxed. William Richmond, born in 1763, was a black boxer. Born in Virginia, he moved to Staten Island, New York, and while there he gained his freedom and become the first black professional boxer in the country. Richmond was discovered while working in a shipyard as a laborer. Hugh Percy, a British commander, was impressed by his performance in a fight with a sailor. Richmond's talents took him to England, where he became a cabinetmaker. He continued boxing while in England, though largely for self-defense, but was a semiprofessional boxer by 1800. Richmond earned the nickname "Black Terror" after knocking out an Englishman in less than 30 seconds. He fought before thousands, among them members of the aristocracy, and boxed until he was more than 50 years old.[10]

Tom Molineaux was also a well-known black boxer during the early part of the nineteenth century. He began his career boxing other slaves. Plantation owners would place bets on the fights. Molineaux's talent really paid off. He once defeated a slave from another plantation and was given, as a reward, $500 and his freedom. He also ended up in England and was trained by Richmond.

Black boxers came from many parts of the globe. George Godfrey was a black Canadian boxer in the late 1800s. Godfrey worked for a time as a porter in Boston, Massachusetts. At the age of 26, he started fighting competitively. "Old Chocolate," as he was called, eventually earned the title of World Colored Heavyweight Champion.

George Dixon was another black Canadian boxer. George "Little Chocolate" Dixon fought as a featherweight. He was the first black to win a world boxing championship. He is considered one of the best fighters in the history of the bantamweight and featherweight divisions. He was a professional boxer for 20 years.

Few boxers in the early part of the twentieth century were as well known as Jack Johnson. Jack Johnson was born 1878 and became the first black heavyweight champion of the world. A native of Galveston, Texas, Johnson did not have a lot of formal education. At the age of 19 he became a professional fighter, and he rarely lost a fight. "In 113 fights, over the next 35 years, he lost only eight. He is still considered one of the great counter punchers of all time. A 1903 victory over 'Denver Ed' Martin established Johnson as the unofficial Black heavyweight champion. John L. Sullivan and Jim Jeffries refused to fight Johnson, claiming that to do so would sully the sport's reputation." Johnson would eventually get the chance at a title fight:

On December 26, 1908, finally given the opportunity to compete for the heavyweight championship in a fight in Sydney, Australia, Johnson dethroned the reigning champion Tommy Burns. Johnson defended his championship against five white fighters over the next two years. Responding to the call of legions of white fans anxious to restore boxing's traditional racial hierarchy, Jim Jeffries came out of retirement to challenge the Black champion. Billed as "The Great White Hope," Jeffries fought Johnson in

"The Fight of the Century" on July 4, 1910, in Reno, Nevada. Johnson soundly beat Jeffries.[11]

Jack Johnson was known as much for his boxing as he was for the fearlessness with which he routinely violated the social norms of the day. He was committed to living life by his own rules, no matter what anyone else said or thought, and this appealed to the sensibilities of more progressive blacks. For a time, Johnson's every move seemed to attract the attention of the mainstream press and of government officials. Little, if any, attention seemed to be devoted to Johnson as long as he was fighting black boxers, while Johnson's fights with white opponents were covered with regularity.

For example, on February 20, 1907, the *New York Times* included an article about Johnson's victory over Peter Felix, a black boxer from Australia. The article contained only 21 words: "Jack Johnson, an American colored pugilist, to-day defeated Peter Felix, the colored heavyweight champion of Australia, in two minutes of fighting." A year later, an article about Johnson's desire to fight heavyweight boxing champion Tommy Burns was several hundred words long. The article, which again identifies Johnson's race but not the race of Burns, relates that Johnson went to London with his manager to issue a challenge to Tommy Burns. Before an audience of "sporting newspapers" Johnson issued the challenge to fight anywhere for a prize set by Burns. They fought in 1908 and Johnson became the first black heavyweight champion. Subsequent articles featuring Johnson were reflective of the times. Johnson was known for cheating on his wives and for abusing women, but he was hated because of his violation of miscegenation laws and his refusal to be treated like a slave. The treatment of Johnson by the mainstream press and by the society at large made him a "reluctant hero."

But it was Johnson's desire to be accepted as a total person that brought members of the black community and the black press to see him as a hero, says Denise Morgan. Morgan makes a distinction between two kinds of heroes, the linked fate hero and the reluctant hero. Reluctant heroes are "those who have difficulty reconciling their sense of individuality with membership in a subordinated community." These individuals have what Morgan describes as a complex relationship with the black community. On the other hand, linked fate heroes understand that they have "a responsibility to one another because their shared racial identity can be both an excuse for their political and economic subordination, as well as a source of political and economic power."

Morgan adds that reluctant heroes, by doing well in their chosen fields, play an important role in debunking the myth that blacks are inferior to whites. Johnson made his statement through his excellence in the boxing ring. At the same time, the reluctant hero reinforces the myth of white superiority by severing ties to the black community. Reluctant heroes often try to mute their blackness and focus on their individual needs as opposed to the needs of the larger community. Johnson's decision to date and marry white women exclusively, his refusal to fight black boxers after becoming champion, and his denouncing of black women as unfaithful were cited as evidence of the fact that Johnson had turned his back on the black community. In fact, his choice of white women as marital partners was perceived as his attempt to "associate himself with those on the upper rungs of the racial hierarchy rather than to dismantle that hierarchy."

Many blacks rallied around Johnson despite concerns about his loyalty, or lack thereof, to the black community. Even if Johnson did not see himself as a representative of the black race, blacks saw him as such, particularly as "he became the target of a racially motivated criminal investigation," says Morgan. Everyone but Johnson—blacks as well as whites—saw his personal life and professional career as embodying the ongoing racial struggle in America. Given the preeminence of scientific racism and biological determinism, blacks saw Johnson's success against white fighters as a blow to the contradictory idea that blacks were simultaneously a physical threat to whites *and* cowardly by nature. Indeed, Morgan shows that "the myth of black biological inferiority substantially affected all areas of life—including sports. In boxing it was widely accepted that black men made poor fighters because they were cowardly and had weak stomachs which made them susceptible to body blows." Additionally, it was taken as fact that whites had more stamina than blacks because they came from colder climates and would therefore outlast black fighters in bouts that routinely included dozens of rounds.[12]

Like other black athletes of his day, Johnson had to mask his talents so that he would not give credence to the caricature of black fighters in the imagination of many whites of the day. Johnson deemphasized his offensive weapons and instead emphasized his defensive style, a move some believed helped him get the title fight that led to him becoming the first black world heavyweight champion. Even if Johnson strategically decided to appear less threatening, blacks and whites see him as a threat.

For whites, Johnson's victories threatened the racialized social system that had privileged whites and disadvantaged blacks over time. For blacks,

Johnson's victories were viewed as placing the entire race at risk. Johnson was calling into question the issue of black rights. In the past, efforts to challenge the dominant racial ideology were met by violence aimed not only at an individual actor but against blacks as a whole. Blacks feared Johnson's victories might further enrage whites and increase acts of domestic terrorism against blacks throughout the country. In many ways, Johnson was attempting to live his life in a way many members of the black community had hoped to live but never thought possible. While members of the black population did not feel that integration and interracial marriages were essential to racial progress, they did believe that the basis for barring interracial marriages was erroneously rooted in the belief of the biological inferiority of the black race. Johnson's refusal to be viewed as less than a whole person whose choice of partners is dictated by others should, in theory, have been embraced by a population aware that they were living in a very color-conscious society. The goal, after all, was to eliminate such perspectives and be treated as full-fledged citizens of the United States, respected for their humanity and not singled out for degradation, humiliation, torture, and terror because of their race. Neither blacks nor whites were truly ready for a color-blind approach to life, and as a result Johnson was convicted of violating a law that was not even in effect at the time he was said to have violated it. Johnson was convicted of violating the Mann Act. The Mann Act was passed to curb prostitution involving white women, which was also referred to as white slavery. The Mann Act was never meant to address any other type of relationship. However, it was used against Johnson. Johnson could not be defeated in the ring by a great white hope, so the law was used to defeat him. To make matters worse, the Mann Act was passed on the very date authorities claimed Johnson violated it! Johnson was convicted of violating the Mann Act and sentenced to jail. While he was out on bail, Johnson escaped to Canada. He lived in exile for years, wandering in foreign lands. Upon his return and completion of his sentence, he was received by many in the black community, and at the same time rejected.

Instead of embracing Johnson's philosophy of refusing to be treated as a slave and to demand respect for his rights to life, liberty, and the pursuit of happiness, many moved more cautiously, to avoid unnecessarily waking the sleeping giant, better known as racism. Therefore subsequent fighters, such as Joe Louis, had to go to great lengths to appeal to white audiences by, for example, not gloating after defeating a white opponent and not being seen in the company of white women. Had more blacks adopted

Johnson's approach, the outcome could have been quite bloody or radically transformational.

There are some problems with the notion of Johnson as a reluctant hero that are not unique to Johnson, but are inherent in Morgan's general description of a reluctant black hero. In many ways, the hero, in this case Johnson, is blamed for society's unwillingness to see blacks as on equal footing with whites. The reluctant hero is chastised for trying to enjoy the rights and privileges that so many blacks, and sympathetic whites, have fought and died for. The idea that enjoying such rights means that one does not identify with the historic struggle of the black community—a key element in some definitions of the black community—is really counterintuitive. Johnson should not be penalized for challenging the status quo in this manner. In fact, many movements in the black experience in America have started with individuals who have tried to exert their humanity and their rights, and their lives have served as an inspiration to many others. Over time this can develop into a collective effort not only to enjoy benefits as individuals, but to bring about systemic changes. In the case of slavery, for a time individuals sought to free themselves. Efforts to free individuals were gradually replaced by efforts to dismantle an entire system, to turn society upside down by ending slavery altogether. Individual acts of defiance tend to precede collective efforts to bring about social change.

Moreover, the idea of Johnson as a reluctant hero implies that Johnson's race is a mutable trait. This suggests that Johnson's blackness is voluntary, even symbolic, and can be abandoned or embraced at will. Morgan said that Johnson "created the impression that blackness is something to be avoided." Johnson did not create this impression; this idea has been at the heart of the racialized society pattern that was in place long before Johnson's birth.

Many blacks, including those in the black press, understood that what Johnson experienced, in and out of the ring, was about much more than boxing: it was another chapter in the ongoing struggle for blacks to gain political power and civil rights. Whether Johnson saw himself as part of the black community was not relevant to whites or to blacks, because the society in which he lived saw him not for his talents or business savvy but as a black man in a society where black men were supposed to know and stay in the place where Booker T. Washington claimed blacks must start, the bottom.[13] Johnson refused to see himself in this manner, just as W. E. B. DuBois, in his critique of Washington, did not believe any members of the black community should view themselves, or their position in a society that their ancestors helped build, in such a manner.[14]

Between the 1940s and the 1950s, in the decades following Johnson's fall, the popularity of sports such as boxing increased as more and more Americans had televisions. Although the number of boxing fans increased, the number of local boxing clubs decreased. The number of professional boxers also decreased as the media favored "sluggers" over other types of fighters. College sports and professional baseball also saw declines at first, but over a relatively short period of time the financial benefits became clear as, in the world of sports and beyond, television became a popular medium for the masses all across the United States.

This period saw the integration of Major League Baseball and the integration of many other sports and social institutions. Integration was a consequence of many factors, including the involvement of blacks in World War II. Blacks made important contributions abroad and at home. The famous "Double V" involved fighting fascism throughout the world, and racism in the United States.

Sports and the Media after the 1950s

One could argue that it was between the late 1950s and the 1960s that the relationship between media and sports was solidified. The passage of the Sports Broadcasting Act bolstered the negotiating power of leagues. The Sports Broadcasting Act of 1961 "allowed sports leagues to pool broadcast rights."[15] Television networks were able to purchase broadcasting rights from teams and then earn money by charging businesses money to advertise to blue-collar workers, who historically make up the largest class of workers and consumers in the country.

The late 1950s and the 1960s were also a tremendous period of social change in America, which television made more immediate to a mass audience. It was during this historic period that many important events took place. The "separate but equal" doctrine was dealt a swift blow with the historic *Brown v. Board of Education* case in the Supreme Court. This decade also saw the brutal murder of a 14-year-old boy from Chicago, Illinois, named Emmett Till. The lynching of Emmett Till helped to spark the civil rights movement, as did the decision made by blacks throughout Birmingham, Alabama, not to ride segregated buses for more than 300 days. Leaders of the movement were able to use television to bring their social-justice message to the living rooms of people around the world. Athletes like Bill Russell were prominently featured in the movement.

By the 1970s and 1980s, we see the world of sports embracing the media to an even greater extent than in the past, and we see the media embracing the sports world. This era saw the creation of *Monday Night Football*. The number of television programming hours devoted to sports grew from 787 in the 1970s to 1,700 by the mid-1980s, and "the symbiotic relationship between sports and the various media continues to change."[16]

Throughout American history, there were formal and informal rules about what blacks could and could not do in all areas of public and private life. Those in positions of authority dictated, or attempted to dictate, every aspect of black economic, political, cultural, and reproductive life. As with any means of social control, these rules and regulations were reinforced through sanctions, positive as well as negative, to increase the likelihood of conformity. Black athletes were not immune. They were expected to adhere to the social mores of their times. Some did, and some did not. Historically, the expectations for blacks were narrowly prescribed and best illustrated by looking at commonly held stereotypes and caricatures. Ferris State University maintains the Jim Crow Museum of Racist Memorabilia in Big Rapids, Michigan, which provides insightful information about the various types of stereotypes that have developed over time, some of which are applicable to the representation of black athletes, male and female. The following caricatures are particularly relevant: the brute and the sapphire.

Black Caricatures: The Brute and the Sapphire

David Pilgrim describes the brute caricature as the portrayal of black men as "innately savage, animalistic, destructive, and criminal—deserving punishment, maybe death. This brute is a fiend, a sociopath, and an antisocial menace. Black brutes are depicted as hideous, terrifying predators who target helpless victims, especially white women." Boxer Mike Tyson serves as a classic textbook example of the brute caricature:

> Mike Tyson, the former heavyweight boxing champion, has embraced the brute image. Tyson was marketed as a sadistic and savage warrior who was capable of killing an opponent. His quick knockouts bolstered his reputation as the world's most feared man. Joyce Carol Oates wrote, "Tyson suggests a savagery only symbolically contained within the brightly illuminated ring" (Souther, n.d.). She wrote this a decade before Tyson was convicted of several

criminal charges, including the rape of a beauty pageant contestant, and later, the battering of two motorists. After his boxing skills had diminished, Tyson gained greater notoriety by biting the ear of an opponent during a bout. In a news conference Tyson said, "I am an animal. I am a convicted rapist, a hell-raiser, a loving father, a semi-good husband." Referring to Lennox Lewis, the heavyweight boxing champion, Tyson said, "If he ever tries to intimidate me, I'm gonna put a fu—ing bullet through his fu—ing skull" (Serjeant, 2000). Tyson benefited from the brute image. His boxing matches were "events." Spectators paid thousands of dollars for ringside seats. Tyson became the wealthiest and best known athlete on earth. In his mind, he was a twenty-first century gladiator; to the American public, he was simply a black brute.

Tyson is a violent and emotionally unstable man, but he is more than a one-dimensional brute. He has donated thousands of dollars to civic, educational, and humanitarian organizations. Without media fanfare, he has visited hundreds of hospitalized patients, especially seriously ill and injured children. He is smarter than his public image, and has worked diligently to "deepen" his intellect. Yet, he was marketed, with his permission, as a crude savage. Americans see him as an affirmation of the black brute caricature, and he has, especially in recent years, embraced the stereotype outside the boxing ring. Tyson can no longer distinguish the (Iron Mike) myth from the (vicious criminal) madness, and many white Americans cannot separate Tyson's criminal behavior from his blackness.[17]

The sapphire caricature involves commonly held stereotypes about black women. The sapphire caricature portrays women as "rude, loud, malicious, stubborn, and overbearing." Black women through this prism are often portrayed in the media as "tart-tongued and emasculating, one hand on a hip and the other pointing and jabbing (or arms akimbo), violently and rhythmically rocking her head." Black women through these distorted lenses are said to be "mean-spirited and abusive." Black men usually bear the brunt of their hostilities, although black women are believed to always have "venom for anyone who insults or disrespects her." The generic black woman always complains and is always bitter and unhappy. "The Sapphire Caricature is a harsh portrayal of African American women, but it is more than that; it is a social control mechanism that is employed to punish black women who violate the societal norms that encourage them to be passive, servile, non-threatening, and unseen."[18]

First Lady Michelle Obama is often characterized by the media in terms of the sapphire caricature, particularly by members of the media who are ideologically worlds apart from her husband's administration. There is evidence of the sapphire caricature in the world of women's sports too. One need only reflect back on the media coverage surrounding tennis great Serena Williams. Chris Chase, a writer for *USA Today*, describes a confrontation between Williams and a line judge during a U.S. Open match in 2009, as well as other events occurring between 2009 and 2012. He writes, "In the past three years, Serena Williams has threatened to shove a ball down a lineswoman's throat and threatened a chair umpire during major matches at the U.S. Open." Reflecting a recent string of victories and "recent wave of good will," Chase contends that Williams should use the opportunity to apologize for her behavior in the past, but adds that anyone who knows Williams knows that she will never do that. Chase notes that Williams has had a number of opportunities to apologize, but has not. When asked about the 2009 incident involving Shino Tsurubuchi, Williams remained unapologetic. Not satisfied by her explanation that she was "stressed" and "angry" or her repeated claims that a foot fault had not occurred, as indicated by Tsurubuchi, he writes, "What Serena fails to mention—what she always fails to mention—is that no one criticized her for questioning the foot fault call. They criticized her for threatening to shove the [expletive] ball down the lineswoman's [expletive] throat."[19]

Adam Goldberg filed an article with the *Huffington Post*, writing about a fine Serena Williams received in 2011. The matter was described as "verbal abuse" of the chair umpire. Goldberg and other media outlets lament how Williams's "outbursts" overshadowed the winner of the match, Australian Samantha Stosur.[20]

Ann Killion, writing in *Sports Illustrated*, observes that outbursts are not new in the world of sports and describes some of the outbursts she has witnessed, including the head butting of opponents, spitting on opponents and officials, and "tackling aged bench coaches." She observes that Serena Williams's encounter with the lineswoman in 2009 does not really compare to the actions of some other elite athletes, but less attention is devoted to those actions. Killion attributes the double standard to gender. We are more accustomed to witnessing such actions by male athletes than female athletes, due in large part to the lack of attention paid to women's sports relative to men's sports. The writer does not address the role of race, as if race is neutral in this case, but it is apparent that it is not only the fact that Williams is female that the reaction to her was so visceral, but also the fact that she is black, and dominant in a sport where blacks have historically been underrepresented. And yet Killion goes on to say that Serena "came off last weekend as unhinged as Mike Tyson."

To equate Serena Williams with the popular image of Mike Tyson is a far stretch, but is in keeping with the sapphire caricature. Killion summarizes the relationship between sports reporters who cover tennis and Serena Williams this way: "They don't much like Williams, never really have. The muckety-mucks don't think she's properly respectful of the sport. The tennis media thinks she's a phony and condescending."

Killion looks at Williams's actions in this case in the context of what she calls tennis's current "Golden Age of Sportsmanship," in contrast to previous eras that featured regular outbursts and tantrums. A host of nonblack players are cited as embodying the preferred cultural norms for the tennis world:

> Roger Federer is inordinately gracious—well, except for hating on the replay system and cursing the chair umpire in his loss to Juan Martin del Potroon Monday. Rafael Nadal is usually all class. So maybe the way Williams behaved reverberates more loudly these days, especially when she's playing as popular and lovable an opponent as Kim Clijsters.
>
> Maybe Serena's era was really a quarter century ago, when McEnroe and Connors and Nastase were roaming the court. When tennis champions routinely acted like boorish fools.[21]

Federer is still consider "gracious" despite cursing a chair umpire, while Serena Williams's career appears to be forever tainted by the stain of her reaction to calls she determined were unjust. Clijster is described as "loveable" and "popular," words that are not often used to describe Williams, despite her long list of accomplishments on grass and clay courts. Few, if any, black female athletes are referred to as "lovable" or even "popular." In the same year Cheryl Miller won an Olympic gold medal, Mary Lou Retton also won a gold medal. Retton, a petite white gymnast, graced the cover of the Wheaties box, but Miller, a lanky black woman, did not. Race messages are all around us, even on our breakfast tables.[22]

With regard to Serena Williams, much has been made of her body. In fact, Williams's features were mocked by a fellow tennis player, Caroline Wozniacki. Wozniacki, The Root reports, "stuffed her tennis outfit with padding in what many are interpreting as an imitation of Serena Williams' body, and 'made many in the audience laugh as she swung her tennis racket while displaying her fake assets.'"[23] While some, including Williams, have defended the Danish athlete, others argue that it was reminiscent of long-held stereotypes of black women throughout American history. Wozniacki's poor impersonation of Williams reminded many of another

caricature, the Jezebel caricature, intended to mock women of African ancestry. "The Jezebel images which defame African women may," according to
David Pilgrim of the Jim Crow Museum, "be viewed in two broad categories:
pathetic others and *exotic others*. Pathetic others include those depictions of
African women as physically unattractive, unintelligent, and uncivilized.
These images suggest that African women in particular and black women in
general possess aberrant physical, social, and cultural traits. The African
woman's features are distorted." This description clearly reflects the image
that Wozniacki set forth of Williams, which the media then represented and
reproduced, asking whether Wozniacki was just having fun or being racist.[24]

Conclusion

The relationship between the media and sports is important and has
evolved over time. The media are dependent on sports for their success
and profitability, and sports are dependent on the media for the same reasons. Neither can operate in a vacuum. Both institutions shape, and are
shaped, by racial ideology, and as such they serve as important agents of
racial socialization. The mass media communicate the rules of society for
athletes, spectators, coaches, owners, and so on. Media representations—
and misrepresentations—of blackness impact sports participation and
often lead to the identification of sports as either white sports or black
sports. The dominant racial ideology is maintained and perpetuated
through this process of racialization, and societal changes—such as population and economic changes—can lead to manifestations of racism at the
individual and institutional levels. Black athletes tend to be treated unfairly
in the media, and the values of fairness, justice, and equality are not always
applied to black athletes in the manner they are applied to white athletes.
The same may be said of blacks and whites as a whole.

In the next few chapters, the process by which certain sports come to be
associated with blacks and others with whites is explored in greater detail.
The process of racial socialization and manifestations of racism—both
covert and overt—in some of the nation's most popular sports is explored
at various levels including professional, collegiate, and amateur. We now
turn our attention to the role of racial socialization in participation in
American football, as well as the manner in which racism is manifested,
and to the variance between what we say we value and how we act at the
individual and institutional levels.

Chapter 4

Race Thinking and Minority Athletes in Football

Few events can, year after year, captivate the attention of millions of Americans from all walks of life. Super Bowl Sunday is such an event. According to *Los Angeles Times* writer Chuck Schilken, almost 110 million people tuned in to watch the Baltimore Ravens take on the San Francisco 49ers in the 2013 Super Bowl. New Orleans, the host city, received a nearly $500 million economic boost.[1] Mark Waller of the *Times-Picayune* wrote of the same game that, in all:

> $262.8 million in direct spending by visitors for the 47th Super Bowl, $217.2 million in chain reaction spending from businesses and workers serving the visitors, the temporary creation of 5,672 part-time and full-time jobs bringing $154 million in new income to those workers, $21 million in tax revenue for state government and $13.9 million in tax revenue for local agencies in the New Orleans area.[2]

Clearly, football is big business, and has been that way for some time. As such, football plays a very important role in communicating the ways of society for people with membership in various social groups, including black and white athletes. In this chapter, we examine the racial socialization of black and white athletes as it relates to football. The overrepresentation of blacks and whites in certain positions is among the topics explored. Manifestations of racism, which often increase or decrease as population, economic, political, and even cultural changes take place in the larger society, are also examined. These manifestations of racism and unequal treatment call into question whether the playing field is truly level for black athletes when compared with their white counterparts. Youth, collegiate, and professional sports are considered. This chapter begins with a brief history of the game of football in America.

American Football before the 1960s

American football has its roots in the sport of rugby. Walter Camp is credited with establishing the rules of the game back in 1879. He instituted several key rules that helped distinguish the sport from soccer and rugby. Camp forever changed the game by establishing the line of scrimmage. He called for 11 players instead of 15. He created two positions, quarterback and center. He is also responsible for the forward pass, numerical scoring, and the standardization of scoring. The first football game, predating Camp's rules, was played in the fall of 1869 in New Jersey and featured Princeton and Rutgers. The teams played on a field much larger than the 100-yard football fields of today, with no officials and more than 20 players on each side.

The sport slowly grew in popularity, and other universities, including Columbia, Harvard, and Yale, soon had teams. By 1875, the round, soccer-like ball was replaced by an egg-shaped rugby ball. A judge for each of the teams, and a referee, served as the officials for the contests. In the next year, changes to the goal posts were made, which included elevating it to its present-day height of 10 feet. The number of players per team went from 25 to 15.

After Camp's revisions to the sport, especially "the first-down rule of 1882," which required the marking of yard lines on the fields and led to the term gridiron. It also inspired the first planned play strategy and verbal signals. With these changes the game spread more rapidly, and some 250 colleges were participating by the beginning of the twentieth-century.[3]

The game of football certainly had its critics. The game was brutal and resulted in a number of deaths and injuries. By the early 1900s, some institutions bowed to public pressure and banned football on their campuses. Over time the game became safer with the inclusion of a number of safety measures and improved protective equipment.

Football, although enjoyed by many, was largely segregated during the first few decades of the twentieth century. The National Football League (NFL) was established in 1920, and like most leagues at that time, was not open to black players and remained that way for many decades to come.

The 1920s were an important time in the history of race relations in America. Around this time, immigration was cut off from areas of Europe that were considered undesirable, including southern, eastern, and central Europe, which had over the preceding decades sent millions to urban areas. The 1920s was also a time when blacks were moving en masse from the southern to the northern states to seek employment opportunities in factories that were once off limits to them, and to seek a better quality of life, free from the threats that came with living in the Deep South at this time. This period was also marked by a booming intellectual renaissance that saw the emergence of a class of black thinkers and artists, many of whom offered scathing critiques of American idealism and realism. It was a time characterized by profound changes that had an impact on race relations in general and race and sports in particular. The 1920s saw some of the worst race riots in American history—such as the Tulsa Race Riots—while institutions and organizations like the NFL drew the color line and worked to maintain its existence at all costs. George Marshall, owner of the Washington Redskins, led the movement, which resulted in an absence of black players in the league from 1933 until 1946.

Black players did, however, excel on college football teams—although in very small numbers. The presence of a small number of black players on a college football team was not seen as a threat to the sport or to the larger dominant racial ideology. Jackie Robinson, who would go on to integrate Major League Baseball, was an extraordinary athlete at UCLA, along with teammates Woody Strode and Kenny Washington. Strode and Washington would go on to break barriers of their own in the game of football. Like Robinson, Strode and Washington faced a great deal of racial discrimination from fans, opponents, and even teammates, but during their three seasons in the game, they never experienced the kind of success that Robinson attained. They did, however, pave the way for other black players in the sport. By the early 1960s, each team in the NFL had at least one black player.

American Football after the 1960s

Although the overt policy of limiting the number of black players per team was eventually eliminated, unequal treatment in football based upon race was still a factor. On both the professional and college levels, some areas of the game integrated more rapidly than others. R. T. Bowen remarked in a 1982 article that it was not until 1969 that the colleges in the Southern Conference permitted black players. The conference was made up of elite college football programs in Louisiana, Kentucky, Tennessee, Alabama, Georgia, Mississippi, and Florida. The schools were motivated primarily by a desire to remain competitive on the national stage, not necessarily because of a larger commitment to integration or broader social justice issues.

A decade later, the conference saw increases in the numbers of black players. The changes in this "last bastion of segregated college sports" were part of a larger trend taking hold in the world of sports.[4] For instance, the number of black quarterbacks in the NFL was on the rise.

It is not a coincidence that the number of black players—even in the most hostile environments—increased after the 1960s. The 1960s saw the greatest period of social change in modern history with the civil rights movement. The civil rights movement directly called into question the gap between American idealism and realism in all areas of sports, and black athletes like Bill Russell, Jim Brown, and Muhammad Ali were at the center of the battle. Black athletes during the civil rights and black liberation movements often used their celebrity status to draw attention to their own plights but also to the plight of blacks as a whole.

William Rhoden writes about the fact that athletes of this era understood that they had a mission that extended far beyond the athletic venue. The goal was to seek justice, fairness, and equality for a group of Americans that had historically been treated as property and then as second-class citizens.[5] The victories associated with the civil rights movement and the consciousness-raising of the black liberation movement led to the legislative destruction of racial barriers—even if actual racial progress was slow, stagnant, or in some cases, regressive.

While teams were welcoming more black players, the positions at which these players could excel were limited, and their opportunity to hold authority positions both on and off the field was also limited. The segregation into certain positions is called stacking. A number of studies have documented the presence of stacking. Stacking is "the disproportional allocation of persons to central and non-central positions on the basis of race and ethnicity."[6] Stacking is the result of larger racial and ethnic stratification patterns in society that base the ranking of individuals and groups upon physical and/or cultural characteristics such as skin color, language, or country of origin. Just as racial and ethnic classifications have social meanings, positions on the football field also have social meaning. Some positions are associated with qualities and characteristics that society has historically claimed are attributable to certain racial and ethnic groups due to either innate abilities or environmental facts. Perceptions about which racial groups were better suited for various positions have been evidenced in a number of ways. Murrell and Curtis conducted content analyses to determine how media outlets treat black and white quarterbacks in the NFL. They compared news coverage of three black quarterbacks and

TABLE 4.1   Percentages of Football Players in Selected Positions by Race: 1990–2010

Position	% White 1990	% Black 1990	% White 2000	% Black 2000	% White 2010	% Black 2010
Offense						
Quarterback	92	8	78	21	83	16
Running Back	7	90	13	86	12	86
Wide Receiver	14	86	10	90	15	84
Tight End	49	51	56	41	54	43
Offensive Tackle	51	46	48	30	51	48
Offensive Guard	64	48	32	50	51	43
Center	87	13	70	25	87	9
Defense						
Cornerback	4	96	7	93	2	98
Safety	17	83	13	87	15	84
Linebacker	31	66	22	76	26	71
Defensive End	28	72	25	73	21	76

Source: Table created by the author using data from: Lapchick, R., Costa, P., Sherod, T., and Anjorin, R. (2012). *The 2012 Racial and Gender Report Card: National Football League.* http://www.tidesport.org/RGRC/2012/2012_NFL_RGRC.pdf (accessed June 24, 2014).

three white quarterbacks and found that the successful performance of black quarterbacks was attributed their natural abilities, while the successful performance of white quarterbacks was due to hard work, a strong work ethic. The media play an important role as an agent of socialization in football in that the "media not only report but also project images and convey evaluations"[7] (see Table 4.1).

Black Collegiate Players and the Navigation of Athletic and Academic Identities

Racial socialization in sports impacts players in a number of other ways including identity formation and the perpetuation of race, gender, and social class inequality. Research has shown that for some black athletes, including football players, success in sports and academic excellence seem incompatible. Black players often demonstrate difficulties navigating between their athletic and academic identities. The low graduation rate of black male athletes is one example. A host of factors contribute to how black athletes see themselves, including during the recruitment visit when the player's role on campus is presented (see Table 4.2).

Black male athletes in high-revenue-generating sports like football quickly come to realize the significance of their sport in generating television and radio contracts, ticket sales, corporate sponsors, donations, and enrollment. They quickly learn that athletics is big business. In 2003, the Big Ten Conference invested $500,000 in the recruitment of student-athletes.

Black football players, research shows, have a substantially lower graduation rate than their white counterparts. This may show that white players not only may be better prepared than their black counterparts for college, they may also be under less pressure to perform, and they may see their athletic and academic identities as more closely tied than their black counterparts. Evidence of this can be found in the six-year graduation rates for black and white football players. Less than half, or 49 percent, of black football players graduated in six years compared to 61 percent of white players in 2005.[8] These data show the tragedy of sports participation for black athletes who, as a result of not receiving equal access to educational resources, are often ill-prepared, or at the very least, less prepared than many of their white counterparts. Yet explanations for the graduate gap often point to deficiencies with the player rather than the system that produced the inequality to begin with.

More recent data are available for graduation success rates for the 70 teams in the 2012–13 NCAA Football Bowl Subdivisions (FBS) bowl

TABLE 4.2   Graduation Rates at Selected Schools for Black Male Student-Athletes

Rank	University	Grad Rate Across Four Cohorts
1	Iowa State University	30
2	University of South Florida	31
2	University of Arizona	31
2	University of Arkansas	31
5	Florida State University	34
5	University of Florida	34
7	Indiana University	36
7	Arizona State University	36
7	Mississippi State University	36
10	University of Minnesota	37

Source: Harper, S. R., Williams, C. D., and Blackman, H. W. (2013). *Black Male Student-Athletes and Racial Inequities in NCAA Division I College Sports*. Philadelphia: University of Pennsylvania, Center for the Study of Race and Equity in Education.

games, and it further highlights how unlevel the playing field is and how disadvantaged black football players are relative their white counterparts. The results showed that 7 percent of the teams graduated at least 90 percent of black football student-athletes, compared to 24 percent of teams graduating that many white football student-athletes. Only one school, University of Georgia, had identical graduation rates for black and white football student-athletes at 69 percent, which was 11 points lower than the graduation rate at the institution for all student-athletes. The results also revealed that black football student-athletes had higher graduation rates than white football student-athletes at only 2 of the 70 schools, Notre Dame and San Jose State. Ninety-seven percent of black football student-athletes graduated at Notre Dame compared to 93 percent of white football student-athletes. At San Jose State, the graduation success rate was 56 percent for black football student-athletes compared to 45 percent of white football student-athletes.

In nearly one-fifth of the teams, less than half of black football student-athletes graduated. There were no teams with a graduation success rate lower than 50 percent for white football student-athletes. The gap between black and white football student-athletes in graduation rates was more than 20 points on some teams. In fact, 38 of the 70 teams reported racial disparities in excess of 20 points, which represents more than half of all teams. Over 20 percent experienced a gap of more than 30 points. In fact, two schools, Iowa State and Ohio University, had graduation success rates that were more than 40 points apart. The graduation success rate for black football student-athletes at Iowa State was 45 percent; for white football student-athletes it was 88 percent. At Ohio University, the graduation rate for black football student-athletes was 56 percent, and 97 percent for white football student-athletes.[9]

Other key findings from the report *Keeping Score When It Counts: Assessing the 2012–2013 Bowl-Bound College Football Teams' Graduation Rates* include the finding that the academic success of student-athletes increased over the past year, but that the gap among some schools, as shown previously, is disturbing. The authors of the report point out that the NCAA created a measure that the study uses to hold "each team accountable for the success of student-athletes in the classroom and their progression towards graduation. Individual teams are penalized if they fall below an APR score of 925, which is an expected graduation rate of 50 percent of its student-athletes." Louisville and Louisiana at Monroe have scores that do not meet the minimum standard and will likely face penalties.[10]

A report from the University of Pennsylvania, *Black Male Student-Athletes and Racial Disparities in NCAA Division I College Sports*, is also quite alarming, particularly where graduation rates are concerned. The schools with the lowest black male student-athlete graduation rates include Iowa State University, University of South Florida, University of Arizona, University of Arkansas, Florida State University, University of Florida, Indiana University, Arizona State University, Mississippi State University, and University of Minnesota.

Northwestern University and University of Notre Dame, on the other hand, had the highest black male student-athlete graduation rates at 83 percent and 81 percent, respectively. The report also looks at the overrepresentation of black male student-athletes when compared with black males in the undergraduate student body by conference in revenue-generating sports, like basketball and football. Although distinctions are not made for football and basketball separately, the findings are worth reporting here.

The report includes recent data for the Atlantic Coast, Big East, Big Ten, Big 12, Pac 12, and Southeastern conferences. Of the 12 schools in the Atlantic Coast Conference, 1 institution had a graduation rate below 50 percent. Boston College had a graduation rate of only 45 percent for black male athletes in basketball and football. Duke University had a graduation rate of 50.3 percent. University of Miami and Florida State University had the highest graduation rates at 75.7 percent and 75.4 percent, respectively. Black male student-athletes in this conference did not do as well as all student-athletes, nor did they do better than black male students overall.

Three of the 16 schools in the Big East Conference reported graduation rates for black male student-athletes in revenue-generating sports that were below 50 percent. The graduation rate for black male student-athletes was 49 percent at Georgetown University, 45.6 percent at University of Notre Dame, and 43 percent at St. Johns University in New York. Given the numbers presented in the report on bowl-bound teams, it can be shown that black male student-athletes at University of Notre Dame on the basketball team are not faring nearly as well as similar athletes on the football team.

The Big Ten reported some of the poorest graduation rates for black student-athletes in revenue-generating sports. Less than 40 percent of black male student-athletes in football and basketball graduated from University of Iowa and Northwestern University. Less than half of such athletes at University of Wisconsin gradated. Graduation rates were lower for black male student-athletes in football and basketball than for all student-athletes. Black male student-athletes in football and basketball had lower graduation rates than all black male undergraduates at most institutions, except at University of Iowa, University of Nebraska, and Pennsylvania State University.

The Big 12 conference did not have any institutions graduating less than half of black male student-athletes in football and basketball, although Kansas State University barely made the cut with 50.8 percent of black male student-athletes in revenue-generating sports graduating. Graduation rates were lower for black male student-athletes when compared with all student-athletes at each of the institutions with the exception of Texas Christian University, where there was a 0 percent difference. It should be noted that there was just a 1 percent difference between black male-student athletes at Texas Tech University and all student-athletes. Black male athletes in this conference had lower graduation rates than all black male undergraduates at Baylor, Iowa State, University of Kansas, University of Oklahoma, and University of Texas, but higher graduation rates than all black men at Kansas State University, Oklahoma State University, Texas Christian University, and West Virginia University. These disparities point to unjust and unequal attention and treatment that black athletes receive relative to whites, not just at the college level. These numbers also reflect the cumulative disadvantage that black athletes, and blacks as a group, face when compared with whites in terms of educational opportunities.

Black male student-athletes in the Pac 12 had relatively lower graduation rates, with none of the institutions graduating more than 56.2 percent of black male student-athletes on the basketball and football teams. This conference is the only one in the study to hold this dubious distinction. About a third of such players graduated at the University of Utah. About 35 percent graduated from Stanford University, and the graduation rate for Washington State University was 40.2 percent. University of South Carolina had the highest graduation rate for black male student-athletes in basketball and football. For the most part, the difference in graduation rates for black male student-athletes relative to all student-athletes was in, or near, the double digits. Black male student-athletes fared better than all black males where graduation rates were concerned at 4 of the 12 institutions: Arizona State University, University of Oregon, Washington State University, and Oregon State University.

As noted previously, the Southeastern Conference was the last to integrate college football, but some of the institutions are doing much better than schools in conferences that integrated earlier. Vanderbilt University had the lowest percentage of basketball and football team graduation rates at 43.3 percent, while University of Mississippi and Mississippi State University had graduation rates for this population that were just shy of 80 percent. Black male student-athletes, in general, had lower graduation rates than all student-athletes at each of the institutions, with the exception of Vanderbilt University, where graduation percentages were 74 percent for both populations. Black male student-athletes had higher graduation rates than all black undergraduate men at University of Alabama, University of Mississippi, and University of Tennessee. Graduation rates were the same for black male student-athletes and all black male undergraduates at Auburn University.[11]

Tomika Ferguson outlines an identity progression model that explains how black athletes develop a sense of self. This involves a preencounter, a salient encounter, and identity congruence. The impact of being a student-athlete can be beneficial or detrimental.[12] Kwame Agyemang and colleagues echo these sentiments in a pilot study involving four black male athletes at a predominantly white institution.[13] They place the pilot study between two points of contention in the literature on race and sports. From the functionalist perspective, participation in sports for black male athletes at these institutions can best be understood as beneficial and wholesome. On the other hand, in the tradition of conflict theories such as that of Harry Edwards, Agyemang and colleagues assert that the best way to understand the experiences of black male athletes at historically white institutions is as "exploited and ripped off and dumped once their eligibility has expired." Although preliminary, the scholars found that psychosocial detriments exceeded psychosocial benefits.[14]

This revelation is evidenced not only among athletes but also in other areas of the sports-industrial complex at the collegiate level. In addition to the issues of stacking players and coaches into limited positions, and barring individuals from high-level front-office positions, scholars have written about the connection between social capital, race, and promotion, particularly as it relates to coaches; however, these findings may also apply to promotions in other positions within the industry. Jacob Day and Steve McDonald conducted a study involving 320 assistant college football coaches and found that social capital, or resources embedded in networks, matter and that it varies by social groups. Social capital is more important for white males than for others. They also found that since many occupations remain highly segregated, "race and social capital play important roles in the promotion process, particularly in a highly segregated occupation such as college football coaching."[15] Assistant college coaches benefited most from having access to a lot of individuals who could provide career help, and white assistant coaches tended to have more ties. Moreover, the study showed that it was not enough for black coaches to simply have contacts, but black coaches with different-race contacts fared better than black coaches with same-race contacts. It is easy to see how the problem persists, as black coaches have historically been, and often still are, excluded from white networks. The exclusion of black coaches from these key networks limits their access to these positions, but it also segments within the larger white imagination that coaching is an occupation where whites excel and blacks do not, and that this is based upon merit rather than a restricted set of networks that exclude blacks.

Why do such seemingly archaic views about race persist in America? How can a nation with a black president have an unlevel playing field in any area of social life, but especially in an area that appears to be the athletic equivalent of the Horatio Alger myth, the idea that anyone can make it in America, if they try hard enough?

Writing about the death of Joe Paterno, David J. Leonard discusses a fear among some in the dominant racial group of a loss of white masculinity. Paterno, despite the horrific sex scandal involving his assistant coach, Jerry Sandusky, was represented in the media, especially in death, as the "embodiment of the underprivileged white masculine body that in the end contributed to the criticism and demonization he experienced in life and death." He was, says Leonard, considered the exact opposite of what many Americans see as "trash-taking, spit hurling, head-butting sports millionaires." Leonard says Paterno allowed members of the dominant group to go back to a time in America's history when sports heroes were white males. "He is constructed as a clear alternative to black athletes who are routinely depicted in the popular press as selfish, insufferable, and morally reprehensible."[16]

A study conducted some 20 years before Leonard's piece provides some insight as to how sport and people associated with it help to perpetuate inequalities based upon race, gender, and social class. Douglas E. Foley, conducting an ethnographic study of a small South Texas town, explored community sport as a potential site for counterhegemonic cultural practices. He specifically examined how football socializes future generations of youth. While some see sport as an ideal place to challenge inequality, Foley makes the case that even high school football reproduces race, class, and gender inequality. White ruling class ideology and patriarchy are maintained, even when disadvantaged groups seek to resist. In fact, sports are a less progressive site for challenging the status quo than critical sport theories may suggest.

Foley unequivocally describes sports as a socialization process. He asserts that sports take place within a historical community that has a social structure, or established pattern, which should be the focus, and not merely a group of people participating in a given sport. Using reproduction and resistance perspectives, Foley examines how messages of race, class, and gender are communicated through the medium of football through rituals, rites, and ceremonies that symbolically stage class, gender, and racial inequality. Foley concludes that there is a need to understand sports within a historical context, along with the significance of structural dominance. Football is, after all, according to Foley, "still central to the socialization of each new generation of youth and to the maintenance of the adolescent society's status system. In addition this ritual is also central to the preservation of the community's adult status hierarchy."[17]

Racial Inequality in and around the Gridiron in the NFL

Racial socialization impacts not only impacts players but also other areas of the game. Sports, as agents of socialization, communicate what is expected of individuals in society based upon their racial group. Social meaning is attached to certain racial groups, and the adoption and internalization of such messages may lead to discriminatory treatment toward racial and ethnic minority groups, including stacking players in certain positions, or stacking coaches and imposing a color line and/or glass ceiling on the sideline, courtside, or in the front office.

Paul Kooistra and colleagues described how this occurred by examining racial equality within the labor market of professional football. The researchers distinguished between protected and marginal players and suspected that discrimination was greatest among nonwhite marginal players and marginal white players. They contended that marginal players were more likely to be white because a quota exists for nonwhite players, which led to discrimination by race. The researchers also argued that racial composition of the community was related to the racial composition of a given team because teams rely on the interest of fans. "Consequently, there may be subtle pressures to favor placing white players on rosters with whom the dominant white audience would identify that potential source of discrimination, together with a continuation of other long-standing patterns of structural discrimination . . . plus personal prejudices, may lead to racial discrimination in professional sports."[18]

Kooistra acknowledges potential critics who might claim that football has all the structures in place to ensure that it is more racially neutral than most sports. For one, because players wear heavy equipment, it may difficult to identify the race of any given player. Also, football has a longer history of integration than some other sports, and it is highly visible and therefore open for much media scrutiny. Moreover, some might say that everyone associated with a given team, regardless of their respective roles, has a shared goal: to win. Despite these arguments, Kooistra maintains that evidence of racism in the game persists. One need only look at the under-representation of blacks in management positions and other positions that are said to "require leadership qualities, emotional stability, and greater responsibility," qualities that the historic narrative about blacks claims are characteristics that blacks simply do not possess.[19]

Data from *The 2012 Racial and Gender Report Card: National Football League* showed that 67 percent of players in 2011 were black, 31 percent were white, 2 percent were Asian, 1 percent were Latino, 1 percent were other, and 1 percent were international. About a decade earlier, in 1999, percentages of blacks and whites playing in the NFL were about the same. In 1990, 61 percent of players were black and 39 percent were white. In 2012, by contrast, 74 percent of individuals employed in management were white and 8 percent were black. In that same year, 9 percent of individuals in management were Asian, 5 percent were Latino, and 3 percent identified as other. In 2000, 77 percent of management employees were white, 14 percent were black, less than 3 percent were Latino, and 7 percent were Asian. Management clearly does not reflect the racial composition of the players. An examination of the data for the majority owners looks much worse. Between 1997 and 2011, 100 percent of the majority owners were white. Of the 32 majority owners in the NFL in 2012, only 1, representing 3 percent of the majority owners, was nonwhite and identified as Asian.

The number of black head coaches in the NFL has increased over time. However, the increase has been slow and not reflective of the racial composition of the players. In 2012, 16 percent of head coaches in the NFL were black, compared to 81 percent white. In 2000, just 10 percent of head coaches were black. In 1990, there was a single black head coach, representing 4 percent of all NFL head coaches. The report lists the names of only 18 black individuals to ever serve as a head coach in the NFL, and in some cases the coaches served as interims. The list includes Art Shell, Tony

Dungy, Herman Edwards, Lovie Smith, Jim Caldwell, Mike Tomlin, and Dennis Green, who had some of the best records with teams like the L.A. Raiders, Indianapolis Colts, Chicago Bears, and the Minnesota Vikings.

Moreover, research shows that black assistant coaches comprised about one-third of all assistant coaches in the NFL in 2011. While 67 percent of assistant coaches were white, 32 percent were black. A decade earlier, only 28 percent of assistant coaches were black and 71 percent were white. In 1991, 54 of the 343 assistant coaches were black, which amounts to 16 percent of all assistant coaches, while 84 percent were white.[20]

Although there has been an increase in the proportion of assistant coaches in the NFL who are black, there remains a great racial disparity. This disparity has led some to call for a "move beyond examinations on average rates of promotion to focus on how structural differences in the labor market interact with race and social capital to reproduce racial inequality."[21] One consequence is that coaches, like black players, may get stacked into positions that do not lend themselves to mobility within the league.

Stereotypes about blacks, communicated through the process of racial socialization at all levels of society, impact the access of minorities to jobs with significant levels of authority. Jomills Henry Braddock and colleagues examined the 2000–2006 football seasons and the influence of race on assignments to coach-central positions, appointments as offensive or defensive coordinators, and the hiring of head coaches. Researchers found that race has direct and indirect effects on managerial authority in the NFL. Research has also shown that the same challenges that blacks face in corporate America are evident in professional football. As in corporate America, blacks in the NFL have racialized job functions, limited access to job authority, and receive less return for their investments in education and work-related experiences; blacks thus face structural barriers to attaining high-level positions.[22]

One need only look at the racial composition of the CEOs and presidents in the NFL between 1997 and 2012. In each of these seasons, 100 percent of individuals in these positions have been white. General managers and directors of player personnel were also more likely to be white than any other race or ethnicity over the past few decades. In 2012, 81 percent of individuals in this position were white compared to 19 percent black. In 2001, 94 percent in these positions were white while 2, or 6 percent, of the 64 general managers and directors of player personnel were black. In the earliest decade for which data are provided here, which is 1993, 10 percent of managers/directors were black.

A smaller proportion of blacks rose to the level of vice president in the NFL between 1993 and 2011. In 2011, 92 percent of vice presidents were white, 8 percent black, and 1 percent Latino. In 2001, only 7 percent were black, 92 percent white, and 1 percent Latino. Eight years earlier, 93 percent of vice presidents were white, 7 percent were black, and none were Latino. More than 80 percent of senior administrators from the early 1990s to 2011 were white. During the same time period, 90 percent of individuals employed in the category of "professional teams: administration" were white.

Even the racial composition of team physicians reflects the underrepresentation of blacks in football, particularly in the NFL. In 1992, there were 67 team physicians and only 1 was black. There were no black team physicians at all in 1993–95 and just one in 1996 and in 1997. There were never more than two black physicians between 1993 and 2007. Between 2007 and 2011, the number of black physicians was five or six, and never accounted for more than 5 percent of all physicians. The percentage of Latino physicians never rose above 2 percent between 1993 and 2011. The percentage of Asian physicians ranged from 0 percent to 5 percent during the same time period. The percentages of head trainers who were black has been slightly higher, at least reaching double digits, but very few head trainers were Latino or Asian between 1992 and 2011. Most head trainers, more than 80 percent in most years, were white.

Blacks were even underrepresented among on-field officials in the NFL. In 2013, there were 120 officials. Over 80 percent of officials in 2003 were white, compared to 18 percent black. The first Latino official appears in the data in 2004, and there is no evidence of anyone of Asian ancestry among the officials. The percentage of black officials reached 25 percent in 2009. In that same year, the percentage of white officials is 73. By 2012, 32 officials, representing 26 percent of all officials, were black.[23]

Conclusion

Race has historically played an important role in society, including in the world of sports. Evidence of the historic and continuing significance of race in sport is apparent in a number of ways, including racial disparities in the types of positions blacks and whites play, racial disparities in coaching opportunities, and even racial disparities in graduation rates of college athletes. The exclusion of blacks from the NFL in the early part of the twentieth century impacted participation in the sport, as opportunities to play were limited to only a few spots on predominantly white teams or to very limited spots on teams at historically black colleges and universities. Shifts in the black population from the South to the North, and shifts in the social, political, and cultural American landscape during the1960s, led to the integration of football on a much larger scale even in the Deep South. Despite advancements made in the sport where race relations were concerned, evidence remains of the unjust treatment of blacks relative to whites in the sport, which have served to perpetuate ideas about sports participation by race and the overrepresentation of blacks as athletes in selected positions and the underrepresentation of blacks in key decision-making occupations within the sport. These observable racial differences are reflections of the racial stratification that exists in our society and in the game of football.

In the next chapter, we will look at the process by which black and white athletes come to know what is expected of them in the game of baseball and how those messages are communicated beyond the ball field to the society as a whole. We will explore the manifestations of racism—both covert and overt—that are particularly evident in times of profound social change, such as changes in the population or changes in the economy. Expressions of injustice, inequality, and unfairness in America's favorite pastime are also explored.

Chapter 5

America's Other Favorite Pastime: Baseball

Few sports have been more closely tied to the issue of race relations in America than baseball. One of the most watched sports movies in recent years tells the story of how Jackie Robinson integrated baseball. The release and popularity of the film has caused many to look at the game and ask a number of questions, including where have all the black ballplayers gone? Why are there substantially more blacks playing basketball and football than baseball? One might expect that given the legacy of great black baseball players, including those forever enshrined in the Hall of Fame, baseball would remain a relatively popular sport for blacks and other people of color. Evidence suggests, however, that young athletes are socialized racially when it comes to sports and that baseball is no longer seen as a black sport. Rather, baseball is viewed as a sport dominated by whites and by players of Hispanic origin who may or may not identify themselves as racially black. There is also evidence to suggest that stacking, or the representation of groups in certain positions, by race and ethnicity is not only evident in football but also evident in baseball. Blacks at the college and professional levels may also hit a glass ceiling or glass walls when seeking careers in this industry. Even the value placed upon trading cards for black and white players may be a reflection of the continuing significance of race in the game. Well-known players like Gary Sheffield are among those who argue that race continues to be significant in one of America's most favorite pastimes.

In examining racial socialization in baseball, we begin with a brief history of the game and an exploration of the Negro Baseball League and some of its major players. The integration of modern-day baseball, by Jackie Robinson, is considered, as are the challenges he and others faced. This chapter examines the extent to which race still matters in baseball, despite claims that we are living in a postracial society. Historic and recent data highlighting the racial and ethnic composition of players, owners, coaches, and front-office staff are also presented, as they provide evidence of the inequality and injustice that has characterized American sports over time. Baseball, unfortunately, is not an exception in this history.

Baseball Prior to the 1940s

Baseball was established in 1839. Abner Doubleday is credited with creating baseball in Cooperstown, New York, but that claim appears to be in dispute:

> Doubleday has often been credited with inventing the game of baseball in 1839 at Cooperstown, New York, now the location of the baseball's Hall of Fame. This claim appears to date from the late nineteenth century, when baseball owners tried to disassociate the game from any connection to the English game of rounders. The assertion that Doubleday invented baseball is almost certainly untrue. Doubleday was not at Cooperstown in 1839; he never referred to the game, much less claimed that he invented it, and his obituary in the *New York Times* did not mention baseball, either.[1]

Despite the controversy, it is clear that baseball was a very popular sport during the first half of the nineteenth century. To set the record straight, a commission was convened to determine precisely when and how the game originated. The Spaulding Commission determined, in a report published in 1907, on the testimony of Abner Graves, an engineer, that the game was invented by Doubleday in the small upstate town of Cooperstown, New York. A man by the name of Alexander Cartwright established the rules in the 1840s that reflect the manner in which the game is played today.[2]

According to the Baseball Hall of Fame, Cartwright was born in New York City in 1820. Considered the "Father of Modern Baseball," Cartwright was a founding member of the first organized baseball club in America. Organized in New York City, the Knickerbocker Base Ball Club of New York City left a lasting impact on the game, as did Cartwright. To his credit, he gave the game "the concept of foul territory, the distance between bases, three-out innings, and the elimination of retiring baserunners by throwing batted baseballs at them."[3]

The myth of Doubleday's contributions to baseball is not the only myth associated with the game. Baseball has long been considered a blue-collar pastime, but this too is a myth. Wendy Donahue, writing in 2005, says golf

and tennis have long been considered white-collar sports, but a closer examination of the first baseball club in New York City highlights the enormous
class divisions that existed at the time the sport was established, and these
class differences endure today. The Knickerbocker Base Ball Club was made
up of nearly 30 men of privilege. The men, who were actually cricket players,
included brokers and merchants. Baseball was very popular, especially in the
Northeast, and during the Civil War people from the North taught
Confederate soldiers in prison camps how to play the game. This helped
spread the love for the game below the Mason-Dixon line. As the number
of new clubs increased, and people were willing to pay to see a game, players
were being recruited and some were even being paid. The shift toward profes-
sionalism in the game had a profound effect, and by 1869 the Cincinnati Red
Stockings, a team made entirely of professionals, played for the first time.

In less than a decade, the National League was established, with William
Hulbert as president, and soon after, the American Baseball Association
was created. The first black player in the major leagues was Moses Fleetwood Walker. He joined the league in 1884. Sidney Gendin offers an in-
depth look into the life and times of Walker. The first black man in the
major leagues was born in 1857, the son of a barrel maker near the town
of Steubenville, Ohio. His father went on to become a physician and sent
Moses and his brother to Oberlin College, where both excelled on the baseball diamond. Although "Fleet" studied physics, Latin, and Greek, he was
much more interested in playing baseball and eventually abandoned his
studies for a career as a professional baseball player.

Walker joined a ball club in Toledo, Ohio, in 1883, which was part of the
American Association. He played catcher. A year later, the National League
accepted the American Association as a co-major league. Fleet was later
joined in the big leagues by his brother, Weldy. Fleet faced racist taunts
by spectators and the press. Like many other blacks, including black athletes, he was often excluded from eating in the company of whites. Fleet
has been described as Jackie Robinson's "accidental predecessor," as the
team he played for became a major league team only after he was on it.[4]

David Zang wrote about Fleet's misfortune after leaving the game.
In 1892, Walker was attacked by a group of white men. He stabbed one
of the men and ultimately faced second-degree murder charges. He claimed
self-defense and was acquitted. He was later charged, according to Zang,
with mail robbery and was sentenced to a year in jail.[5]

Walker was clearly a pioneer in the game of baseball during a time when
many other significant events occurred in the game. According to Ken

Burns's documentary on the sport, the first World Series was held in 1903. Four years later, the first woman to ever play professional baseball, Alta Weiss, took the field. Weiss was a successful pitcher in men's professional baseball from 1907 to 1922. She came from an upper-class family. Her father, a doctor, eventually purchased the team for which his daughter played and renamed it the Weiss All-Stars. Despite her talents, she was always regarded as somewhat of a novelty and used as a promotional gimmick. She went on to graduate from medical school as the only woman in her class. Weiss was not the only woman in the league at the time, according to Robert Elias. There were three other female players, a female umpire, and one female owner. Black women played professionally, dating back to the late 1860s, but not on men's teams.

Ty Cobb, arguably one of the greatest players in the history of baseball, was apparently known as much for his hatred of blacks as for his abilities on the field. Cobb believed that blacks were inferior to whites and took advantage of most opportunities to try and prove his point. He is said to have slapped a black construction worker who admonished him for stepping in some newly laid asphalt. For the assault and battery on Fred Collins, Cobb was found guilty, but received a suspended sentence.

Cobb was said to be a violent man, and much of that violence was directed toward blacks. During the 1909 World Series, Cobb got into a confrontation with George Stansfield, who came to the aid of an elevator operator whom Cobb slapped. Cobb was initially charged with attempted murder. He pled guilty to a lesser offense and settled a civil suit out of court with Stansfield. A few years later, Cobb brutally beat Claude Lueker, a fan of an opposing team, who called him a "half-nigger." This beating led baseball officials to suspend Cobb indefinitely, although his teammates, and others, rallied around him.[6]

Cobb was not the only baseball player who had a problem with blacks in the early part of the twentieth century. The firing of Jimmy Claxton supports this contention. Keith Olbermann describes Claxton as a gifted left-handed pitcher. He played in the Pacific Coast League out of Oakland, California. He was introduced to team officials as "a fellow tribesman" by a Native American fan. The fact of the matter, says Olbermann, was that Claxton was Canadian. He spent his formative years in Tacoma, Washington, son of a white mother and an African-French-Native American father. Once his ancestry became known, he was released.[7]

The 1919 scandal that surrounded the World Series was not the only black eye on the game. The separation of the races in society at large was also evident in professional baseball with the parallel existence of leagues for whites and blacks. In *The Cambridge Companion to Baseball*, Leslie A. Heaphy addresses the rise and fall of the leagues, touching on important moments, and examines life off the field, the roles of black owners, and the move toward integration.[8]

The Negro Leagues

There was no shortage of talent in the Negro leagues. The players were talented and the competition was fierce. While some look upon baseball as the embodiment of a host of American ideals such as democracy, equality, individualism, loyalty, honor, and teamwork, this assumption is flawed, and the history of the Negro leagues provides one of the best examples.

Lori Martin and Hayward Horton chronicle the history of the Negro leagues. Using an overarching framework that draws from critical race theory, colorism, the population and structural change thesis, and the critical demography paradigm, the scholars show that the integration of baseball was not only the historical moment it is recognized as in the media and in academic studies. It was also an event with demographic implications, particularly in rural black communities where blacks owned the local Negro baseball teams and often the facilities where the teams played.[9]

Minnie Forbes, for example, who was recently honored by the Obama administration, is a black female who owned the Detroit Stars team, which she purchased from her uncle, Ted Raspberry. Raspberry was already owner of the Kansas City Monarchs. Other black owners included Abe Manley of the Newark Eagles.

The Negro League Museum describes the league as multilayered with "community teams, college teams, community economics, ownership, wealth consolidation," to name a few attributes.[10] The centrality of racism in American social life, and in the great American pastime of baseball, was particularly evident in the first few decades of the twentieth century.

Although blacks had played baseball since the Civil War, they were not permitted to play against whites. Racism, and racist practices, kept black and white players separated in different leagues. The athletic destinations of players during this time period were determined not purely by performance on the diamond but by the player's skin color.

The official website for the Negro Leagues Baseball Museum reports the presence of some black players on teams with whites in the late 1800s. However, within a few decades, "racism and Jim Crow laws would force them from these teams."[11] By 1920, a league for black players was formally organized. Andrew "Rube" Foster, himself a former player, manager, and owner, was the league's founder. Other leagues included the Southern Negro League, Eastern Colored League, Negro Southern League, American Negro League, East-West League, Negro National League, and Negro American League.

The *Kansas City Advocate*, a historically black newspaper, covered the opening day of the National Negro Baseball League on April 27, 1923. The game featured the Kansas City Monarchs against the American Giants of Chicago. The game was held in a venue formerly known as Association Baseball Park. Opening day was a community affair, the paper reported, with the usual "big auto parade," but this time over 300 automobiles participated, including one carrying Foster and several black police officers. Local elected officials were invited to participate, and for the first time, black umpires were to officiate. "Two of the best known race umpires have been selected to start the season."

Despite the excitement and optimism, it soon become clear that trouble was on the horizon for the league. In fact, the National Negro League and the Eastern Negro League met to discuss the mounting struggles. During the meeting, the leagues discussed a series of financial concerns, which led to, among other things, an agreement to cap salaries. Attendees claimed, "The high salaries, for ball players, the enormous railroad and traveling expenses, the large cost of parks, has been the financial ruin of several cities." After careful deliberation, the leagues adopted a salary limit of $3,000 per month. In an earlier series of disputes, players left teams to join teams in the opposing league. The Negro leagues simply did not have the resources, or access to the human, social, economic, or cultural capital, necessary to compete on equal footing with the white-owned major leagues. The wealth inequality exemplified in the ownership of black-owned teams in the Negro leagues and white-owned teams in the major leagues were indicative of the wealth inequality between blacks and whites in society at large. Impacted players were, under the agreement reached by the leagues, to return to their team of origin or risk expulsion from both leagues for a period of five years.

Not only was there evidence of wealth inequality between some of the owners in the Negro leagues and in the major leagues, there was evidence of income inequality too, which mirrored the income inequality that existed in the society at large between the dominant racial groups of the day. Black players, even the star players, earned much less than their white counterparts. According to John Holway, whites in the major leagues earned $2,000 in 1905. On average, whites in the minor leagues earned $500 compared to $466 for blacks in the minor leagues. In the decades that followed, similar patterns were observed.

Research has shown that although "salaries varied from individual to individual, and teams differed in their methods of pay," player paychecks fluctuated with the economy. "During the 1920s, monthly salaries averaged about $230, but during the Depression of the 1930s they fell to $170." The researchers also found that "the average annual salary was probably about $5,000 to $6,000 in the 1920s and about $7,000 in the 1930s."[12]

Players from the Negro leagues supplemented their incomes by barnstorming, playing exhibitions in small towns throughout the country. In an article for MLB.com, Justice B. Hill describes how unwelcome the players were in hotels and how they were forced to live out of their suitcases or sleep on buses or in the stadiums where they played. Hill describes the motivations behind the willingness of these players to endure exclusion from areas of public accommodation, as well as racial taunts. It was both economical and political.

"Their incentive to barnstorm was for the extra money they earned from exhibition games against whites and other black teams. The games against whites were cash cows, often drawing thousands of fans to these small towns to watch the great Negro League players." The games gave an economic boost not only to the players but also to the towns. "On the meager salaries from the Negro Leagues," wrote Hill, "the players valued the extra pay. They had the added satisfaction of showing fans in these small towns how well blacks played the game." Hill sums up the article with the observation, "Black players had to remain mindful of the color line. Not even money would let them cross it."[13]

The Depression, mismanagement, and the death of Rube Foster have been cited as factors contributing to the decline of the Negro leagues, but few events had an impact like that of the integration of Major League Baseball in the modern era by Jackie Robinson. Luix Overbea wrote on this very subject matter on July 8, 1949, in the paper *Plaindealer*. Overbea described the many empty seats in the stadium where "the Giants, now the hottest team in Negro baseball," played. Across town, over 40,000 people went to see Jackie Robinson and the Brooklyn Dodgers take on the Cubs. "Of this massive crowd, at least one third was Negro." Blacks were cautioned against "killing the goose that lays the golden eggs." Negro baseball was the goose and the players were the golden eggs. Journalists and others sought to remind fans that the whites had refused to recognize black players for many years. One individual is quoted in Overbea's article as having said, "If Negro baseball dies there will be no other means to prepare Negro players for the majors."[14] Perhaps the prediction was right, at least in part, and may help to explain the disappearance of blacks from baseball. Without the Negro leagues, black players had nowhere else to go, and if the major leagues decided to focus recruitment efforts elsewhere, such as internationally, what would become of the black player? Black players and spectators had always hoped for the opportunity to prove that they were just as good as whites, both on and off the field. Racism kept this from happening for many years, and capitalist interests, not the desire to right historic wrongs, were the driving forces behind the integration of baseball.

According to Heaphy, the day Jackie Robinson entered the big leagues marked the beginning of the end for the Negro leagues. Much has been written about Robinson's ascension into the big leagues. Roger Kahn wrote about Robinson's experiences. He describes the cries of "jungle bunny" Robinson endured.[15] Alvin Dark, a player for the New York Giants, was said to have compared Robinson to Adolf Hitler. Just how Robinson came to break the color barrier in professional baseball has been misrepresented, says Kahn. He describes how Branch Rickey, president of the Brooklyn Dodgers, wanted to integrate baseball long before Jackie Robinson came along but faced resistance from the other club presidents. Rickey was aided by the passage of a new law in New York.

This law, the Ives-Quinn bill, was signed on March 12, 1945, in response to pressures from Jewish groups that were facing unequal treatment at various prominent medical schools. The law required fair employment practices, which leaders of the American Jewish Congress and the National Association for the Advancement of Colored People found significant in their ongoing quests for social justice. Rickey was willing to use the new law as leverage to persuade the other club owners to integrate the game. Jackie Robinson was not Rickey's first choice.

According to Kahn, Silvio Garcia was the first choice, but the Cuban-born player was disqualified because he allegedly dodged the Cuban military draft. Don Newcombe was the second choice, but Newcombe was still a teenager and the thinking was he would not be able to withstand all of the prejudice and discrimination that was certain to come his way. Robinson was next on the list. He was asked how he would respond to being a target. He invoked his Christian faith, remarking he would simply turn the other cheek. Robinson was soon presented with a contract and a copy of a book by Giovanni Papini called *Life of Christ.*

Robinson was given the following tasks by Rickey: "As a baseball player, you give it your utmost, and as a man, you give continuing fidelity to your race and to this crucial cause that you symbolize." Robinson also had to agree to play for a year in the minor leagues. He could not hold back the tears after his team won the International League pennant and a mob of whites followed him, not to lynch him but to get his autograph. To Robinson this was a sign of enormous change.

Rickey desired to bring Robinson up to the majors, but some players on the Dodgers signed a petition stating they would not play if he were a teammate. The team manager chastised the signers of the petition and spoke of Robinson's talent and what he could do for the team. He also warned the players that more black players would follow. He admonished them, "Unless you wake up, they're gonna run you right out of the park." Robinson eventually made it to the majors and his team won more than half of the National League pennants and a World Series, the first for the club. However, the integration of baseball occurred incrementally. Robinson would be joined by players such as Roy Campanella, a star in the Negro leagues and the first black catcher in the major leagues, but it would be several years before many clubs would welcome a black player. After Robinson walked away from baseball, he was not offered a position with any team, although his knowledge of the game was well known.[16]

Some Negro league owners resented what they considered to be the abandonment of the league once the doors and windows of opportunity opened in the major leagues. The integration of Major League Baseball was the final nail in the coffin for the storied history of the Negro leagues. Nevertheless, the Negro leagues provided blacks with many opportunities they otherwise would not have enjoyed. The integration of baseball eventually led to a rediscovery of some of America's greatest, yet relatively unknown, baseball players of all times. It would pave the way for other great nonwhite players, like Hank Aaron, who broke Babe Ruth's home run record in 1974, Tsuyoshi Shinjo, the first Japanese player in a World Series (in 2002), and so many others.

Baseball after the 1940s

While racial progress is evident in the game of baseball and in society as a whole, there remains a great deal of evidence that race continues to matter in the sport: Stacking, or the segregation of players into certain positions based upon race, occurs, and people of color are underrepresented in ownership and decision-making positions. Data from *The 2012 Racial and Gender Report Card* by Richard Lapchick show that the percentage of blacks in baseball has decreased over time, while the number of some other nonwhites, like Latinos and international players, has increased. In 1990, 17 percent of players in Major League Baseball were black. About 13 percent were Latino and 70 percent were white. A decade later, 13 percent were black, 26 percent Latino, and 60 percent white. As we ushered in the age of Obama in 2008, the numbers were 10 percent black, 27 percent Latino, 60 percent white, and 2.4 percent Asian, and almost a third of players were international. In the most recent year for which data are available, 2012, blacks had dipped below 10 percent, to 8.8, 27 percent were Latino, 61 percent were white, 1.9 percent Asian, and about 28 percent were international.[17]

There is evidence to suggest that stacking occurs in baseball as in other sports, with nonwhites playing noncentral positions. In baseball, one can think of the pitcher and catcher as central positions. Between 2005 and 2011, the percentage of white pitchers went from 69 to 66 percent while the percentage of black pitchers remained the same, at 3 percent. One-third of pitchers were Latino in 2011, up from 26 percent in 2005. There was a 1 percent decrease where Asian pitchers were concerned. About 3 percent of pitchers were Asian in 2005 and only 2 percent were Asian in 2011.

Most catchers, between 2005 and 2011, were white. In 2005, 62 percent of catchers were white compared to 1 percent black, 36 percent Latino, and 1 percent Asian. By 2011, the percentages of white and black players declined, while the percentages of Latino and Asian catchers increased. Fifty-six percent of catchers were white, 0 percent were black, 40 percent were Latino, and 2 percent were Asian.

There was more diversity in the infielder and outfielder positions between 2005 and 2011. Less than half of infielders and outfielders were white in 2005. By 2011, more than half of players in these positions were white. The percentage of black players was greater among outfielders than infielders. In 2005, 11 percent of infielders were black, but by 2011 that number had decreased to 8 percent. About a quarter of outfielders in both 2001 and 2011 were black. Conversely, the percentages were highest for infielders who were Latino. In 2005, nearly 40 percent of infielders were Latino. About 35 percent of infielders were Latino in 2005. Approximately one-fifth of outfielders in 2005 and 2011 were Latino. Asians made up about 2 percent of infielders and 3 percent of outfielders in 2005 and 2011.

Stacking may be the result of many factors. It may best be understood, as in the case of football, as a result of the social stratification of people by race and ethnicity in the United States. Racial socialization and stacking have been linked. Some contend that there are more costs associated with training for certain positions, such as pitcher, and that given the relative disadvantaged positions of racial and ethnic minority groups, it is not likely they will have the needed resources to train adequately and therefore select other positions on the field. Some young athletes prefer same-race idols, which may help to perpetuate the problem of racial stacking in sports.

Baseball has long been considered a white sport. The desire to keep the sport white is evident in data for positions in and around the field. In 1990, almost 80 percent of central-office personnel were white, 14 percent were black, and 7 percent were Latino. None were Asian. By 2000, 74 percent in this category were white, 14 percent black, 14 percent Latino, 2 percent Asian, and 1 percent Native American. By 2011, the percentage of people of color was nearly 32 percent, but the overwhelming majority of staffers were white.

While the Negro leagues offered blacks opportunities to own amateur and professional teams, ownership by blacks in the major leagues has proven to be much harder. In 2005, 31 of the 32 owners were white. There was one Latino owner in that year. In 2012, 96.4 percent of owners were white, less than 2 percent were black, and one majority owner (1.8 percent of the total) was Latino.

Blacks and other racial and ethnic minorities seem to have problems crashing the glass ceiling where team managers are concerned. For much of the 1990s, nearly 90 percent of managers were white. By 2000, 83 percent were white, 13 percent were black, and 3 percent were Latino. Twelve years later, 83 percent of managers were white and even fewer managers were black. Two of the 30 managers were black, none were Asian, and 3 were Latino.

Between 1993 and 2012, white coaches made up between 69 and 80 percent of all coaches. The percentage of black coaches ranged between 12 and 18 percent. Latino coaches never constituted more than 21 percent, which was substantially higher than in the 1990s, when the percentages of Latino coaches was mostly in the single digits.

Very few people of color served as the CEO/president in professional baseball between 1999 and 2012. In 2004, one black person served in this capacity, but for every other year, 100 percent of the individuals who had the title of CEO/president were white. Likewise, between 1994 and 2012, over 80 percent of general managers/directors of player personnel, senior administrators, team professional administrators, vice presidents, physicians, and head trainers were white.[18]

Racial disparities in pay are a problem throughout society, so it is not surprising that some researchers have uncovered a similar problem in baseball, but recent research suggests improvements in this area. In his book *Raceball: How the Major Leagues Colonized the Black and Latin Game*, Rob Ruck points to the fact that in 2010, 15 of the 20 highest-salaried players in professional baseball were black or Latin. More concerning is another issue Ruck addresses, that of the disappearance of the black baseball player. Ruck observes, "Not too long ago, African-Americans played a much bigger role in baseball. In the mid-1970s, a quarter of all players were black Americans. Today, it's one in 10." His book explores how this happened, a subject matter that other scholars have also tried to address.[19]

The Disappearance of the Black Baseball Player

David Ogden and Randall Rose believe they know how to explain the disappearance of the black baseball player. Based on their research, they contend that structural theory helps explain why baseball is no longer viewed as culturally relevant for blacks in America. The theory addresses how the structural properties of social systems influence, and are influenced by, practices that make up those systems.

Baseball, Odgen and Rose acknowledge, is not, as it was in the past, at the top of the list of leisure activities for blacks today. They suspect that this has not been the case for some 60 years. Back in the day, baseball was big business. The researchers go as far as to say that baseball became the first black national business. Today, basketball is king. To understand the shift we must, say the authors, examine the "process by which individuals and cultures come to embrace some sports while letting go of others." They say there is a "circular interplay between social interactions and the social structures on which individuals draw to produce and reproduce these interactions/sets of situated practices." There are three distinct dimensions of interaction: (1) understandable communication, (2) exercising power, and (3) sanctioning of each other through rules of significance, resources of domination, and rules of legitimation.

Structural theory sees the individual as knowledgeable. At the same time, the individual is not completely aware of the consequences, intended or unintended, of his or her actions. It also sees individuals as encompassed in a web of social structures with varying levels of equality. The following elements mediate each other in helping to mold interaction practices of individuals: (1) economics, (2) peer and family influence, (3) mass-mediated messages, (4) cultural identity, and (5) the general environment. Ogden and Rose speak very little of the role of structural barriers and see racial socialization as a by-product of rather than central to understanding how sports are social constructed and racialized.

Ogden and Rose see the roles of agents of socialization as largely ancillary, as opposed to integral, components of the structural foundation of society, particularly as it relates to racial formation. This is evidenced by the authors' characterization of parents who direct their children toward, and away from, particular sports. Parents, they suggest, "feel that basketball is one of the more important leisure activities for their children and that basketball is a sport that best fits African Americans." The association of blackness with sport is reduced to a feeling as opposed to an outcome based upon a host of complex processes involving various social institutions communicating messages about what it means to have membership in selected races. The authors do, however, acknowledge the role of other agents of racial socialization, what they call other forces, which include peer pressure, schools, and the mass media.

Ogden and Rose go on to assert that basketball can be understood as a form of self-expression, which reproduces the sport as a cultural form, in a way that baseball no longer does. Long gone are the days when baseball "provided structures through which African American culture was celebrated and on which African Americans built routines, found ontological security, and constructed desirable identities." Ogden and Rose's view oversimplifies the complexity of the black community and places baseball at the center of black life for decades. Although baseball was an important part of black life, few would argue that it was the social lynchpin around which all black community life existed, particularly given that it was male dominated and that the relative exclusion of black females must call into question the extent to which baseball held such a prestigious place in the lives of blacks over the course of several decades.

Baseball, at some point in time that is not identified by the authors, "ceased to be embedded in the structure of African American culture," which meant, according to Ogden and Rose, that blacks were faced with trying to understand their place in the world. Throughout American history, it has always been clear where that place was within the white imagination and the white power structure. The presence, or absence, of the Negro leagues was no match for a racialized social structure that was in place before Cartwright ever wrote down one baseball rule, and that has persisted despite the election of the nation's first president of color.[20]

Conclusion

In this chapter, the history of baseball and many of the myths that have surrounded the game, from the game's inventor to the idea that baseball, better than most sports, embodies many core American values, were explored. The rise, fall, and legacy of the Negro leagues were chronicled, along with an account of the declining interest in baseball among blacks. Some believe that integration destroyed the Negro leagues, and an integral part of black culture, while others see the loss of the Negro leagues as inevitable because the consistent message communicated through various agents of socialization, where race and ethnicity are concerned, has been the supposed superiority of whites and the alleged inferiority of nonwhites, especially blacks.

Existing evidence supports this book's claim that institutions such as sports—in this case baseball—play an important role in determining sports participation by members of various races based upon access to the leagues, teams, positions, and occupations both on and off the field. Thus racial socialization—or the process by which we learn the ways of society for blacks and whites—is apparent in baseball and is manifested in the overt and covert ways in which racism is manifested. The unequal treatment of black baseball players during the Jim Crow era and in the so-called postracial era is often highlighted during periods of social change, including changes in population and economic, political, and cultural changes.

In the next chapter, racial socialization and basketball are explored. Again, we will look at the how the process of communicating what is expected of black and white athletes occurs here and how manifestations of racism are expressed as sports and the nation experience various forms of social change.

Chapter 6

The New Plantation?: Racism on the Hardwood

One of the more widely held stereotypes about race and sports is the belief that basketball is a black sport. A surprising number of people believe that blacks are biologically predestined to be good, or even great, at basketball. Great athletes, therefore, are born and not made; this idea of black supremacy in basketball is held by many blacks and whites alike, young and old. Evidence of this assumption can be seen all around us. The film *White Men Can't Jump* brought the issue of black supremacy in basketball to the big screen. In the film, Sidney Deane, played by Wesley Snipes, teamed up with Billy Hoyle (Woody Harrelson) to hustle playground players out of their money. The pair capitalized on commonly held racial stereotypes about the physical superiority of blacks, especially in power performance sports like basketball. Sidney, who was black, would let the players he just defeated select his next teammate in an attempt to prove that he was so good that he could win with anyone. Without hesitation, the defeated players would select Billy, who was white, to team up with Sidney. What the defeated players did not know was that Billy, a former college player, was very good at the game. Sidney and Billy would split their winnings, until they eventually turned on each other.

The overrepresentation of blacks in basketball and the prevailing notion that "white men can't jump" is an issue that has garnered the attention of academics, players, spectators, and general observers of the game. This overrepresentation is due to a number of factors, including the perception on the part of blacks that avenues of upward social mobility for blacks are limited, as well as the reality the blacks are often treated unfairly and unjustly in their interactions with individuals and institutions. Access (or the lack of access) to other sports in neighborhood-based sports programs, and/or the availability of school-based sports programs, are other factors to consider. The high visibility of black male sports role models in basketball relative to other sports is another reason. Data collected by the Institute on Race and Ethnicity point to significance of race in basketball.

Richard Lapchick's research shows that over the past few decades, more than 70 percent of players were black. For example, during the 1989–90 seasons, 75 percent of professional players were black and 25 percent were white. By the mid-1990s, 82 percent of players were black and 18 percent were white. During the 1999–2000 seasons, 78 percent of players were black and less than 1 percent of players were Latino. Over 70 percent of players in the NBA during the 2004–5 seasons were black, 23 percent were white, 2 percent were Latino, and less than 1 percent were Asian. Almost one-fifth of players were from countries other than the United States. Nearly 80 percent of players in the NBA during the 2009–10 seasons were black, 18 percent were white, 3 percent were Latino, 1 percent were Asian, 1 percent identified their race as "other," and 18 percent were international players. In the 2011–12 seasons, 78 percent of players were black, 18 percent were white, 3 percent were Latino, and less than 1 percent were Asian or other. About 17 percent of the league players were international.[1]

More than half of Division I male basketball players between 1991 and 2010 were black. The percentage of white players declined from about 34.5 percent during the 1991–92 seasons to 30.5 percent during the 2009–10 season. On average, about 60 percent of Division I male basketball players during the same time period were black. The percentage of Latino male basketball players in Division I has increased slightly over time. During the 1991–92 seasons, less than 1 percent of players were Latino, but by the 2009–10 seasons, almost 2 percent of players identified as Latino. Less than 1 percent of male basketball players in Division I were American Indian or Asian.

Racial and ethnic differences were also observed in the Women's National Basketball Association and in Division I women's basketball. During the 1999–2000 academic year, almost 54 percent of players where white, 35.7 percent were black, 1.5 percent were Latino, and less than 1 percent of players were Asian or American Indian. By the 2007–8 seasons, blacks comprised half of all women's basketball players at this level. Approximately 43 percent of players were white, 1.3 percent were Latinos, 0.3 percent were American Indians, 1.1 percent were Asians, and almost 4 percent were international players. The percentage of nonwhite players increased between the 2008–9 seasons and the 2009–10 seasons. Only 40 percent of players identified their race as white.[2]

A larger proportion of black women are in the WNBA than in Division I programs. In the year 2000, for example, 65 percent of WNBA players were black, 33 percent were white, and 2 percent were Latina. Five years later, 63 percent of players were black, 34 percent were white, and 1 percent were Latina. About one-fifth of all players were from outside the country. Almost 75 percent of WNBA players in 2012 were black, 16 percent were white, and 9 percent were international athletes.[3]

History of the Game Prior to the 1950s

Basketball has not always had such large numbers of players of African ancestry. The role of segregation and integration in the development of the game, like race relations in America in general, is dynamic. The game of basketball, which is now watched by millions of people across the world, was invented by James Naismith. Naismith, who was born in Canada and was one of four children, overcame a great deal of tragedy in his life. Naismith's parents died when he was just 10 years old, leaving the children orphaned. Naismith and his siblings lived with their grandmother until her death, and then with an uncle.

Naismith grew up to become quite a gifted athlete, excelling in rugby and gymnastics. He also excelled in his studies, graduating from McGill University in Montreal with degrees in philosophy and Hebrew. In an effort to continue his education, Naismith secured employment as the director of physical education at McGill. The job helped pay for his studies in theology at Presbyterian College. He was a frequent visitor to the Young Men's Christian Association (YMCA), taking and teaching classes and competing in sporting activities.

Naismith was asked to come up with a new game and, as they say, the rest is history. Building upon a game he played as a child, Naismith developed a sport that could be played during the cold winter months and that would not interfere with the already established football and baseball seasons. Naismith's childhood game, Duck on a Rock, included the use of peach baskets and a soccer ball. Basketball quickly became popular. The first college game was played in 1897, and today hundreds of millions of people enjoy the game.

Basketball, like baseball and football, was segregated. Kareem Abdul-Jabbar observed that the American Basketball Association, established in 1925, prohibited black players. Blacks played for selected college teams, but they were not permitted in the professional ranks until 1942. As they had done in other sports, blacks created their own opportunities. Few, other than true students of the game, have ever heard of the Black

Fives era. The official website provides a timeline that contains important dates in history. Shortly after Naismith invented the game, St. Phillips Protestant Episcopal Church established a black basketball club called the St. Christopher Club. St. Phillips, one of the most prestigious black churches of the day, was located in the Tenderloin District in New York City. The club served as a religious activity for black men, and grew to include other activities as well.

The center of black basketball in the Northeast, according to Black Fives researchers, was True Reformer's Hall. The Hall, located in Washington, DC, was purchased and managed by blacks in 1903. During that same time, the Colored Branch of Washington, DC, YMCA boasted more than 600 members and occupied True Reformer's Hall.

Researchers at George Washington University describe True Reformer's Hall as a source of great pride for the local black society. Built by a group of blacks calling themselves the United Order of True Reformers, the hall is described as "one of the great symbols of community and its history."[4] The building also housed a tailoring and design school, a drugstore, and the Silver Slipper Club.

Basketball grew in popularity due, in large part, to a black physical education instructor named Edwin Henderson. In 1904, Henderson returned from a class at Harvard University, where he had been introduced to the game. He taught basketball to segregated students in public schools, organizing teams and events. Shortly thereafter, Henderson created the first all-black athletic conference, the Interscholastic Athletic Association (ISAA). Henderson was inducted into the Basketball Hall of Fame in 2013 for his contributions to the game. The Smart Set Athletic Club of Brooklyn and the St. Christopher Club of New York City established the first independent all-black basketball teams. Parallel sports institutions were not uncommon at this time. The exclusion of blacks from white leagues did not deter blacks from competing, but it did severely limit where and when they played.

The Smart Set Athletic Club was comprised of well-educated and affluent blacks from the largely white Stuyvesant Heights section of Brooklyn. Many of the club members belonged to St. Augustine's Protestant Episcopal Church and they played at the Fourteenth Regiment Armory. Members of the club also participated in track and field and tennis. A separate group, called Spartan Girls, was established for black women. "There were as many as 50 or 60 separate African-American basketball clubs in the first 50 years of the 20th century."[5]

The first official basketball game featuring two all-black teams was played in Brooklyn in 1907 and featured the St. Christopher Club and the Marathon Athletic Club. An all-black Olympian Athletic League was established during that same year. The league also included the Alpha Physical Culture Club and the Jersey City Colored YMCA. Fitness was viewed as a way to combat diseases like tuberculosis and pneumonia, which were contributing to relatively high mortality rates for blacks during this period.

A Colored Basketball World's Championship was soon created. The 12 Streeters, part of the Twelfth Street Colored YMCA and made up mostly of Howard University students and alumni, were undefeated in 1909 and were the first champions. A year later, most players left and formed a varsity team, coached by Henderson, which won the Colored Basketball World's Championship. The New York All-Stars, a semiprofessional team, was also created, and its players received payment for playing.

Basketball continued to grow in popularity, especially among blacks. By 1922, "two white sports promoters in Harlem form[ed] the Commonwealth Five, an all-black team playing out of the Commonwealth Sporting Club and Casino, using guaranteed full-year contracts, thus making it the first fully professional African American basketball team." A year later, the Commonwealth Five played the New York Original Celtics, representing the first time a black basketball team played "against a mainstream acknowledged World Champion."[6]

The first black-owned professional basketball team was also established in 1923. Called the New York Renaissance Big Five, it was named after the newly opened Renaissance Ballroom and Casino in Harlem. The team would go on to win the Colored Basketball World's Championship in 1925.

In 1942 four black players—Bill Jones, Case Jones, Al Price, and Shannie Barnett—signed contracts to play for the Toledo White Huts of the National Basketball League (NBL). Later that season, six black players signed with the Chicago Studebakers, also in the NBL. It would be five years before Jackie Robinson famously broke the color line in Major League Baseball.

The National Basketball League was created in 1935 and was the first major professional basketball league in North America. In his book about the league, Murray Nelson describes it as the top professional league in the country for more than a decade. An outgrowth of the Midwest Conference, the NBL had its ups and downs. Like many other American social institutions, the NBL was impacted by global conflicts.

World War I led leagues to close because "the armories that were used for many games were unavailable and the railroads, which served to make these professional player itinerant independent contracts, were national-ized and the access to their lines were somewhat restricted."[7] After World War I, many Americans had more free time and greater economic security, allowing both rich and poor to devote more time to leisure activities such as basketball. The teams often reflected a great sense of community pride. Team names were often based upon the race or ethnicity of the group or the trade with which members of the team were associated. Later, the eco-nomic crisis that would come to be known as the Great Depression had a profound effect on all areas of social life as well, including sports. Teams played fewer games and often played only locally.

Few know that professional games during the 1920s and 1930s were played in cages. Robert Peterson documents these early days of basketball: "At the time, the cage made good sense. Front-row spectators sat even closer to the court than they do today, and Naismith's original rules sad that when the ball went out of bounds, the first player who got to it could throw it back in."[8] Teams in the Northeast were more likely to play in cages, which were replaced with rope netting, but high school, college, and Amateur Athletic Union (AAU) teams never played in cages.

The Harlem Globetrotters were among the teams playing on the barn-storming circuit. Segregation in areas of public accommodation and overall attitudes about the need to keep blacks and whites separate—even in sports —placed constraints on black basketball players even when they played on all-black teams. The Globetrotters organization was founded by Abe Saperstein. Although Saperstein played basketball, he was not considered a stand-out. Nevertheless, he did acquire an all-black basketball team he called Savoy Big Five, which he later changed to the Harlem Globetrotters. The team members showcased their abilities early on, so much so that it became difficult for other teams to compete with them, so many opted not to try. Saperstein decided to add a "fancy, comedic" style to attract opponents. The addition of the now-famous antics of the Harlem Globe-trotters served many purposes. Not only did it add a form of entertainment to the game, it also helped many white Americans to see the all-black team as less of a threat to white spectators and opponents when given the oppor-tunity to play white teams. The team did not appear as a threat to the racial order of society as long as the images of black masculinity did not fall into the same tradition of the stereotypical images of black men as brutes and criminals, such as those seen in the popular 1915 film *Birth of a Nation.*

Involvement in World War II left the league with only a few teams, as many players were off fighting in segregated units. After the war the league flourished again, with not only more teams but, arguably, some of the best professional players. The NBL and its rival league, the Basketball Association of America (BAA), merged to form the National Basketball Association (NBA) in 1949. A year later, Chuck Cooker, Earl Lloyd, Nat Clifton, and Hank DeZonie became the first four black players in the NBA, just a few years after Robinson integrated baseball.

Several years earlier, in 1944, historic changes were taking place on the college hardwood too. In a particularly historic game, the North Carolina College for Negroes faced the Duke School of Medicine. Few contests between blacks and whites took place in the South before the 1960s, Peterson observes. The contest was not advertised, and some speculated that "if the police had found out about the game, they could have winked at it, or made it hard for the players and possibly arrested them. No one really knows."[9]

The inability to predict how law enforcement might respond to the presence of whites and blacks playing against each other in a basketball game speaks volumes to the state of race relations prior to the 1960s. What exactly were the fears? One possible concern was that race riots could break out as virtually every other aspect of social life was segregated by race, reminding whites of their privileged status and blacks of their alleged inferiority. The potential for race mixing, which could lead to violations of miscegenation laws that banned sexual relationships between whites and nonwhites, was another fear. The use of the law and enforcement as forms of social control helped to communicate the ways of society for black and white residents and athletes. Manifestations of racism were noticeably more overt during this time period than in more contemporary times, and so were resistance efforts. The fight for civil rights that involved individuals from many racial and ethnic groups troubled some whites, including some whites in the Deep South. Any opportunities these troubled individuals had to show that they were not embracing what seemed like an unstoppable wave of change were capitalized on, even if those opportunities occurred on the basketball court.

Segregation in basketball was evident at this time in many other places and at many other levels. Steve Fry, writing for the *Topeka-Capital Journal* in 2009, tells of the segregation on basketball teams in Topeka, Kansas, in 1949. Although black and white athletes played football, baseball, and track and field together, basketball at Topeka High School was segregated. White players played on the Trojan basketball team and black players played on the Rambler basketball team. "There were separate cheerleaders for the basketball teams, blacks didn't have equal representation on the student council, separate school parties were held for black couples and white couples, and black students didn't use the school swimming pool," writes Fry.[10]

The Ramblers played against other black teams from area high schools. As they traveled, the team members would find lodging with local black families and eat at churches and school gyms. The black players ate food that was provided by community residents. This remained the norm until three black players were placed on the Trojan junior varsity team in 1950, and the first black player joined the varsity team a year later. According to Fry, no one fully understands why the basketball team was segregated when other teams were not. Calls to integrate the two teams came in 1949 from Dean Smith, a member of the Trojan basketball team who would go on to become a legendary coach of the North Carolina Tarheels. The school principal, Buck Weaver, "worried about the social interaction at the large dances after the game, declined" to integrate the team.[11] Again, the fear of blacks and whites interacting as equals, on or off the court, posed a threat to the racial social order and would challenge the dominant racial ideology, which placed whites in a place of dominance and blacks in a place of subordination. It was important to communicate to blacks and whites their rightful place in society, and sports were as good an opportunity as any other to get that message across.

Basketball after the 1960s

Many point to the historic NCAA tournament game of 1963 between Loyola-Chicago and Mississippi State as "a vehicle to challenge segregation" that "helped to forever change college basketball and civil rights in this country." Mississippi State players had to sneak out of town late at night before Governor Ross Barnett could serve papers that would have prevented the players from playing.[12] Again, there were still great fears about what would happen if blacks and whites played against each other and if black and white spectators interacted socially after the game.

Cheryl Corley of National Public Radio describes college basketball in the early 1960s as predominantly white. Only two or three black players appeared on the court at any one time. By 1964, Loyola started four black players. Jerry Harkness, the Loyola team captain, remembers the hate mail he and other players received, as well as the pressure on the team from the black community, which saw a win for the team as significant for the race.

Black basketball players, like other black athletes before them, were not seen simply as individual athletes with talents that should be on display for the world to see. Rather, they were considered living symbols of the contradictions in America between what we say we value and what we actually value. Every victory for a black athlete was understood as a victory for the entire race over a racialized system of oppression.

Corley describes Governor Barnett as a segregationist who would use whatever power necessary to preserve the racial social order of the day. Barnett saw it as his duty to preserve the forced separation of people based upon physical characteristics, namely skin color.[13]

Evidence of the continuing significance of race in the nation and in basketball is abundant, even in the post–civil rights era. Some scholars assert that "the racial politics of the early 1970s caused the ABA to fold. According to racist logic, professional basketball was drug infested simply because it was too black. The specter of drug abuse within the league was used as evidence of the inherent depravity of the black males who dominated and thus threatened the existence of professional basketball."[14]

The American Basketball Association (ABA) was established in 1967 and had as many as 11 teams. The ABA was the "freewheeling alternative to stodgy NBA."[15] The players wore afros, talked trash, and played a brand of playground basketball that was largely absent from the NBA. The ABA had a 30-second shot clock while the NBA had a 24-second shot clock. The ABA instituted a three-point shot, which the NBA later adopted, and a highly successful dunk contest, which featured Julius "Dr. J" Irving. The NBA played with a red, white, and blue ball, but did not get the same kind of attention as the NBA because they did not have the television contracts that were key to the NBA's prominence.

Nelson George paints a similar portrait of the ABA in his book *Elevating the Game*. The motivation for starting the league, according to George, was to make money, but the league was doomed to fail because it lacked network television network support. It did, however, succeed in creating jobs for black athletes. In George's words, "The idea of riding the ghetto-to-millionariedom express with a brief stop at a university, became central to the sports industry and it was fueled by the pro basketball experience." He adds that during the 1970–71 season, 44 athletes earned at least $100,000, 3 of whom were black. Today's athletes, regardless of their chosen sport, enjoy their multimillion-dollar salaries due to the bidding war sparked by the ABA, a league "dominated by Black athletic aesthetic."[16]

Black Athletic Aesthetic: From Magic to Jordan

Black athletic aesthetic, for Nelson George, is "our music put into physical motion." It is the infusion of "black style" and "improvisation" into the game of basketball, which was personified by Dr. J. in the 1970s, Magic Johnson in the 1980s, and Michael Jordan in the 1990s. These individuals, along with many others, helped save the game. Dr. J's dominance led to the merger of the ABA and NBA, which helped to save a sinking ship. Magic Johnson's rivalry with Larry Bird helped the NBA at a time when it was experiencing legal problems, regular brawls, and bad press related to cocaine use among players. The narrative surrounding Bird was that he was hardworking, dedicated, and team oriented. Bird made people feel nostalgic about the American Dream and the dominance of whiteness and white players, while Johnson's narrative focused on his natural abilities and showmanship. Together, Bird and Johnson were said to have helped cleanse the league. Jordan, according to Nelson George, was viewed as a safe model of black masculinities for the 1990s as he appeared to exemplify good family values off the court and excellence and improvisation on the court.[17]

In his book *Reflecting Black: African-American Cultural Criticism*, Michael Eric Dyson discusses Michael Jordan within a broader context. He says of Jordan, "He has attained unparalleled cultural status because of his extraordinary physical gifts, his marketing as an icon of race-transcending American athletic and moral excellence, and his mastery of a sport that has become the metaphoric center of black cultural imagination." Dyson describes Jordan's impressive career as informative in three key areas: the culture of athletics, expressions of black culture, and commodification in an advanced capitalist system.

Dyson notes that the marginalization of blacks in the world of sports has historically reflected two competing forces, "the presumed lack of sophisticated black cognitive skills and the fear of superior black prowess." More recently, however, "the physical prowess of the black body would be acknowledged and exploited as a supremely fertile zone of profit as mainstream athletic society literally cashed in on the symbolic danger of black sports excellence."

Black athletes like Jordan have "often acquired a social significance that transcended the internal dimensions of game, sport, and skill. Black sport became an arena not only for testing the limits of physical endurance and forms of athletic excellence—while reproducing or repudiating ideals of

American justice, goodness, truth, and beauty—but it also became a way of ritualizing racial achievement against socially imposed barriers to cultural performance," argues Dyson. Jordan's performances reflected the influence of black culture as evidenced in his improvisation, stylization of the performed self, and what Dyson calls his edifying deception, for his "ability to flout widely understood boundaries through mesmerizing and alchemy, a subversion of common perceptions of the culturally or physically possible through the creative and deceptive manipulation of appearance."

The marketing genius that is the signature of the Jordan brand is reflected in the sneaker, Dyson adds, which simultaneously reflects the black urban style and our nation's broader culture of consumption. Dyson summarizes the link between Jordan, basketball, and black athletic aesthetics this way:

> Basketball is the metaphoric center of black juvenile culture, a major means by which even temporary forms of cultural and personal transcendence of personal limits are experienced. Michael Jordan is the center of this black athletic culture, the supreme symbol of black cultural creativity in a society of diminishing tolerance for the black youth whose fascination with Jordan has helped sustain him. But Jordan is also the iconic fixture of broader segments of American society, who see in him the ideal figure: a black man of extraordinary genius on the court and before the cameras, who by virtue of his magical skills and godlike talents symbolizes the meaning of human possibility, while refusing to root it in the specific forms of culture and race in which it must inevitably make sense or fade to ultimate irrelevance.[18]

Dyson clearly understands the complex relationship between race and sports in historical and contemporary times, and demonstrates how these complex processes are personified in the greatest to ever play the game of basketball.

Dyson's remarks on society's waning tolerance for black youth is true even today. News outlets are unfortunately filled with stories about unarmed black youth killed by largely white males for doing things that most teenagers do. Trayvon Martin was enjoying the NBA All-Star weekend and decided to go to a local store during a break in the action. Like many other young black males, Martin was likely fascinated by black male athletes like Jordan and LeBron James of the Miami Heat. On his last night on earth, he was exercising his right as a free person to walk through the community where he was visiting his father. Tired of a rash of break-ins allegedly involving young black males, self-appointed neighborhood guardian George Zimmerman pursued Martin, and at the end of their brief encounter Trayvon Martin lay dead. His hoodie became a symbol for young black males everywhere, as well as the threat each faces because their very skin deems them suspicious.

Jordan Davis—killed at the hands of Michael Dunn—was in a car with a group of other young black males enjoying some music that Dunn thought was too loud. The encounter ended with Davis's death and attempts on the lives of the other youth in the car.

Both of these cases, which are by no means isolated, highlight the diminished tolerance of black youth. The devaluation of young black males could easily cause them to feel hopeless and to live life without purpose. The fact that young black males can turn on the television or go online or check their phones and see black male athletes showing the world their strength and abilities continues to sustain them.

The LeBron Jameses of the world remain "iconic fixtures" in the society at large. James and other black professional basketball players remind viewers of the potential that lies within all of us to be great and to exceed what we thought possible. Ironically, these ideals do not translate off the court. The prevailing wisdom is not that black males have the ability or the potential to do well in society, but rather that the athletic realm is one of the few places where black males excel and are allowed to excel, but only within certain prescribed roles (for example, as players but not as coaches, managers, CEOs, or owners). The belief on the part of young black males that their opportunities are limited off the court, coupled with their sense of the "diminishing tolerance" society has for them, leads many to see basketball not only as a black sport but as one of few legitimate means to achieving success.

The process by which we learn what is expected of us as members of a society—based upon our membership in certain racial groups through sports—is also evidenced in other ways. Racial socialization is a continuous and enduring process that endured not only the most significant period of social change in America—the civil rights movement—but also the retirement of Michael Jordan from the game, and even the election of the nation's first black president.

Race, Color-Blindness, and the Decision

Three recent events in NBA history that received a lot of media attention helped highlight the relationship between race and sports and the role of sports as an agent of racial socialization: LeBron James's decision to leave the Cleveland Cavaliers, the NBA lockout during the 2011–12 season, and the media frenzy surrounding Jeremy Lin.

Once, maybe twice, in a generation an athlete emerges in a sport and fundamentally changes the game. Michael Jordan was that athlete in the NBA, and when he retired there was a search for the next great player. There was speculation that Kobe Bryant might take the throne, and then of course, there was the king, King James. James—who never played a day of college basketball—is an athlete who has captured the imagination of a broad spectrum of Americans and is an icon for many young black males. His story of being raised by a single mother is one that many can identify with, and his story of making it to the professional level despite seemingly insurmountable odds gives hope to the next generation of ballplayers. In many ways, his story is their story, or at least the story with the end that many long for.

According to ESPN, LeBron James was born and raised in Akron, Ohio, where he attended St. Vincent-St. Mary High School. He led his team to a state title in his first and second years. By his sophomore year, he was chosen to the USA Today All-USA First Team. He was the first sophomore player to ever receive that honor. James made his first appearance in *Sports Illustrated* and *ESPN the Magazine* by his junior year at St. Vincent-St. Mary's. The skill James demonstrated very early on led some to conclude that his raw natural abilities were responsible for his level of play, as opposed to his cognitive ability and commitment to training.

In his senior year, he was selected to the All-USA First Team for the third time, and the title of Mr. Basketball of Ohio was bestowed upon him. He earned Most Valuable Player (MVP) honors in a number of prestigious and highly competitive games, including the Jordan Capital Class, the EA Sports Roundball Classic, and the McDonald's All-American Game. But his appearances in the postseason all-star games rendered him ineligible for the NCAA. Here was a young black male forced to take a path to the NBA—direct from high school—that few have taken. Since his success, young black males struggling in underresourced schools with little hope of earning a college scholarship can hold fast to the belief that anything is possible because King James showed that it could happen.

James, the first overall pick in the 2003 NBA draft, began his career in his home state of Ohio with the Cleveland Cavaliers. Playing at home is the dream of many aspiring young athletes. He won the NBA Rookie of the Year honor and made history in virtually every year he was with the Cavaliers. After the 2009–10 seasons, James became a free agent. He met with a number of teams, including the Cavaliers, Knicks, Clippers, Bulls, Heat, and Nets, but in many ways James's situation was much different from that of other free agents. One need only look at the economic impact of James on the league, on the franchise, and on the city of Cleveland to understand the stark contrasts.[19]

Writer Robert Schoenberger of the *Cleveland Plain Dealer* described LeBron James in 2010 as "more than a sports superstar. He's a one-man economic engine that drives the lane, fills the bars and puts Cleveland on national TV." Schoenberger and many others tried to estimate the potential economic impact prior to James's announcement that he was leaving Cleveland. The loss to downtown businesses was estimated at $48 million, and the loss to the region at $150 million if the team missed out on at least 10 home playoff games. Schoenberger also estimated the value of LeBron to the franchise at $100 million.[20]

The *Huffington Post* took a look at how Cleveland has fared since James's departure. Total attendance dropped after James left. The Cavaliers went from 2nd in total attendance in the league in 2010 to 19th just two years later. The loss of LeBron James was most felt in the overall value of the franchise, which fell more than 25 percentage points in January 2011 and another 7 percent in 2012, but the team did manage the third-highest profit in the NBA with over $30 million. The *Huffington Post* attributes the relatively high profit gain "to help from a $30 million payroll cut and no luxury tax." Businesses situated near the home of the Cavaliers claim commerce has not suffered, as some had expected, largely due to fan loyalty and the influx of exciting new players.[21]

Whatever the economic impact, LeBron James's decision to leave the Cleveland Cavaliers will be remembered more for how he left and not enough for the reaction of Dan Gilbert, the team's majority owner, to his departure. Much of what Gilbert wrote to the Cavalier fan community could be found in a textbook on racism in the twenty-first century, were such a textbook to be written. There are few stereotypes about blacks, in general or in particular, that are missed by Gilbert in his address, and yet his words are coded in such a way that anyone saying they are racist comments would be accused of overreacting, of making something out of nothing, of reading too much into it, of playing the race card. This is no game, however; this is racism in the twenty-first century in the NBA. Let us look closely at what Gilbert says—and at what he does not say.

Gilbert addressed his statement not only to professed fans of the Cleveland Cavaliers but to all of northeastern Ohio. Clearly James's decision was about more than just the team. It was about more than just one player. It was much bigger and had significance beyond the hardwood. James's choice to leave Cleveland and play for the Miami Heat would economically impact the regional economy and profit margin of the owner and all the other stakeholders that benefited from his presence, but his attempt to decide what was in his own best interest from a business standpoint showed that he was, in his own way, challenging the status quo. James was demonstrating his ability to live life as a total person, not merely as a basketball player. He demonstrated a willingness to make a decision based upon what was best for him and his career and not for an owner who could let go of him at will.

LeBron James's deliberation about where he would spend his playing days was symbolic of long-held American ideals of individualism, success, and self-determination. At the same time, it signaled a threat to the racialized social system that dictated that decisions are to be made by those in positions of power and authority, such as the owners. Given that almost all of the majority owners in the NBA are white, whites have had, as they do in the broader society, the decision-making authority. Here LeBron James was threatening to upset the established pattern of racial hierarchy by making his own decision in his own best interest, and the fear was that players with similar levels of star power would follow suit. It is not a coincidence that the rules regulating some movements of player personnel changed soon after James's decision, as evidenced by the unwillingness of the owners to support an agreed-upon trade involving Chris Paul.

Gilbert refers to James as "our former hero." As long as LeBron James acted in such a way as deemed fit for someone of his race, he was regarded favorably. The minute James flexed his economic muscle he was described as a deserter turning his back on the very place he spent his formative years. The characterization of black people, especially black males, as untrustworthy is an enduring stereotype. Blacks were kept out of military service or segregated in noncombat roles because common beliefs held that black males lacked the courage and trustworthiness to fight under the American flag, despite the fact that blacks have been found in some capacity in virtually every major battle for which Americans have bled and died.

Moreover, Gilbert describes James as "narcissistic." James announced his decision on live television. Gilbert described the event as "self-promotional," which is ironic given that the promotion of LeBron James's image and ascension as "king" of professional basketball was fine when it sold tickets and Cavalier memorabilia. James's own efforts, however, to determine his worth in the NBA market were viewed in largely negative terms by Gilbert and others.

Gilbert employs some other commonly held stereotypes about blacks in his description of LeBron James in the days following the decision. He describes James as lazy, disloyal, and lacking motivation. He juxtaposes this image of James and the black males he represents with "the ownership team and the rest of the hard-working, loyal, and driven staff at your hometown Cavaliers" who, he adds, "have not betrayed you nor NEVER will betray you." Terms like *betray* are repeated throughout the statement, demonstrating Gilbert's intent to drive home the point that James is a traitor not only to his teammates but to the broader society when he should be grateful for what the city and team ownership have done for him. Nowhere is there even an acknowledgment as to what LeBron James had done for the game of the basketball, for the region, or for the franchise. Gilbert goes out of his way to talk about how much the people in the region and the team's fans gave, and how much they deserve, implying that LeBron James's gains were in some way undeserved.

Gilbert used the aforementioned words to conjure up negative images of black people, especially black males, in an effort to gain the support of disgruntled fans and nonfans who were already feeling frustrated by with their own economic standing and then were inundated with around-the-clock coverage of a young black male quibbling—not negotiating—over more money than most Americans of any race will ever see in a lifetime.

The disgruntled owner of the Cavaliers goes out of his way to paint James and the black males who identify with him as outsiders, or the "other." He again uses the terms *shameful, selfish,* and *betrayal* to describe James before concluding his statement. He again implies the treasonous quality of James's decision. He says, "If you thought we were motivated before tonight to bring the hardware to Cleveland, I can tell you that this shameful display of selfishness and betrayal by one of our very own has shifted our 'motivation.'" Gilbert accuses "some people," referring to James and to others like him, of thinking "they should go to heaven but NOT have to die to get there." In other words, Gilbert is acknowledging the challenges LeBron James faced in Cleveland, but he is not taking responsibility for failing to build a team around James that was good enough to win a championship. Instead he implies that James wanted the glory of a championship without putting in the required work.

Gilbert also questions LeBron James's role as a model for youth. In the years James was a Cavalier, there were no statements from Gilbert raising questions about this. After his decision to leave the franchise, Gilbert warned parents—likely white parents—that he is not a good example for children. While James was marketed regularly as the chosen one, the one who would take over the void left by Michael Jordan's retirement, Gilbert claims here that the title was self-imposed and he says that James's "disloyalty" and betrayal of the state where he spent many years "sends the exact opposite lesson of what we would want our children to learn. And 'who' we would want them to grow-up [sic] to become." Given that Gilbert has painted James and the black males he represents as the "other," one can infer that when he uses the terms we and our that he is talking to and about whites.

Additionally, Gilbert describes James's decision as "heartless" and "callous." These terms have been used to describe and dehumanize blacks since the days of slavery. Black masculinity has often been associated with criminality and violence. Black males in particular have historically been viewed as individuals incapable of controlling their urges, and as a result have a propensity to commit crime and an insatiable desire for white women. Gilbert describes James as lacking feelings and emotions, which are essential traits that distinguish man from beast.

Gilbert essentially calls upon the fans and the people of the region to unite, to harness their energies and work toward the shared goal of showing LeBron James and others who might consider following suit that their perceived power pales in comparison to the power of individuals with membership in the dominant group.[22]

The characterization of James by Gilbert is of course not new. It is a page taken from an old American playbook in which the rules say blacks are inherently inferior to whites and must know their place. "Their place" is in subjugation to whites and to white authority and privilege. Electing to take one's talents to South Beach does not fit this model.

When people like Rev. Jesse Jackson say that Gilbert's letter is offensive and the personification of a slave master mentality, some find it easy to dismiss. Jackson and other legends of the civil rights struggle are not unaccustomed to being called outside agitators, or even racial ambulance chasers. It is a convenient tactic to deflect attention from the real culprit, in this case Dan Gilbert. One need not take Jackson's word for it, however; one need only take a look through the pages of history and examine racial stereotypes and caricatures of black people. The words chosen by Gilbert can be found in the description of any number of stereotypes about blacks, dating back to antebellum America, and the fact that James's likability dropped among blacks and whites is not evidence that the response to his decision, or the way in which he delivered it, was race-neutral. Blacks often believe the lies told about them, even if they claim to see those representations in other blacks and not in themselves. Take a look at the exhibits at the Jim Crow Museum of Racist Memorabilia at Ferris State University and you will find many of the artifacts in the homes of people of African ancestry.

Gilbert's representation of James fits into the brute (discussed in chapter 3) and coon racial caricatures. David Pilgrim of Ferris State University characterizes the coon caricature as "one of the most insulting of all anti-black caricatures," described as lazy and easily frightened. Gilbert portrays James as both in his description. Pilgrim adds, "The coon caricature was born during American slavery. Slave masters and overseers often described slaves as 'slow,' 'lazy,' 'wants pushing,' 'an eye servant,' and 'trifling.' The master and the slave operated with different motives: the master desired to obtain from the slave the greatest labor, by any means; the slave desired to do the least labor while avoiding punishment. The slave registered his protest against slavery by running away," which one could interpret is the meaning underlining Gilbert's comments about James wanting to go to heaven but not have to die to get there.

"Slave owners," says Pilgrim, "complained about the laziness of their workers, but the records show that slaves were often worked hard—and brutally so." Professional athletes, regardless of their God-given talents, do not get to where they are without putting in a lot of hard work both during and outside of the playing season.

The idea that LeBron James's decision to exercise his rights as a free agent was one of the worst forms of betrayal brings to mind the shock that some slave masters felt when slavery officially ended and their slaves were finally allowed to live as free people. Some slave owners were surprised that their former slaves did not want to remain with them:

> The supporters of slavery claimed that blacks were a childlike people unequipped for freedom. Proslavers acknowledged that some slave masters were cruel, but they argued that most were benevolent, kind-hearted capitalists who civilized and improved their docile black wards. From Radical Reconstruction to World War I, there was a national nostalgia for the "good ol' darkies" who loved their masters, and, according to the proslavers, rejected or only reluctantly accepted emancipation. In this context, the conceptualization of the coon was revised. During slavery almost all blacks, especially men, were sometimes seen as coons, that is, lazy, shiftless, and virtually

useless. However, after slavery, the coon caricature was increasingly applied to younger blacks, especially those who were urban, flamboyant, and contemptuous of whites.[23]

The latter description of the coon caricature is consistent with perception of black male basketball players, at all levels, especially in recent decades. For some, it is hard to fully understand how individuals making millions of dollars could be in any way equated with the horrific institution of slavery. This is of course due to a general lack of understanding about what racism is and is not.

Sportswriter J. A. Adande's analysis of the role of race in the NBA illustrates the poor understanding of how racism is best defined. In an article on ESPN.com, Adande responds to comments made by LeBron James in an interview with CNN's Soledad O'Brien. O'Brien asked James if race played a role in the reaction to his decision to leave Cleveland. Adande acknowledges that race will be a factor "as long as the NBA features predominantly black athletes playing for predominantly white owners who are selling their sport to predominantly white ticket buyers." Not only does Adande acknowledge the continuing significance of race, he also identifies basketball as a "their sport" or a "black sport."

Adande also contends that it is only natural for people to want to root for people of the same race, and says of whites preferring to root for whites, "It's no different than black people who previously didn't care about the difference between a serve and a volley rushing to the TV to cheer for Venus and Serena Williams. We all do it to some degree, be it with athletes or even 'Price Is Right' contestants. We tend to support those representing our racial group." But Adande also says, "It's not racism. I prefer the term . . . tribalism. . . . It's not hatred of others, it's about comfort within your own, with a natural reluctance to expend the energy and time to break across the barriers and understand another group."

It clearly is not the same for blacks and whites, and, contrary to Adande's assertion, this is not "natural." It is the result of learned behaviors that are communicated through various agents of racial socialization. Victorious black athletes have come to represent more than champions in their respective sports. Much like the Double V campaign, which saw black soldiers in World War II fighting against fascism abroad and racism at home, black athletes and their supporters see victorious black athletes— particularly those who are underrepresented in their sports or who defy commonly held racial stereotypes and notions of black inferiority—as victors over their natural opponents as well as the racialized social structure into which they have been born.

A large part of the problem is that there is a general lack of understanding as to what racism is and what racism is not. Some people, including Adande, are under the mistaken notion that for something to be racist or be a manifestation of racism, it must be clothed within a white hood bearing the letters KKK, or that there must be a noose hanging from a tree, or the body of an innocent man chained to the back of a truck. Given this misunderstanding about what racism is and is not would cause some, like Adande, to observe, "The color of LeBron's skin won't prevent him from making $14.5 million to play basketball for the Miami Heat this season. It didn't prevent him from signing endorsement deals with corporate titans Coca-Cola, McDonald's and Microsoft while in his early 20s. It didn't keep people of all races from buying his jersey. Racism has yet to come into play in LeBron's professional life. That doesn't mean he can exist in a racial vacuum."

Adande apparently cannot grasp the role that race and racism play in the commercialization and commodification of blackness, as defined in works by Michael Eric Dyson and others. Instead they see responses linking Dan Gilbert's comments to an enduring system of oppression as "an overly exaggerated reaction."[24] Adande would benefit from reading the works of social scientists who have defined racism in a way that explains how even the millions of dollars these young athletes possess is not enough to buy out of the American racialized social system.

Racism is a multilevel and multidimensional system of a dominant group's oppression scapegoating the race or races of one or more subordinate groups. One cannot separate the history of racism in America from the representations of people of color today any more than one can separate the history of racism in sports, including in basketball, from the modern-day athlete.

Race, Color-Blindness, and the Lockout

Understanding racism in this way lends itself to the type of analysis found in an essay by David J. Leonard entitled "Not a Question of Courage: Antiblack Racism and the Politics of the NBA Lockout." Regarding the lockout of the players by the owners, player Carmelo Anthony said that players have been relatively silent about the labor negotiations because "athletes today are scared to make Muhammad Ali type statements." Leonard places the seemingly controversial comments within an appropriate historical context, one that is "very much tied to the larger history of the NBA and race." He cites the reaction of the league to the infamous fight involving Metta World Peace, formerly known as Ron Artest. "The NBA implemented a series of draconian policies that sought to both appease white fans and corporate sponsors who were increasingly uncomfortable with its racial optics, all while disciplining the players to comply and embody a different sort of blackness." The lockout can, within this context, be understood as yet another effort to "capitalize on the perception of NBA players as thugs, as criminals, as greedy, and underserving anti-role models," wrote Leonard.[25]

Those who fail to account for race in the NBA and in the society at large often point fingers at people of color in the industry for injecting race into matters that are presumably devoid of race. Greg Wilson of NBC, writing about Bryant Gumbel's description of NBA commissioner David Stern as a "plantation overseer," claimed that Gumbel "goes racial as pro basketball talks falter." This tactic is of course not new, but is reflective of what some scholars have dubbed the new racism, where extraordinary measures are taken to explain away racial disparities using nonracial terms and explanations. So the overrepresentation of black players in the NBA in the context of predominantly white owners and decision makers, and the treatment and representation of players by them and predominantly white writers, is not viewed primarily as a manifestation of the persistence of racism in American society, and anyone who attempts to assert that is "going racial."[26]

Race, Color-Blindness, and Linsanity

The effect of racial socialization on professional basketball players is evident in the treatment of other groups as well as blacks, but the overrepresentation of blacks in the league means that much of the attention is directed at them, and their treatment relative to whites, in and around the game. However, reactions to the play of former New York Knick Jeremy Lin showed how racial socialization in sports impacts other people of color, including those of Asian ancestry.[27]

Marc Lamont Hill argues in a piece called "The Linsanity Sham: Why Jeremy Lin Really Can't Play" that Jeremy Lin is capable of playing in the NBA, but is not worthy of the praise bestowed upon him during the 2011–12 season, including comparisons between him and Hall of Fame players like Shaquille O'Neal. Hill provides quantitative evidence to support his contention and then he shifts to what he calls "the thorny issue of race." After private conversations with players within the league, Hill tells his many readers that most teams and players were not that concerned about Lin and found it hard to accept that "an Asian player under seven feet could dominate an NBA game. As a result, they simply let him play with little resistance, allowing him to temporarily thrive on the 'soft bigotry of low expectations.' "[28]

The racial narrative surrounding people of Asian ancestry in the United States has not been built upon the same constructs that have supported the racial narrative concerning other people of color, namely blacks. Asians have been stereotyped in many ways, some of which might be considered positive, comparatively speaking. However, scholars such as Lisa Sun-Hee Park have shown that the idea that Asians are a model minorty is more a myth than a fact. In this view, Asians are the model minority and, unlike other racial and ethnic minority groups, they are generally hardworking, college educated, and law abiding. The myth represents Asians "as exemplary models for other minorities based (usually) upon measures of income, education, and public benefit utilization rates." Individuals within a so-called model minority are often placed on a pedestal and "mistakenly regarded as normative representatives" of the group.[29]

Park is not alone in critizing the model minority myth. Miranda McGowan and James Lindgren identify several other problems for groups labeled model minorities.[30] The designation of model minority, according to Martin, masks the discrimination faced by group members. "While reinforcing the American Dream, the idea of a model minority ultimately blames members of other minority groups for their problems, many of which may be the consequence of structural, economical, or political changes that have a deleterious impact on some minority groups and not others. It also divides members of the model minority from other minority groups."[31]

In a recent interview, Jeremy Lin discussed the role that he thinks race has played throughout his basketball career, at various levels. Lin told Charlie Rose on *60 Minutes* that his race played a role in the fact that he was not heavily recruited out of high school, nor was he drafted out of college. Lin made it to the NBA after a stint in the NBA Summer League. Commissioner David Stern admits that Lin's race was likely a factor as to why he was not drafted, according to a report by Mike Mazzeo of ESPN.[32]

Lin did however develop quite a following, including "his Christian following, his Asian American following and his Harvard following, and he did it while playing in the center of the basketball universe."[33] These groups are not immediately associated with the NBA's legions of players or fans. Lin quickly became the cause célèbre of the moment because his very presence deviated from the athletic norms of the sports-industrial complex we have come to expect. It is not surprising that his status as a premier player in the league was short-lived. The attention he garnered had the desired effect—to increase the profit margins of the respective owners and to draw attention to a player who represented what many black athletes do not in the imagination of many fans—a humble, highly intelligent, hardworking athlete, deserving of praise.

Conclusion

In this chapter, a brief history of basketball in America was offered, ranging from the invention of the game to more contemporary issues related to race, such as LeBron James's self-determination as a free agent and the NBA lockout. Despite the integration of college and professional teams, the race-based ghettoization of selected positions in the sports-industrial complex is still very much alive. Understanding racism as a social system impacting all levels of society in various ways helps us to better understand claims that race continues to be a significant determinant of the life chances and opportunities of people of color, especially blacks, even when members of the group are making millions of dollars or hosting meetings in the most powerful place on earth, the Oval Office.

Sports are clearly "among the most potent institutions in the production, maintenance and contestation race in the modern world,"[34] and this is particularly evident in basketball, where a large majority of players are black. Clearly, the process by which we learn the ways of society according to one's racial identification involves agents of socialization like sports. Through sports, messages about the participation of blacks in basketball are clear. Blacks are welcome to participate in the game, but must know their place and not attempt to exert more power and authority than allowed by the dominant group—or there will be repercussions. The repercussions include taking some of the very characteristics of the black male athlete that were used to generate profits and using them to dehumanize the black athlete, and the larger black population, in the hope of reminding members of the white majority of the so-called natural tendencies of blacks to be disloyal, selfish, heartless, and callous. Clearly, these manifestations of racism—both overt and covert—may increase at a time when society is undergoing great changes. At a time when average workers are struggling to find or hold on to jobs, it is not surprising or coincidental that the image of the undeserving spoiled black athlete reemerges. A collective call to admonish the black athlete for not being more appreciative of what the franchise and the country has given him or her goes out and finds fertile ground without regard for what the black athlete has given to the franchise.

Chapter 7

Black-Free Zones: Black Athletes on the Course and on the Court

Blacks are underrepresented in more sports than they are overrepresented. The list of sports where there are relatively few people of color, including blacks, is quite numerous. "There are proportionately many more whites who play basketball and football in high school and college than there are blacks who play tennis or golf at those levels."[1] Few, if any, NASCAR or IndyCar drivers are black. Moreover, data show that middle- and upper-class white communities have a higher rate of sport participation than predominantly black communities. "Racial ideology causes many people to overlook this fact. They see only black men who make high salaries in high-profile sports and assume that blacks have 'taken over' sports, that discrimination is gone, and that the nation is not colorblind."[2] An examination of two sports in which blacks have been underrepresented both historically and in contemporary times will further illustrate the ideas set forth in this book: that social institutions, like sports, play a key role in communicating the ways of society based upon our historically biracial classification system and population, and structural changes matter in determining the extent to which manifestations of racism will be overt or covert.

Racial Socialization and Golf: The Early Years

Most Americans, whether they are fans of golf or not, know the name Tiger Woods. Woods was a household name even before the very public split with his wife put his story on pages outside the sports section. Few Americans know that Tiger Woods is the latest in a long history of golf participation among blacks dating back to the late 1800s. Charlie Sifford and Lee Elder were among the better known golfers of the 1960s and the

1970s. Others, like Teddy Rhodes, Bill Spiller, Nathaniel Starks, James Black, and Joe Roach, were less well known.

Blacks, up until the middle of the twentieth century, were excluded from participating in the Professional Golf Association of America (PGA). The PGA, on its official website, describes the organization as the largest working sports organization, with more 27,000 members. Established in 1916 in New York City, the purpose of the association was to increase equipment sales. During the organization's first year, the first ever PGA championship was held. The championship was canceled in 1917 and 1918 due to World War I. The PGA Championship resumed in 1919. The fee for entry in the championship was $5, and the organization had more than 1,300 members. Dues increased from $10 in 1928 to $50 in 1929.

The PGA established a fund to support members who were unable to work in 1940. The association paid out over $4,600. A year later, the group celebrated its 25th anniversary with over 2,000 members. The Golf Hall of Fame was also established at this time. The PGA Championships were again canceled due to war. About a decade later, membership was almost doubled, and shortly thereafter a major television network purchased the broadcasting rights for PGA Championships that would last for four years. As a result, PGA membership reached almost 10,000 by the mid-1980s. Missing from the rich history of the PGA is information about important dates and events involving people of color. This is because for much of the organization's history, blacks were excluded altogether or placed in very restrictive roles.

As they had done in other cases, in sports and other aspects of life, blacks created their own association. For example, black professional golfers played throughout Florida. Blacks made other important contributions to the game. Dr. George F. Grant, for example, was one of the first black dentists as well as one the first black golfers. Using his dental skills, he invented an improved golf tee, which he patented in 1899, that is still the basis for golf tees today.

John M. Shippen Jr. also made an important contribution to the sport of golf, even though the clear message at the time was that golf was a white sport. Shippen, at the age of 16, became the first professional black American golfer. In 1896, he was one of two nonwhite players in the second-ever U.S. Open. The other nonwhite player was Oscar Bunn, a Native American. Shippen learned the game from Scottish golfer Willie Dunn who owned the Shinnecock Hills course in Long Island and taught local young people how to caddy and play. Shippen also worked as a laborer in the construction and expansion of Dunn's course.

Members of the Shinnecock club entered Shippen and Bunn in the U.S. Open. Shippen's European opponents did not like the idea of playing non-white opponents and walked out. When informed by officials that the competition would proceed with or without them, the European opponents returned. Although Shippen finished fifth, he led on day one and received national attention. After 1896, Shippen was prohibited from participating in many professional golf competitions due to his race, but he continued to play professionally on mostly black courses. He went on to run a business, as many golf professionals did at that time, including making and selling golf clubs.

In 1925 black golfers formed the Colored Golfers Association of America. The organization held a tournament in Stow, Massachusetts, in 1926 that was very successful: "The tournament was a proving ground for gifted minorities and a place where Black golfers came together in a show of strength and harmony in a segregated America."[3]

The African American Registry, in its brief history of blacks and golf, found that most blacks learned to play the game of golf as caddies. It was estimated that there were over 5,000 golf facilities in the late 1930s and less than 10 allowed black players. However, wealthy blacks in places like Polk County, Florida, created their own spaces to enjoy the game of golf. Wealthy blacks purchased land in places like American Beach, near Amelia Island. Prior to the purchase of the land, it was not uncommon for whites playing on segregated courses, such as Cleveland Heights Golf Course and Carpenter's Home Golf Course, to pull local children out of classes in nearby high schools to serve as caddies. Caddies could play on the segregated courses once a week and would be allowed the use of inadequate equipment. LaFrancine Burton, writing in the *Ledger*, points out that "learning how to play golf under such circumstances led to the remarkable skills possessed by some of the early golfers."[4] Many black golfers enjoyed much success professionally playing against other professional black golfers. The black association, however, folded due to a lack of adequate funding and by the 1980s was no longer hosting tournaments. As in other sports, once blacks moved toward the predominantly white league, the black leagues folded.

Legal battles in sports increased during the post–World War II period, and golf was no exception. Lawsuits related to golf came about owing to the popularity of the sport in the black community, an increase in black militancy, and the lack of available private and public golf courses that were open to blacks. One of the more publicized cases involved black golfers William Spiller, Ted Rhodes, and Madison Gunter.

William Spiller, according to sportswriter Jimmie Tramel, was a native of Tulsa, Oklahoma, and one of its most famous residents. Spiller was born in 1913 in Tishomingo. He was a good athlete in high school and went on to earn a degree at Wiley College in Texas. Spiller eventually made his way to Los Angeles, where he developed a love for and expertise in the game of golf. Tramel, in an effort to increase awareness about Spiller's legacy, tells us that Spiller played in the Los Angles Open in 1948. The Los Angeles Open was one of only a handful of tournaments that permitted blacks to compete.[5]

"Many black golfers of that era took a pacifist approach and were willing to embrace equal rights in increments. Not Spiller," says Pete McDaniel, author of *Uneven Lies*. "Not only was he radical by nature, he was also intelligent. So he could argue pretty much his own case and he knew his rights and he knew his rights were being broken. That was unbearable for him. He was a civil rights activist long before it was fashionable simply through the game of golf and the game he was determined to play no matter what."[6]

This combination of a commitment to the game and a commitment to social justice is a recurring theme in the history of race and sports and of efforts of blacks and other relatively disadvantaged minority groups to resist institutional and individual efforts to limit their ability to live as free people. In the late nineteenth and early twentieth centuries, blacks and whites were not far removed from the period of slavery, in which laws dictated the movements of enslaved and freed blacks. Reconstruction and the decades that followed were a period of adjustment, to say the least, and that period was characterized by efforts to find innovative ways to maintain control over the black population, including control of its labor. Blacks like Spiller and Jack Johnson sought to live their lives as autonomous people. Blacks—including athletes—wanted to enjoy all of the rights and privileges their ancestors and supporters had fought so hard and long to secure, but the broader society was simply not ready for that. As blacks resisted, or as whites felt that the threat of resistance was imminent, manifestations of racism were evident in the many race riots that took place across the nation and in the tightening of restrictions in other areas of public life, such as in the realm of sports.

With society experiencing so many changes in such a relatively short period of time, it was not surprising that racial antagonism either grew or became more pronounced. The nation was not that far removed from a time when blacks were considered property and were prohibited from assembling in relatively large numbers for fear of revolt. Americans could remember when blacks were not permitted to read, write, or bear arms. The racial hierarchy that had been a feature of American society since the beginning was seemingly being threatened, and efforts to achieve some degree of normalcy meant that individuals and institutions went to great lengths to show that even though laws had changed, not much else had. It is not surprising, then, that efforts to reinforce long-held stereotypes about what was acceptable for black and whites—even in the world of sports—were all the more prevalent. Evidence of this enduring legacy can be found in the experience of black golfer Ted Rhodes.

Ted Rhodes was another highly skilled golfer, but limited in what he could accomplish because of the bold, seemingly impenetrable color line drawn by the PGA and many private and public clubs. In honor of Black History Month in 2007, Rhonda Glenn of USGA told the story of Rhodes's trials and triumphs. Born in Nashville, Tennessee, Rhodes worked as a caddy when he was just a youngster. Blacks were often relegated to such roles of servitude. Young blacks carrying the bags of whites seemed more in line with the dominant racial ideology of the day, which claimed whites were superior and blacks were inferior. To see black males carrying the clubs of white players and following their every command was one way of showing the caddy and everyone else on the course—and in the broader society—what was appropriate for blacks and whites.

Rhodes worked at Belle Meade Country Club and Richland Country Club. Glenn describes the clubs as exclusive. Blacks were prohibited from playing there, but Rhodes honed his skills, says Glenn, using a two-iron someone had thrown away. Rhodes did not play on the plush greens that wealthy and middle-class whites had access to; instead, he practiced on local baseball fields. Rhodes did what many blacks had done in the past—he made do with what he had and excelled anyway. Despite having access only to inferior schools, neighborhoods, training facilities, and courses, Rhodes and other black athletes succeeded by virtue of their commitment to the sport and their realization that any victory would be a symbolic one for all blacks against a social system that did not see them as worth of equality, fairness, and justice.

In addition to working as a caddy, Rhodes worked as part of the Civilian Conservation Corps before joining the Navy. A World War II veteran,

Rhodes settled in Chicago, Illinois, where he became friends with another legend in American competitive sports, Joe Louis. This relationship had a profound impact on Rhodes's life. Louis loved the game of golf and hired Rhodes to be his player partner and his personal instructor. Rhodes and Louis were quite the team, defeating "entertainers, athletes, and professional golfers."

Louis sponsored Rhodes and assisted him in networking with individuals who could help take him to the next level. Ray Mangrum, brother of Lloyd Mangrum, a U.S. Open Champion of the mid-1940s, did just that. The challenge was finding a place where Rhodes could play. Rhodes played in tournaments sponsored by the United States Colored Golf Association, but the purses paled in comparison to those in PGA tournaments. Glenn reports that the United Golf Association (UGA), as the United States Colored Golf Association is now called, had awards "that often provided as little as $100 to the winner." In the early part of the 1900s, by comparison, the first-place prize for the PGA Championship was about $500 and by the 1930s the first-place prize was at least $1,000.[7]

The costs of segregation in sports and in the broader society were and still are great. Not only were black athletes not able to earn the kind of money their white counterparts earned, many suffered the emotional scars that came with the indignity of being treated unequally. Even black athletes with service experience—athletes willing to lay down their lives for their fellow Americans—could not count on being treated as equals.

Between 1946 and 1947, Rhodes was victorious in six United Golf Association tournaments, including the Joe Louis Open in Detroit. His best year, according to Glenn, was 1948, when Rhodes competed in the LA Open at Riviera Country Club. Spiller also competed there. Both golfers finished high enough to qualify for the Richmond Open, to be held in California.

Rhodes, along with Spiller and Madison Gunther, attempted to gain entry into the event, but were turned away by the clause excluding nonwhites. Again, the message being sent to the black golfers and to the society as a whole was that there was a difference between blacks and whites and the difference was such that the groups should remain separate for fear that the alleged purity of the white race might be—in the view of some people—compromised.

The three, with the help of Jonathan Rowell, filed a lawsuit. Rowell wrote to Thurgood Marshall, then of the National Association for the Advancement of Colored People (NAACP), seeking support with the case. In the letter, Rowell provided Marshall with the facts of the case and insight as to how he planned to proceed. He informed Marshall that he filed a complaint in Superior Court for the County of Contra Costa, where the Richmond Golf Club was located. He identified the following code: "All citizens within the jurisdiction of this state are entitled to the full and equal accommodations, advantages, facilities, and privileges of . . . places of public accommodation or amusement."[8] Rowell let Marshall know that he argued that the three black golfers were trying to gain entrance into a profession tournament and that this was in keeping with the spirit of the code. On their behalf, Rowell reported that he would be seeking $5,000 in damages— $2,000 for actual damages and the rest for humiliation, stress, and anguish.

A suit would also be brought against the PGA in the amount of $100,000 each for Rhodes, Spiller, and Gunther because the PGA essentially operated as a monopoly and provided economic opportunities for golfers, and the three black players were denied the right to compete for those economic benefits. Rowell believed there was a precedent for this in *James v. Marinship*, 25 Cal. 2nd 721. According to the opinion of the court, this case dealt with:

> an appeal from an order of the Superior Court in Marin County awarding a preliminary injunction which, among other things, restrained defendants from discharging or causing the discharge of plaintiff and [25 Cal.2d 725] other Negro employees because they are not members of a labor union with which their employer has a closed shop agreement, but which will not grant Negroes full membership privileges. The basic question presented is whether a closed shop may be enforced by a labor union together with an arbitrarily closed or partially closed union membership.

The judgment was affirmed.

Just before the case was to come to court, the PGA vowed to do away with their discriminatory policy and the three men dropped the lawsuit. A year later, after enjoying much success playing against black golfers, Rhodes attempted to enter a PGA tournament in Iowa, but was denied. Rhodes left his mark on the game. He was a mentor to Lee Elder, who in 1975 became the first black person to play in the Masters.

Racial Socialization and the Reluctant Black Golfer

Few people have had the kind of impact on a professional sport that Tiger Woods has had on golf. Few who follow the sport can forget seeing Tiger Woods on the course with his dad by his side. Julia Wang of *People*

magazine edited a piece on Woods, and notes that he began his golf training at the young age of 10 months in the late 1970s.[9] He did what most kids
do: he imitated someone else, in this case his dad playing golf. Seeing that
his son took an interest in the game, his father taught him. By 1990, Tiger
Woods was on the Junior Amateur circuit, winning world title after world
title. As a 10th grader, Tiger Woods became the youngest person ever to
play in a PGA tour event. A few years later, he entered Stanford University,
but left after two years to play golf professionally. In no time he had
million-dollar endorsement deals with major companies such as Nike. He
was winning awards and gracing the cover of sports magazines. By 1997,
he became the youngest person ever to win the Masters. Woods continues
to be a dominant player, but suffered the tragic loss of his father in 2006.
Within about three years, Tiger Woods began making the headlines for
all the wrong reasons. He was accused of cheating on his wife with multiple
women after a very public incident near his home. After some time away
from the game, Woods staged a comeback.

An examination of the scholarly literature on Woods speaks less to his
skills on the golf course and more to how he is identified racially and how
he identifies himself. While efforts to communicate the ways of society
for blacks and whites are not without its problems, there is a general consensus as to who is considered black and who is considered white. Tiger
Woods tries to tackle the racial classification system by refusing to conform
to it. However, demonstrating almost total disregard for the way that
Woods self-identifies racially, he is still referred to as a black golfer by other
golfers, fans, and sports journalists.

In an article, Leilani Nishime discusses how Woods's refusal to identify
solely as black, in favor of a more multicultural identity, brought him support from many other multiracial individuals, but diminished his support
from blacks, some of whom believed he was attempting to distance himself
from the racial group.[10]

Ellis Cashmore, writing in 2008, sees Tiger Woods as a "colorfree
emblem of a new America in which racism is dead and there are no barriers
to progress for any member of its citizenry—a new racial order." Cashmore
goes as far as to define Woods as "a new kind of white person." Said
another way, Cashmore contends that:

> Woods effectively invites consumers not to challenge racism directly, but to
> buy commodities that externalize success and in this way avoid confronting
> the racism that continues to bedevil most of America's black population.

So it is not Woods the individual here, it is the representation of Woods to media. He becomes a "personalized reproduction of America. It is a place where the racism that was such a source of torment throughout the twentieth century has now almost disappeared."[11] Cashmore's reference to "niggas" in the article is inappropriate, and his claim that racism is dead is contradictory to statements and data presented in the article, and made about persistent racial and ethnic inequality. Tiger Woods's declaration concerning how he plans to identify himself racially informs the ongoing debate in communications, and in other social sciences, namely, whether to consider racial categories as an imagined social construct or as a material reality.

Although Cashmore seems to believe American society has entered a postracial era in which people of color have the option of identifying, or not, with their racial and ethnic group, despite highly visible racial markers like skin color, the PGA has identified ways to address what it continues to see as a race problem in the sport by administering programs aimed specifically at children, college students at historically black colleges and universities, and minority business owners.

PGA Plans for Diversity

The PGA publishes a document outlining diversity efforts, the goal of which is to increase participation and employment opportunities for women and people of color.

The National Golf Foundation found that participation rates were lowest among blacks for each of the years under study and that there has been a decline in participation rates over time for blacks and whites, while the opposite trend is observed in reference to Asian and Hispanic golfers.

The National Golf Foundation found a connection between household income and minority participation in golf for 2010. For each group, participation rates increased as income increased. Incomes and participation rates were higher for whites, Asians, and Hispanics at all income levels when compared with the black population. Continued discrimination in the sport or lack of interest among golfers and nongolfers may be to blame.

A number of strategies were outlined to get the number of nonwhites up. The PGA says it raises awareness about careers in golf at junior golf tournaments that feature minority players and at historically black colleges and universities. Additionally, the PGA says its partners provide scholarships to minorities through the PGA Minority Collegiate Golf Championship to defray the cost of attending the PGA Professional Golf Management Program, which includes an internship opportunity.

The golf association boasts that it has provided over $10 million in funding to youth development programs across the country that include minority youth. These programs include Midnight Golf and Urban League Youth Golf. Scholarships have also been provided for minority students interested in attending an institution of higher learning that offers the PGA Golf Management University Program. Just a few years ago, according to the PGA, the University of Maryland Eastern Shore became the first historically black university in the nation to offer the management program.

A commitment to increasing minority representation among vendors at PGA-sponsored events is also under way. The association aims for 25 percent of vendors and suppliers at major championships to be certified as minority- and/or women-owned companies.

Real Tennis and Racial Socialization Prior to the 1960s

The PGA, scholars, and fans of golf are not the only ones addressing these issues. While Lee Elder was winning the hearts and minds of some by becoming the first black golfer to play in the Masters, Arthur Ashe was breaking down stereotypes and dispelling myths with his brilliant tennis and becoming the first black to win Wimbledon. Like golf, tennis too has a long history of sour race relations in America.

Paul Gittings provides an overview of the sport in a 2010 article for CNN. Tennis, said Gittings, is not a new sport. The game may date back to ancient Egypt. It was played in Italy in the fifth century, with players using their bare hands. By the twelfth century, tennis had become more defined and was played in an enclosed courtyard. Like golf, tennis was very popular with the wealthy. Francis I of France was said to have enjoyed tennis immensely and even built tennis courts and promoted tennis beyond the aristocracy. Henry VIII was said to have been a very skilled tennis player. He too built courts, including a court at the Royal Palace, which is still in use today.[12]

Tennis grew in popularity and was played widely in the seventeenth and eighteenth centuries. The rules of tennis have not changed much since the 1890s. During this era, four grand slam events were established: Wimbledon in 1877, the U.S. Open 1881, the French Open in 1891, and the Australian Open in 1905. The biggest changes in tennis occurred with the reward levels and the professionalization of the game in the late 1920s, around the time Althea Gibson was born in South Carolina.

Althea Gibson, a black woman, grew up in Harlem in New York City. She was known for her athletic abilities early on in life. She often preferred playing against males and she excelled in several sports, including tennis. One of her greatest challenges was getting adjusted to the cultural expectations of a game that was historically dominated by wealthy whites. Given the limited opportunities for women and for blacks, Gibson was not originally offered the opportunity to compete against whites; instead, she competed like many other black athletes in predominantly black leagues. Gibson excelled in events held by the American Tennis Association (ATA).

The ATA was established to create better relations among black players and to host a national championship. The association also encouraged the establishment of more black clubs and the coordination of schedules so referees could be assigned to matches. Overall, ATA's goal was to promote the game among blacks.

Most ATA tournaments were played at historically black colleges and involved a great deal of celebration and ritual in addition to the athletic contests. It is noted that tournaments often included parties, card games, and fashion shows.

Not originally a fan of schooling, Gibson would go on to earn her high school diploma and then graduate from Florida A&M, where she received a scholarship in tennis and basketball. "By the 1950s the white sports world was beginning to open its doors to black athletes." Gibson found support from many places, including from other professional athletes like boxers Sugar Ray Robinson and Joe Louis. A white tennis player, Alice Marble, went as far as publishing a letter in *American Lawn Tennis Magazine*, on Gibson's behalf. Marble called upon the U.S. Lawn Tennis Association (USLTA) to let Gibson play based upon her talent and her right to be treated like any other professional female player. Marble was instrumental in creating a climate that led to the end of the so-called color barrier in tennis.

Gibson, like other black athletes of her era, faced discrimination both on and off the court. "When she played USLTA-sanctioned events, referees called her for mistakes, or faults, while letting the white players get by."

After leaving the game, Gibson went on to teach physical education at Lincoln University in Missouri, and even joined a travel team sponsored by the U.S. State Department and traveled to Southeast Asia. Her career peaked in the mid-1950s with a win at the French Open, her first major, and by becoming the first black player to win at Wimbledon in 1957. No other black tennis player would win at Wimbledon until 1975, when Arthur Ashe was victorious. More than 30 years after Gibson's victory, another black female tennis player, Zina Garrison, finally appeared in a final at Wimbledon. An additional 20 years passed before another black female, Venus Williams, would win there.

The tragedy is that an individual as talented as Althea Gibson, who had such a profound impact on American society and American sports, was never able to enjoy the quality of life that her white counterparts enjoyed. Gibson also tried her hand at golf, at running a tennis and basketball circuit, and even a career as a singer and actress.[13]

Racial Socialization and the Obligation of the Black Athlete: The Case of Arthur Ashe

Although blacks remained underrepresented in tennis, there were a number of standouts. As noted previously, Arthur Ashe won Wimbledon in 1975, but his contributions to the sport and to the nation go far beyond that victory. In a 1970 interview, Richard Shapiro describes Ashe's attempt to raise awareness about apartheid in South Africa. Ashe tried to get a visa to play in the South African Open, but racially mixed competitions were outlawed. His actions led the tennis association to consider action against the South African government. Ashe recognized that he would be alone in the tennis world in his efforts to address race relations internationally. Ashe described tennis players as apolitical.

As a black player, Ashe saw his role as very different from other tennis players. He faced discrimination and recognized a shift was taking place. During the interview Ashe says, "Most of the discrimination I now find is of the institutionalized variety like trying to get taxicabs or rent apartments."

The tennis great also commented on the underrepresentation of blacks in the sport he dominated. He cited access as an issue. He said tennis is not a big sport in public schools. Most teaching, said Ashe, takes place in private facilities where blacks were refused entry.

Ashe clearly saw his role as an educator and an opinion leader. Tennis put him in a position where he could draw attention to critical issues in a way that few others could. In the interview with Shapiro, he asserts:

Black individuals in similar positions to myself, who have access to the mass media, have the ability to dish out the truth on issues especially to tell the public the truth of black history. One of the unfortunate aspects of the current struggle is that the wrong people have the right information.[14]

Donald Dell, remembering the life and legacy of Arthur Ashe, said, "He knew he was representing his race at all times." He described the toughest challenge in life as "being born black in America"—this from a man who endured two open-heart surgeries and HIV/AIDS.[15]

He achieved what he set out to do. He authored the three-volume series *A Hard Road to Glory*, which chronicled the history of the black athlete in America. While he celebrated the legacy of black athletes, he created quite a controversy encouraging black parents to send their children to the library and not to the playground. He described sports as the opiate of the black masses.[16]

Racial Production in the Post–Civil Rights Era: The Williams Sisters

No black male tennis player has been able to achieve what Arthur Ashe did, but black female tennis players Venus and Serena Williams have transformed the tennis world in fundamental ways. Much has been written about the Williams sisters. Minority participation in the sport as players and as spectators has increased as a result of their presence and dominance.

The now-legendary sisters learned to play tennis on public courts in Compton, California. Venus and Serena, the daughters of Oracene Price and Richard Williams, demonstrated talents and skills beyond what their ages and training would, under ordinary circumstances, predict, but these future stars were extraordinary. Venus, the elder of the two sisters, went on to win singles competitions at Wimbledon five times, the U.S. Open twice, and an Olympic gold medal. By the 2012 season, she had 43 single titles and 19 doubles titles, which include three Olympic gold medals with her sister Serena. By the 2012 season, the duo had won five Wimbledon titles. Venus is second only to Serena on the prize money list, according to Tennis.com.

Serena Williams is said to have the best serve in all of women's tennis. She won her first major title in singles play in 1999 when she was just 17 years old. Over the course of her time on the tour, which spans almost two decades, she has won 43 career championships, including 13 Grand Slam doubles titles. She is the fifth woman in tennis history to have held all major titles simultaneously and has won nearly $35 million in prize money, which is more than any female athlete has earned in the history of any sport.

Venus and Serena are not only among the most talented players in the game, they are in many ways also the most controversial players. Many have written about these bright stars and their inner circle, dealing with subjects ranging from their father, Richard Williams, and his role as their coach, to their religious faith, to their hairstyles and game-day attire. Delia Douglas is among the scholars to examine the role of the sisters in tennis and in American society as a whole.[17]

In an article entitled "Venus, Serena, and the Women's Tennis Association: Where 'Race' Enters," Douglas writes about their appearances at Indian Wells in 2001 and the French Open in 2003. Applying the structures of feelings concept, Douglas considers how dominant cultural meaning and values are adapted and expressed through the atmosphere produced at the aforementioned sporting events. The researcher draws upon critical race theory and critical whiteness studies in the analysis. Using these concepts and perspectives, Douglas argues that we can gain a better understanding of how "white racial subjectives are conceived and communicated in daily life."[18]

Douglas describes the controversy surrounding Indian Wells, where Venus withdrew due to an injury, but many suspected that the Williams family was trying to control the outcome of the contest. She describes the audience response as hostile. John Jeremiah Sullivan of the *New York Times* wrote about the same incident: "The flash point was that Venus withdrew from a semifinal match against Serena. She didn't feel well enough to play. Tendinitis. It's often reported that she did this with only minutes to go before the match." Sullivan goes on to say, "Two days later, when the family returned to the court for Serena's match against the big-hitting Belgian Kim Clijsters, the crowd began to boo. Both Richard and Serena assert that they heard the word 'nigger.' The booing continued throughout the match, which Serena won in a display of all but inexplicable poise—or really something more like fearsomeness, when you witness it. But the most astonishing and little-remarked moment occurred before the match even started, when Richard and Venus walked down to their seats in the players' box. The booing intensified." Sullivan adds that the boos were directed at Venus because she "committed the sin," and at Richard, who many disliked "for his frequently asinine Svengali persona," and allegations that he had abused Oracene Price.[19]

Delia Douglas, however, has a different interpretation of the response from those in attendance. Analyzing print media and television, Douglas comments on how the meanings of whiteness and white racial identity are communicated in something as seemingly apolitical as a tennis match. Douglas shows that a tennis match featuring black players is the ideal place because you have black athletes in white space where the crowd may feel that the athletes deserve to be treated poorly. Evidence of this may be seen in violations of protocol and in the identification with white female players. The methods used by the crowd can be understood as the exercise of white racial power to achieve a common goal, and that goal was for Serena to lose. Douglas goes as far as to say that the "symbolic violence signified the undesirability of the Williams family and reinforced the racial barriers."

The reaction of the crowd at Indian Wells in 2001 also helped highlight the significance of examining everyday activities as a means of better understanding how race is considered in the so-called postracial era. The reactions to Serena Williams and her family highlight "how symbolic inclusion can obscure the complex ways in which discriminatory practices and institutionalized power sustain racial injustice and reproduce ideologies of white superiority." Like other black athletes in sports where they are overrepresented or underrepresented, the acceptance of them and their black aesthetic physicality is often symbolic in nature. Black athletes, like blacks in society at large, remain a group that has not been fully accepted, assimilated, or included in mainstream society in meaningful ways, which serve as evidence that fundamental changes in the racialized social structure occurred.

We must, Douglas concludes, analyze that which is "taken for granted . . . namely our rituals, habits, and patterns of thought and interaction, so that we can challenge and respond to the myriad ways in which race and gender (and class) oppression manifest themselves in our everyday lives." In other words, evidence of the continuing significance of race and how racial messages are communicated can be found all around us.[20]

Sullivan, writing for the *New York Times* in 2012, elaborates further on the challenges Venus and Serena Williams face being black players in a predominantly white sport. Sullivan reflects on his finding that Serena Williams finds refuge in France, where she has an apartment. He speculates that she may be trying to get away from many things, including from America, "a country that couldn't decide if she was a goddess or a threat."[21]

Jamie Schultz addressed this very issue in an article that looks at Serena Williams and the production of blackness after she walked onto the court in "the catsuit" during the 2002 U.S. Open. Williams, her attire, and her body were represented in the media in such a way as to demonstrate how blackness is produced in contemporary times.[22] Schultz claims that it was not so much what she wore that brought about debate in the media, but that the suit "accentuated Williams' blackness." Though some media reports were flattering, they overwhelmingly "represented Williams in terms of difference," the effect of which was to "reinscribe whiteness as the normative racialized identity in women's tennis, thereby marginalizing blackness and discrediting ideologies of colorblindness in U.S. sport, media, and society."[23]

One might asked what makes the difference between the experience and reception of players like Althea Gibson and the Williams sisters. The difference is not only in the era in which each played but also in the style of discourse that dominated each era. In Gibson's day it was perfectly acceptable, and in many cases legal, to restrict black players from playing on public and private courts. It was also socially acceptable to use derogatory and inflammatory terms to describe black athletes. In more contemporary times, such practices are less socially acceptable and illegal. Color-blind language has replaced the language that dominated the Jim Crow era. Greater scrutiny of the Williams family and the treatment of the sisters as "others" within the sport are quite similar to the experiences of players like Althea Gibson, but the strategies and tactics used have new guises and appearances.

Conclusion

The overrepresentation of blacks in several high-revenue sports has led some to conclude that blacks have taken over most sports. While black participation in selected sports is quite high, black participation in other sports has declined or is relatively nonexistent. Players in these sports suffer because they are seen as invaders of white space. They are seen as a threat to the racial social order. Tennis and golf are but two sports that historically have been considered white sports, but have seen black players make important contributions, from making equipment to winning integrated championships without the benefits of the training and facilities open to their white counterparts. The reasons for the underrepresentation of blacks in selected sports are multifaceted and are sometimes the same reasons that account for the overrepresentations of blacks in other sports. The common thread, however, is that whatever sport professional black athletes are engaged in, they are subject to the same racialized social hierarchy that has existed around the world for centuries.

Black athletes may experience symbolic inclusion, as blacks in other areas of social life might experience. Each, however, eventually has a personal experience, or learns of the experiences of others, that serves as a reminder that those who have less power and control over their lives than the dominant group are still considered subordinate and receive unequal treatment as a result. The lessons that can be learned from this presentation of the role of racial socialization in athletic determinism, the effects of population and structural changes, and lived experiences in the world of sports are matters discussed in the next chapter.

Chapter 8

Sports and the Myth of a Color-Blind Society

Justice, fairness, and equality are foundational American values. Unfortunately, there have been variations in the extent to which racial groups have been treated justly, fairly, and equally. In the world of sports, black athletes were often the recipients of *in*justice, *un*fairness, and *in*equality. Through the treatment of black athletes over time, the dominant racial ideology—the web of ideas, beliefs, and even institutional practices that proclaimed white superiority and black inferiority—was reinforced and perpetuated down through the years.

The process by which we learn the ways of society for blacks and whites required social institutions—the structures through which the operations of societies are conducted and basic human needs are met—to communicate what was considered appropriate for blacks and for whites. Sports have fulfilled that function in the past and continue to do so now. While a number of historic examples and relatively recent examples were cited in earlier chapters, there are a number of recent events that capture the essence of the arguments set forth in this book: that racial socialization is directly related to the types of sports that blacks and whites have access to and how they are supposed to behave in their respective sports—or in their respective positions; and that challenges to the racial status quo result in manifestations of racism by the dominant group—whites—toward the subordinate group—blacks.

The manifestations of racism prior to the civil rights movement were largely overt, while in the post–civil rights era these manifestations are much more covert but not undetectable. Examples can be seen in the issues surrounding professional football players Richard Sherman, Jonathan Martin, and Michael Sam; in the reaction to LeBron James's decision to wear a black mask to protect his injured nose; and in the celebratory manner of an all-white Michigan high school basketball team. These stories highlight the complex and intimate connection between race and sport, so much so that certain sports come to be associated with blacks and other sports with whites, particularly in the color-blind era.

The terms *color-blind* and *postracial* have appeared in this book previously, but we will now take a more in-depth look at the idea either that race has declined in significance over time or that race is as significant today but only expressed differently. The aforementioned cases—Sherman, Martin, Sam, James, and the all-white high school basketball team—all occurred within the so-called postracial era.

Throughout this book we have seen many, many examples of the unequal treatment black athletes faced. We have seen that their struggle was part of a larger struggle for fairness, justice, and equality that was and is being waged by blacks across the country. During the days of slavery, blacks were considered property. They were governed by rules, codes, and regulations that whites did not have to obey. Every aspect of their lives was controlled. Opportunities for amusement—such as sport and leisure—were meant for the entertainment of the dominant racial group. It was important then, as it arguably is now, for there to be a clear distinction between what was appropriate for blacks and what was appropriate for whites. The ultimate goal was to maintain the color line in life. Forcing black bondsmen to fight one another was just another way for the dominant racial group to show their power—or the ability to exert one's will over others even in the face of resistance.

After slavery ended there were efforts to maintain the racial hierarchy, so blacks became disenfranchised. They were lynched. They were forced or coerced into labor arrangements that, in some cases, forever tied them to the land. Backed by the power of state laws and landmark Supreme Court decisions, blacks and whites were not allowed to ride in the same trains, eat in the same restaurants, swim in the same pools, or play on the same sports teams. As noted previously, some mainstream professional sports organizations had express clauses in their rules and regulations prohibiting membership of nonwhites. White athletes were not afraid to express their unwillingness to play against, or with, black athletes. The purpose, again, was to maintain a separation of the races so there would be no misunderstanding about each group's place in society. When the racial ideology was challenged by organizations and individuals, including black athletes and black athletic associations, concessions were often made, but typically only when they benefited the dominant racial group.

Derrick Bell wrote about the concept of *interest convergence* in his work, which helped lay the foundation for critical race theory.[1] Bell noted that the dominant racial group allows changes when it is in its own interest. Integrating professional sports therefore was done not because it was long past time for blacks to be treated with dignity and respect in sports and in the broader society, but because of competition from competing leagues or bad press—internationally and domestically—that might negatively impact profit margins.[2] In the end, members of the dominant group benefit, and members of racial minority groups, such as blacks, lose. The end of the Negro leagues was one example. The economies that sprung up around the black teams provided jobs and community economic development that could not be sustained after the integration of Major League Baseball because the access to capital that the black community had, relative to whites, was no match.

Even whites who did not have a direct stake in professional sports, and whites who never owned a slave and never held a sharecropping contract benefited—and continue to benefit—from the racial arrangement. In viewing whiteness as property, the benefit to whites who might not be considered elite is referred to as a consolation prize. When whites do not win, they do not lose either, because they maintain their advantage and privilege over blacks. So in the days of slavery, when blacks and whites ran away together, such as in the case of John Punch and several white indentured servants, the punishment the whites received was less severe than that which the lone black man received. The white indentured servants had their service extended for a number of years, but Punch was sentenced to servitude for life. In the case of sport, even after the integration of major professional sports, white athletes who lacked the skill and star power of black athletes were still afforded more privileges than some of the greatest black athletes playing the same games.

Sam Lacy chronicled the experiences of black ballplayers and black writers after integration. He noted that players like Jackie Robinson could not eat in restaurants or stay in hotels with their white teammates. They had to eat or stay in the homes of sympathetic blacks, or on the team bus. The white players were not in a position to make the decision directly as to whether or not baseball would integrate, and they may not have demonstrated any prejudice or discrimination toward blacks, or black athletes, but they nonetheless benefited from the privilege of their racial identity.[3]

Up until the 1960s—and for some time thereafter—it was quite clear where many Americans stood when it came to race relations. Black athletes of the 1960s and the 1970s were at the forefront of the struggle, using their celebrity status to draw attention to the unequal treatment. Muhammad Ali, Jim Brown, Bill Russell, and Kareem Abdul-Jabbar were among the high-profile athletes involved in the movements. The bravery of Tommie Smith and John Carlos on the winners' podium at the 1968 Olympics in Mexico is another memorable moment in which black athletes were concerned not so much with themselves as with the larger struggle of blacks in America.

After the heyday of the civil rights movement and the consciousness-raising black liberation movement, there was a notable backlash against race-specific policies aimed at redressing past wrongs. The backlash was observed in many areas of life: calls to end affirmative action in the 1970s; the co-optation of civil rights language in the 1980s; the nearly undetectable coded language to create, perpetuate, and explain racial differences. This was all evidenced in the world of sports. While predominantly white universities were forced to permit black players, they were often careful not to play too many. The positions in which black players could excel were limited as well. The position of quarterback eluded many standout black players because of the widely held myth that blacks lacked the intelligence to play the position effectively. More important, the quarterback has much of the decision-making power on the field, and relinquishing such power to a black athlete might, some thought, undermine the racial hierarchy that governed the broader society. Black players who demonstrated skill as quarterbacks were often assigned to positions that more closely fit with the general perception of blacks—that they were largely physical beings who lacked the intellect and bravery to command a football team.

The idea that whites benefited more from the integration of sports and of society also finds support when one takes an even closer look at the blacks who benefited most. For example, Jackie Robinson was a standout in multiple sports in college. He was identified as the ideal black person to make the leap into the majors. Surely there were black athletes in the Negro leagues who were better at the game than Robinson, but because they lacked the ability to respond to the anticipated taunts from players, fans, and the press, athletes with stronger skills were not chosen.

The civil rights movement opened the door for largely middle-class blacks to walk onto college campuses and into occupations for which they were already qualified but previously prevented from entering. One of the major criticisms of the movement was the lack of attention to the needs and concerns of blacks who were poor or working class. The very rights that blacks in the South were fighting for were already available to blacks in the North, so while the latter were sympathetic, there appeared to be a lack of connection between the black groups; it could be argued that this was exploited by the dominant group and that victories for the black middle class were seen as victories for all blacks. To be clear, the society as a whole benefited from the civil rights movement, but the benefits were not enjoyed equally. Economically disadvantaged groups did not experience upward social mobility en masse. Due to deindustrialization and the movement of jobs to the suburbs or the disappearance of work altogether, economically disadvantaged groups became even more concentrated and isolated, creating what William Julius Wilson called the *underclass*.[4]

Selected college and professional teams would actively recruit prospective student-athletes from these distressed communities. While it may be said that the student-athletes have the prospect of getting a free college education, it is indeed members of the dominant group who benefit most. With the number of media outlets expanding almost exponentially, so do efforts to capitalize on the skill levels of elite black college and professional athletes, but to do so in a way that maintains the dominant racial ideology, which holds that whites are superior to blacks. Thus the process of racial socialization in sports, of communicating the ways of society to blacks and whites, had to change over time. The role of race is more nuanced, but ever present.

For some, the integration of baseball signaled the end of racism in sports. Many quickly realized, however, that racism was such a powerful force in the broader society that it persisted beyond Robinson. The significance of race in sports continues today. Evidence can be found that the racialization of sports—that is, the association of a given sport as either black or white—is still evident. The manifestations of both overt and covert racism debunk the myth that we are living in a postracial society in which race no longer matters or has at least declined in significance. One need only look at the ways in which black athletes are treated by owners, managers, the press, fellow players, spectators, fans, and even those with no direct interest in sports.

We have seen how institutional barriers have contributed to racial differences in the types of sports played, thus perpetuating wealth inequality and asset poverty in the United States. The relative invisibility of blacks in some sports and the overrepresentation of blacks in other sports is troubling but not surprising. Although racism has been declared dead over and over again, the fact that race remains a power force—and racial socialization a power process—shows how resilient, variable, and socially constructed the racial classification system is in America.

Patricia Hill Collins, in *From Black Power to Hip Hop*, astutely describes "the shift from a color-conscious racism that relied on strict racial segregation to a seemingly colorblind racism that promised equal opportunities yet provide no lasting avenues for African America advancement." With blackness came a host of "economic penalties."[5] Ideologies that serve to rationalize the unequal treatment of people based upon the racial group they belong to are reproduced through the mass media.

This new racism has given rise to a new generation of black athletes, particularly in the post-Iverson sports era that began in the 1990s, when black athletes' endorsement deals with sponsors such as shoe manufacturers became as lucrative as, or better than, actual player contracts. Under these circumstances, players who did not conform to the expectations of the dominant society could suffer financially. Prior to the 1990s, there was an unwritten rule American sports: the majority white spectators would not attend or watch a game in which the majority of players were not white or predominantly white. Black athletes in predominantly white sports or on mixed-race teams could win the loyalty of fans as long as they deemphasized their racial identity in appearance and conduct. This meant emphasizing one's skills and ability to work toward the good of the team and the surrounding community, as opposed to using one's position as a platform for addressing inequalities within the league or society, especially those related to race. Wearing pink in support of breast cancer research was fine, and showing that a league cares by handing out basketballs and shoes was all right, but acts of direct or indirect protest, particularly around issues of race, were not tolerated.

Contemporary black athletes who successfully "mute" their race enjoy success and longevity. Prior to the revelations about his infidelity, Tiger Woods received widespread support from the largely white audience and the general respect of white players on the tour (even though he was the subject of a racist comment following his Masters win, when one golfer joked about the soul food Woods would select as part of his award for winning the tournament). Tiger Woods not only distanced himself from the black label that so many tried to thrust upon him, he created a new racial identity emphasizing his multiracial and multiethnic heritage.

Attempting to mute one's race appears to work most successfully when there are relatively few blacks in the sport in question. Ignoring one's race in a sport that is predominantly black is not a good strategy because individuals with membership in the minority racial group tend to have the greatest fascination with players in their own group, and they show that fascination by purchasing sneakers, jerseys, and other items bearing the player's image or name.

Few black athletes have neutralized the preeminence of their race as successfully as Michael Jordan, who did so among the NBA's largely white fan base. Jordan did not regularly speak out on issues of concern to the black community during his time in the NBA, including the subject of apartheid in South Africa. He did not publicly take sides on political issues, asserting that both Democrats and Republicans bought his shoes. Jordan—and professional black players that followed him—handled the age-old problems that blacks have faced, which W. E. B. DuBois referred to as a double-consciousness: "One ever feels his twoness—an American, a Negro; two souls, two thoughts, two unreconciled strivings; two warring ideals in one dark body, whose dogged strength alone keeps it from being torn asunder."[6]

Professional black athletes since the 1990s have reconciled the twoness largely by conforming to, and not challenging, the dominant racial ideology. Contemporary black athletes seldom challenge the status quo, and when they do, such as in the case of labor negotiations, they are vilified in the press and on social media by their so-called fans.

Black athletes who wish to maintain their racial identity are usually met with some form of resistance. Such resistance is a manifestation of racism that may be overt or covert.

On the one hand, black athletes may very well wish to maintain ties with black family members and friends from before their professional days, but there is an expectation that black athletes should develop ties with other professional blacks, such as teammates and black entertainers. In doing so, black athletes understand that, despite their presence in an integrated professional league, some whites still prefer to maintain a certain social distance between themselves and blacks. Professional black athletes may therefore not be welcomed with open arms into the homes and private clubs of their white counterparts or elite whites even though they are welcome to play for their franchises.

Similarly, when a black athlete conforms to the expectations communicated through the process of racial socialization, he or she can be understood to embrace the hope that sports really have a level playing field. The black athlete embraces the idea that sports and the broader society have moved closer to the goal of judging people based upon their demonstrated abilities and not their race. At the same time, conforming to expectations set by owners, coaches, managers, spectators, and society may reflect a key understanding that race matters as much as it has in the past, if not more. Conformity also indicates an acceptance of the idea that challenging the dominant racial ideology—the belief that whites are superior to blacks—will do more harm than good.

The key problem with black athletes burying their heads in the proverbial sand and carrying on as though sports is a level playing field, and promoting the misconception that there is no gap between American idealism and American realism, is that we are just a news cycle away from an event that reminds us all of just how significant race is in sports and in society. Recent racial controversies involving Richard Sherman, Jonathan Ferrell, Michael Sam, Jonathan Martin, LeBron James, and an all-white high school basketball team in Michigan all reminded us that racism alive and well and that the process of racial socialization continues to communicate expectations regarding sports participation for blacks and whites.

Despite the scholarly literature on race, including the literature on race and sports, it remains unclear precisely when Jim Crow racism allegedly ended and color-blind racism began. Part of the problem is that while examples of color-blind racism are evident in the operation of American institutions, Jim Crow racism is alive and well in the daily interactions of folks, especially whites who receive the consolation prize, described previously. Their concerns about race in America are most evident in social media, which I would argue is where Jim Crow lives today.

Let us now turn our attention to the case of Richard Sherman, which helps to highlight the ways in which racial socialization functions to perpetuate myths about whites and blackness, including black and white sports. We will see clearly from this case study how the use of stereotypes and coded language seeks to play on the anxieties of members of the dominant group about blacks in general, and black athletes in particular, such that interpretations of their actions are quite different than interpretations of similar actions by nonblack athletes.

Stanford University is home to some of the most prestigious academic departments and some of the nation's best athletic programs. Several of the nation's greatest athletes attended or graduated from Stanford, including John Elway, Tiger Woods, and John McEnroe. Richard Sherman of the Seattle Seahawks is a Stanford graduate. Sherman is a high-profile football player known for his many accomplishments on and off the field. Most people know the name Richard Sherman because of the coverage of a postgame interview that he did with reporter Erin Andrews. The discussions surrounding the interview illustrate the theme addressed throughout this book, namely that there is a process of racial socialization that takes place in social institutions, including in sports, whereby expectations for blacks and whites are communicated. Deviations from the norm are met with manifestations of racism, which may be covert or overt and may take the form of stereotypes, the institutionalization of new policies and procedures, and so on, with the express purpose of maintaining the dominant racial ideology that places whites in a position of dominance and blacks in a position of subordination. Changes in the shape, size, and composition of the U.S. population or of the population of players, as well as other social, economical, political, and cultural changes, may lead to the furtherance of these manifestations of racism.

Shortly after the start of 2014, the Seattle Seahawks met the San Francisco 49ers in the championship game of the National Football Conference. The winner would go to the Super Bowl. The game lived up to the hype and was widely watched. The outcome of the game was uncertain up until the final play, when Richard Sherman swatted away a pass that was intended for San Francisco receiver Michael Crabtree. The victory was made sweeter for Sherman because of a long-standing feud he had with Crabtree. According to Sherman, in a show of good sportsmanship, he attempted to shake Crabtree's hand. Crabtree ignored Sherman and then shoved him, pushing him away. Almost immediately after the encounter with Crabtree, Sherman was asked by Andrews to walk her through the final play, which was destined to be a classic. Sherman responded by saying that he was the best corner in the game. He added, "When you try me with a sorry receiver like Crabtree, that's the result you gonna get!"[7]

Sherman's disparaging remark about Crabtree was based upon their previous conflict and Crabtree's unwillingness to take the olive branch offered by Sherman. Sherman, in attempting to do the right thing by bringing an end to the tensions between the two players, was dismissed by Crabtree. The disrespect to Sherman was evident in his comments during the on-field interview.

The All-American corner said during the interview, "Don't you ever talk about me!" Sherman used the opportunity to communicate with Crabtree, who had demonstrated an unwillingness to let bygones be bygones.

Incredulous and perhaps a bit fearful, Andrews followed up with Sherman, asking, "Who was talking about you?" Sherman—in the heat of the moment—added, "Crabtree, don't you open your mouth about the best or I'm a shut it for you real quick!" It is not clear whether Andrews witnessed the exchange in which Crabtree shoved Sherman at the end of the game, but despite the fact that the shove was televised, analysis of the on-field interview focused squarely on Sherman.

The focus on Sherman and the interpretation of his actions reveal the displeasure that many fans, onlookers, and sports journalists felt after watching the interview. The individuals—mostly white—would not characterize Sherman's behavior as that of a model minority athlete. On the contrary, racially coded language was used to describe his conduct. Racially coded language taps into racial anxiety and allows the speaker to deny that he or she is even speaking about race, according to scholar Ian Haney Lopez.[8]

Coded language is used in sports and in the broader society. The use of coded language comprises a new War on Poverty, of sorts, which I wrote about in an op-ed piece for the *New York Amsterdam News*.[9] A term like *inner city* is often a code word for black. Similarly, terms such as *thug* conjure images of violent young black males. Richard Sherman was called a thug after the interview, especially on social media outlets such as Twitter. Twitter, where I like to say that Jim Crow lives, allows members of the dominant group, particularly those who do not consider themselves to be members of the elite, to post what they are thinking anonymously and in real time. At times the posts reflect commonly held stereotypes of groups, including black athletes, and they reflect the web of beliefs and ideas that make up the dominant racial ideology. While it may not be socially acceptable for an organization or leader of an organization to make racially charged comments about an athlete, Twitter makes it open season for average Americans interested in making their views known.

Richard Sherman answered his critics in a revealing analysis of reactions to the interview with Andrews. Admitting that the problems between himself and Crabtree were personal and went well beyond the field, Sherman candidly states, "I just don't like him." He added that his reaction to Andrews's question was just one aspect of who he is as a person.[10] Unfortunately, black athletes are not generally given the benefit of the doubt when it comes to such matters, and in fact there are examples throughout the history of race and sports where the society at large refuses to see black athletes as total persons. Too often black athletes—particularly black male athletes—are viewed as brutes. There are no separations between who the player is on and off the field. The context within which an event occurs is often ignored and the full body of a black athlete's work is seldom considered. Greater deference and understanding is afforded to white athletes, for whom the broader society is more likely to excuse behaviors similar to those of Sherman as naturally occurring in the heat of the battle. Sherman's reaction would likely be described as passionate and adrenaline filled were he a white athlete, but as a black athlete he is labeled using racially charged language.

Sherman noted that individuals used racial slurs, bias, and bullying language in their professional write-ups and Twitter posts. He said that he learned from the experience a number of things about himself, society, and the game he loves. Sherman quickly came to the realization that "the stage is bigger than I thought it was." It seems shocking that a professional athlete playing for an opportunity to participate in one of the most anticipated sporting and social events in the nation would be in awe of the amount of coverage he received. Sherman's candid reaction to all the attention points to just how successful racial socialization is in communicating the ways of society. The roles prescribed for blacks and whites in society are so much a part of our culture that we are often unaware of their influence until we are faced with an event or experience that forces us to see the obvious that has for so long has remained largely invisible. Sherman is therefore not alone in his naïveté, in his belief that football is just a game.

While some Americans, including some athletes, are cautious about interjecting race into a situation because of the potential ramifications for one's career and financial standing, Sherman conceded that race may have had something to do with it. However, Sherman carefully softened the sting of his critique. He questioned whether the reaction would have been the same if he had a more "clean-cut" image, if he did not wear dreadlocks. He added that it is part of human nature that we look negatively upon people who appear different from ourselves, as we all stereotype and label others. This statement minimizes the significance of racism and the racial discrimination he and other black athletes face by asserting that expressions and manifestations of racism by whites are no different from acts of prejudice or discrimination by other groups. Individuals often confuse racism with prejudice and discrimination, and thus interpret issues related to race inaccurately.

Another important observation made by Sherman was that the National Football League always wins when there is controversy. Sherman was likely referring to the old adage that all publicity is good. More people will be drawn to watching the Super Bowl because of all the coverage leading up to it. However, the league and members of the dominant group always win in other ways. The ability to control the image of black athletes is one way to maintain the racial status quo and reinforce the racial ideology that whites are superior to blacks and thus worthy of greater social standing both within sports and in the broader society.

Sherman also expressed an awareness of the ways in which football and society have changed. He said that when football was "raw" and not sanitized "the same things they fined guys for now were the aspects of the game people loved." This begs the question: so what has changed? Yes, there have been increased calls for changes to the rules of the game to improve player safety. What has also changed is the race of many of the athletes and the desire to ensure that the players conform to society's expectations of them as athletes in the sport of football.

The on-field interview with Erin Andrews was not the first time comments made by Sherman elicited a reaction from sports fans, journalists, and society as a whole. Sherman confronted the controversial ESPN personality Skip Bayless. Prior to Sherman's appearance on the ESPN network with Bayless and Stephen A. Smith, Bayless offered his thoughts on how Sherman measured up to similar players in the league. Sherman clearly believed that Bayless did not rank him as high as he thought he should be ranked, but he outright refused to critique other league players, turning his attention instead toward Bayless.

While Bayless may be a popular personality on the network, he is not always popular with athletes, including several black athletes. Those black athletes include Charles Barkley, Jaylen Rose, and Kevin Durant. Bayless once questioned Rose about his proficiency on the court, which resulted in Rose reminding Bayless of a recent controversy in which it was discovered that Bayless had lied about his role on a high school team and that he was not team's version of the legendary player Pete Maravich.

Bayless has made other outlandish and unfounded statements and has received little of the backlash from owners, coaches, sports journalists, and fans that Sherman and other black athletes tend to receive when involved in high-profile media events. For example, with no evidence whatsoever, he has speculated about whether or not Derek Jeter of the Yankees ever used performance-enhancing drugs simply because other players were found using them, and because Jeter has managed to continue to play well despite several injuries and his age. Jeter—whose father is black and whose mother is white—is declared guilty by association and by accident of his birth. Were Jeter a white player such claims would not fly as easily from the lips of commentators like Skip Bayless.

Bayless critiqued Oklahoma City standout Kevin Durant for working out with LeBron James one year during the preseason. Both were potential MVP candidates and frontrunners for the scoring title. Bayless tweeted that Durant needed to wake up. He claimed James was only trying to keep his friends close and his enemies even closer. Bayless portrayed James as untrustworthy and conniving, as a person who would betray someone close to him, and Durant as lacking wisdom and understanding and in need of advice from someone like Bayless. This paternalistic attitude of whites toward blacks is not new and is evidence of Bayless's internalization of the privilege afforded to him because of his racial identification.

Durant's response is significant and powerful. Shortly after Bayless's comments on September 11, 2012, Durant stated that Bayless brainwashes people into thinking he really knows what he is talking about because he is on ESPN. The use of the term *brainwashing* by Durant highlights the fact that few viewers critique what they see and hear in the media. Some individuals believe information shared on what is considered an authoritative and legitimate source like ESPN is the absolute truth. Durant indirectly calls upon individuals in the sports world and the broader society to think more critically and analytically about information presented to them as objective. Durant further refutes Bayless's claim that by training in the preseason with James, James now "owns" Durant. Durant responded, "Nobody owns me." Like athletes in the past, Durant attempts to assert the fact that he is a total person, fully capable of making decisions for himself, that he is not a slave but a free man, free to do as he pleases, although Bayless clearly does not see him as such.[11]

Another recent example of the process of racial socialization in sports is the case of Michael Sam. A former defensive end at the University of Missouri, Michael Sam was said to be on his way to becoming the first openly gay athlete in one of the four major sports in America. Before ever participating in the NFL scouting combine—an opportunity for athletes to showcase their talents before interested teams—Sam, who is black, informed his teammates that he is gay. He later made the same announcement to the American public. Immediately there was speculation in the popular press about whether or not the NFL was ready for an openly gay player. There were also concerns about how the release of the information about Sam's sexuality might impact his overall success in the draft. Before Sam's announcement some believed he would be a third- or fourth-round draft pick. After the announcement the prognostications fell to the seventh round, or that he would even go undrafted.

Objective measures for the lower expectations about Sam's NFL prospects were set forth. During the NFL scouting combine, the 6-feet1-inch, 260-pound athlete had not done as well as expected in the vertical leap, which some say indicates a lack of explosiveness, and his 4.91 time in the 40-yard dash did not rank high among the other defensive line prospects.

The financial cost to Sam could be great. This former collegiate player of the year could take a hit where signing bonuses are concerned. Signing bonuses are typically contingent upon one's place in the draft. First-round draft picks get higher bonuses than second-round draft picks, and second-round draft picks get higher bonuses than third-round draft picks, and so on.

The initial disclosure of Sam's sexual orientation occurred as a result of a team-building exercise in the Missouri locker room. Teammates were asked to share—among other things—something people did not know about them. Sam's race was clearly identifiable. Race, regardless of the other social statuses we hold, remains a master status. It continues to be the most visible marker for determining a host of factors, from the sports you play to how you may be received playing them.

Some observers speculate that Sam will become a trailblazer of gay rights in sports in much the same way Jackie Robinson was a pioneer in baseball. Sam not only will thus have the burden of doing well in his on-field position, but he will carry the load of being a champion of gay rights in a sport filled with expressions of hypermasculinity and, some have argued, homophobia. He will be expected, like Robinson, to accept "his abuse in a kind of heroic stoicism in a sport notorious for its macho culture."[12]

As has been the case for black athletes before, the onus is on the black athlete to shoulder the burden of dealing with the oppressor and not on the oppressor to change. Indeed, black athletes have been hailed for their ability to withstand abuse, but seldom have the abusers been called out and held responsible and accountable for their actions.

The NFL's response to Sam's disclosure of his sexuality is indicative of the gap that exists between American ideals and American realism. According to the NFL's official statement, issued on February 9, 2014, "Any player with ability and determination can succeed in the NFL." History teaches us that this is at the very least is a misrepresentation of the facts. A year prior to the issuance of the statement, the NFL distributed an antidiscrimination policy on the subject of sexual orientation that stated that the NFL had "a long history of valuing diversity and inclusion.

Discrimination and harassment is not consistent with our values and is unacceptable in the National Football League."[13]

These good intentions notwithstanding, historical evidence shows that the NFL and other professional leagues were at the forefront of maintaining the racial color line. In more contemporary times, there have been a number of high-profile incidents involving the NFL and "controversies over homophobia," including punter Chris Kluwe's claim that he was released by the Minnesota Vikings for supporting gay marriage. There were also allegations that prospective players were asked outright whether or not they like women.

What is particularly interesting is the number of stories in recent years about openly gay athletes in the top four American sports and how a disproportionate number of these athletes have been black athletes. Given the continued hypermasculinity in sports such as football and basketball, and given the continued presence and evidence of homophobia in sports that are dominated largely by heterosexual males, it may be more than a passing coincidence that these pioneering gay male athletes are also black male athletes, which may create further distance between whites and blacks in sports in particular and in society more generally. The marginalization of both groups in the larger society will likely be evidenced in the marginalization of these groups in sports as well.

Perceptions of blacks as prone to violence and acts of lust are not new and can have dire consequences. Jonathan Ferrell was a football player at Florida A&M. Ferrell had just moved to North Carolina to be closer to his fiancée. Shortly thereafter he was involved in what is described by NewsOne as a serious car crash. The crash was apparently so severe that Ferrell had to kick out his back window to free himself from the vehicle. Ferrell then walked to some nearby homes and knocked on the doors. A woman answered the door and immediately shut it after realizing it was not her husband. The woman called 911. She perceived Ferrell—the victim of a serious car accident who was seeking assistance—as a threat. She pleaded with the 911 dispatcher to send help right away because she was in the house alone with an infant child. The distraught woman was concerned not only for her safety but that this ex-athlete intended to inflict harm.

One of the officers responding to the call was Randall Kerrick. Assuming that help had finally arrived, Ferrell went in the direction of the officers. One of the officers attempted to taser Ferrell, and when they did not immediately stop his forward momentum, Kerrick fired 10 shots into Ferrell's body. It was beyond the comprehension of the woman who called 911, and of Randall Kerrick, that the black man they saw could be in pain and in need of help. Both interpreted him as a threat. Were Ferrell a white man behaving in the same way under the circumstances, chances are he would still be alive today. In fact, we would be treated to on-screen reunions of the injured motorist who finally got to thank the homeowner and the first-responder who came to the rescue. Blacks in America, however, particularly black males, elicit feelings of fear that can lead to their untimely deaths.

Law enforcement experts say that the use of deadly force by Kerrick against Ferrell was not justified. Ferrell was not armed and video from the dashboard on the night of the shooting shows just that. According to the police chief involved with the case, and according to the attorney for the Ferrell family, the ex-athlete could be seen with his arms stretched out and his hands empty. Kerrick faces the possibility of serving as much as 11 years for the slaying of the unarmed man. The messages communicated about black athletes go far beyond the field of play and can lead to the senseless loss of not just a game but of a life.

Manifestations of racism do not always lead to the loss of a young life, but they can lead to other significant loses. This was particularly evident in the case of Jonathan Martin. Martin once played for the Miami Dolphins and made headlines over accusations that he was bullied and racially taunted by teammate Richie Incognito. Martin, who like Richard Sherman played for Stanford University, broke down the Dolphins' code of silence by sharing with the world what he endured as a player on the roster. According to the report commissioned by the NFL, Martin left the Miami Dolphins team in the middle of the season and immediately sought psychological help. Media speculation that Martin left because of harassment from his teammates grew, and soon the franchise asked the NFL to conduct an investigation. The league's report concluded that Martin was harassed not only by Incognito but also by two other teammates, John Jerry and Mike Pouncey.

Martin was the target of the abuse, but so were an unnamed player and an assistant trainer. "The Assistant Trainer repeatedly was targeted with racial slurs and other derogatory language." The unnamed player "was subjected to homophobic name-calling and improper physical touching." Disparaging remarks were uttered about Martin's mother and sister, and he was "at times ridiculed with racial insults."

Although the investigators found convincing evidence that the trainer and the unnamed player were harassed, they found that "the questions raised in Martin's case were more complex, nuanced, and difficult." Part of the difficulty was that Martin and Incognito appeared to have a relatively good relationship at the onset, one in which they often joked with each other. After consulting a workplace psychologist, the authors of the report found that victims of harassment and workplace abuse may participate in their own abuse as a coping strategy, which was consistent with Martin's locker room actions.

Although sympathetic to the psychologist's interpretation, the report also found that "Martin may have been particularly sensitive to insults from his teammates." Here Martin is viewed as relatively weak. The idea that he is particularly sensitive points to the belief that most players would be able to withstand such insults. The shortcoming, this implies, is with Martin; it is not a matter of an institutional or systemic problem.

In many ways the authors of the report are saying, "Boys will be boys." This type of behavior is expected and accepted: "We accept that the communications of young, brash, highly competitive football players often are vulgar and aggressive." Moreover, the authors say that "profanity is an accepted fact of life in competitive sports, and professional athletes commonly indulge in conduct inappropriate in other social settings." Different rules apply to athletes and to the rest of society, and the same is true for black and white athletes. Even within this context, the authors found some actions out of bounds and "offensive to Martin." Again, the focus is on the individual level for a process that is multileveled and evident on both the individual and institutional levels.[14]

The report even cites the fact that Martin was bullied in middle school and high school, and that this negatively impacted his confidence and esteem. Again, the problem appears to lie with Martin and not with a larger set of processes that communicate to Martin and to others their relatively low status in the social structure.

Reports that Martin thought about suicide on more than one occasion again reflect back on Martin and his inability to take this treatment with the type of heroic stoicism that had been expected of many other black athletes, rather than on the everyday racism that slowly crushes the spirits of many children and adults of color. Although the authors of the report go out of their way to say that this is not the case, the mere inclusion of it as part of their fact finding must be questioned.

Furthermore, the authors of the report find little evidence that Incognito's goal was to force Martin from the team or to "cause him lasting emotional injury," but the authors do not expressly state what Incognito hoped to accomplish. Whatever the manifest reason for their actions, the results were not only that an individual was harmed, but that the dominant racial ideology was reinforced and Incognito was able to use his power and privilege to accomplish these goals.

The situation involving Martin and Incognito is characterized largely as harassment. The term *racist* appears 14 times in the entire 150-page report. Although the "N" word appears almost 40 times in the report, the term *racism* never appears in the report. The term *harassment* appears more than 65 times and the term *bullying* is used over 40 times. The term *race* was used eight times in the report, and was characterized as difficult to resolve. Clearly, the authors of the report are concerned about labeling this a racial issue—which it obviously is. The lead author is a well-respected criminal defense attorney and has represented some of the nation's largest corporations and has served a number of civil rights organizations, but is no expert on race.

The authors of the report demonstrate a clear lack of understanding about race in three key areas: (1) how racial socialization in sports works, (2) how manifestations of racism may be overt or covert in sports, and (3) how manifestations of racism may be exacerbated in times of society change. They conclude that "the extent to which the abuse resulted from racial animus is unclear." Although Martin says the taunting and harassing was at least partly due to race, Incognito claimed that it was not. Incognito admittedly referred to Martin using the "N" word and also used racial slurs in his dealings with an Asian assistant trainer.

Text messages between Martin and his father showed how upset Martin was after Incognito called him the "N" word at a dinner, which refuted claims by Incognito that the term was a term of endearment that he regularly used with Martin. Most troubling for the authors of the report was the involvement of John Jerry and Mike Pouncey. Since Jerry is black and Pouncey is biracial, the authors of the report reasoned that the taunting—in which Jerry and Pouncey participated—could not have been racially motivated and that at least one other person that Incognito treated poorly was white, though most were black. The involvement of Jerry and Pouncey does not mean Incognito did not act upon racial prejudices. The involvement of Jerry and Pouncey involved allegations that Martin was perhaps not black enough. Either way, Martin was targeted in large part due to his race, and his race was used as the focal point for making his workplace hostile and his dream of playing professional sports not worth the mental toll it was taking on him and others. Moreover, in a racialized social system members of oppressed groups are often solicited to participate in the oppression of others with membership in their own group. For example, black slaves often served as overseers of other black slaves under the guidance and direction of slave owners. Some overseers were particularly harsh and brutal toward their fellow slaves, in hopes of gaining favor and concessions for themselves and their families. In the unequal balance of power between the oppressed and the oppressor, it is not uncommon for the oppressed to participate in their own oppression and that of others.

Missing from the discussions of the NFL's report in the popular press is the deeply offensive quality of Incognito's comments about Martin's sister (whom Incognito had never met). The nature of these comments is too graphic to go into here, but the comments became a source of torment for Martin. The sexual exploitation of the black body by white men is not new, nor is the use of the black female body as a tool for demonstrating to black men their lower social status and lack of power to do anything substantively about it.

Another incident that showcases how sports are used to communicate the ways of society for blacks and whites is a recent controversy concerning an injury LeBron James suffered to his nose. James was struck in the nose during a game against Oklahoma City on February 20, 2014. His nose was broken in the victory and he had to sit out at least one game. Upon his return, James did what many other athletes had done. He wore a protective mask. James did not wear the traditional clear mask, but he wore a black mask. He scored a leading 31 points in the victory, but was asked by the league to switch to a clear mask going forward.

James was not the first player to wear a black mask, but on James it caused quite a bit of controversy in the mainstream and social media. What is interesting about this particular matter is that the league did not offer any substantive reason for James not to wear the black mask. Some described the look as "flat out ridiculous." Someone else tweeted, "LeBron James looks like a burglar with mask he's got on." Another Twitter user commented, "If @KingJames isn't scary enough on the court, he's wearing that mask that makes him look like Hannibal Lecter." The coach of the Miami Heat, James's team, described the mask as having "a menacing look."[15]

Reactions to the black mask were both predictable and ironic. As a society we have been socialized to see things associated with whiteness and white people as positive and things associated with blackness and black people as negative, including in sports. Additionally, the institutional practices within the sports world and the private actions between owners, coaches, managers, players, spectators, fans, the media, and corporate sponsors perpetuate this dominant racial ideology, and in a sport in which a majority of players is black it is important for the players not to be seen as such. At the same time, the need to conform to the practices and adhere to the norms even when one disagrees with them means that black athletes in many ways wear a mask every time they play, to hide their true selves.

Black athletes throughout time have had to represent themselves in ways that conform to larger societal ideas about what is appropriate for blacks and whites. Black athletes must remain stoic even in the face of racial inequality. The mask hides the black athletes' true feelings, or their ability to see the reality of their situation clearly. Wearing the mask and being who society wants you to be and not who you really are comes at a high price. It is indeed a great burden or debt that too many black athletes must bear. Despite the personal pain and the effect on the black community at large, the black athlete continues to wear the mask and pushes through the pain, as the society at large seems numb or indifferent to his or her plight and the plight of black people as a whole.

One of the more shocking examples of the ways in which some sports come to be considered as black sports and other sports as white comes from a town in Michigan. On Thursday, March 13, 2014, Howell High School defeated Grand Blanc in a Class A boy's regional final, according to ABC News. The Howell team was all white and the Grand Blanc team was made up of blacks and whites. After the game, players on the Howell team celebrated their 54–49 victory by posting messages on Twitter. Molly Young of Michigan Live.com wrote that the tweets included such statements as "Not only did we beat Grand Blanc but we're all white." "All hail white power. #HitlerIsMyDad." "#kkk."

Howell was home to Robert E. Miles until his death in 1992. Miles, according to Young, was a former Grand Dragon of the Ku Klux Klan and he "hosted KKK cross burnings." The area was home to a number of other KKK leaders, according to neighbors. The four or five students involved in the offensive posts would be subjective to "corrective measures," which were not disclosed by the district.[16]

One could argue that the young white athletes lacked an understanding of history and posted words and phrases that they did not realize had much greater significance. Alternatively, it could be argued that the young white athletes knew full well that basketball is a black sport in which an all-white team is not expected to be competitive, let alone victorious, which made their victory that much more sweet. Given the ties between the township and the KKK, it could also be inferred that at least some of the members of the all-white team felt a sense of duty to promote the dominant racial ideology by defeating the mixed-race team and reinforcing the idea that whites are superior to blacks.

According to Livingston Daily.Com, many in the town of Howell have fallen on hard economic times. Indeed, the basketball coach, Nick Simon, was reportedly laid off from his job as a teacher. In times characterized by structural and economic changes such as the loss of jobs, manifestations of racism are more evident. This was clearly the case in the town surrounding Howell High School and was felt not only by some adults but also by area youth. Through sports, the young players on the Howell High School team learned what was expected of them both on and off the court based upon their membership in a particular racial group.

Although justice, fairness, and equality are foundational American values, they are not enjoyed equally, including in the world of sports. Black athletes are often the recipients of unequal treatment. Sport—as a social institution—communicates what is appropriate for players, spectators, coaches, and owners based upon their membership in a particular racial group. The recent events discussed here demonstrate that racial socialization is directly related to the types of sports that blacks and whites have access to and how they are supposed to behave in their respective sports or in their respective positions within those sports; and that challenges to the racial status quo result in manifestations of racism by the dominant group—whites—toward the subordinate group—blacks.

Chapter 9

Conclusion

To understand why certain sports are associated with particular racial groups requires that we look not only at racial socialization as it is conventionally defined, but also at the process by which the ways of society are communicated to individuals and groups based upon racial identity. Various meanings are attached to the identified racial groups. Additionally, certain rights and privileges are awarded to one group and not to the others. Stereotypes and other manifestations of racism—both overt and covert—are used to perpetuate the belief of group dominance. Challenges to group dominance are met with resistance. Challenges may be direct or may be perceived in changes to the size, composition, and structure of society. Social institutions such as sports are not only built on the aforementioned racialized foundation, they also communicate the racialized ways of society. In the case of sports, this results in the association of certain sports as white and others as black. Changing the perception of sports as either black or white is not easy because this association is just part of the racial divide that exists in the broader society.

It is challenging for players, spectators, owners, coaches, and others to see sports as anything other than a form of entertainment that allows for an escape from daily living. Following a favorite player or team appears on the surface to having nothing to do with race, but who plays which sport is often a direct consequence of race. In addition, the inability of various stakeholders to see the important role of race in sports is not coincidental; rather, it is by design.

Just as there are "walls of whiteness" in many American institutions, there are walls of whiteness in sports. David Brunsma, Eric Brown, and Peggy Placier describe these walls as a force that protects against attacks on white supremacy. Brunsma et al. discuss walls of whiteness within institutions of higher learning, but these walls of whiteness are also evident in the social institution of sports. White owners, athletes, spectators, front-office staff, and even fans are encompassed by a wall of privilege built on the foundation of a racial classification system. Sports, as an institution, do not destroy the walls, but strengthen the brick and mortar through "institutional symbols, cultural reproduction, and everyday practices." The underlying assumptions are that "white supremacy is an ongoing racial project for almost 500 years" and that the United States were founded on the principle of white supremacy. Sports "rearticulate this principle in order to support and foster the civil, political, and social rights of its white constituency." The presence of walls of whiteness in sports is also based upon the assumption that racism impacts not only nonwhites but whites too. The ability of whites "to see beyond the veil of race" is one consequence where whites do not see the economic, social, political, and psychological costs of racism in their own lives and in the broader society.

Mainstream media conveys images and ideas about race, as described in chapter 3, that are often false representations of the experience of people of color. Blacks especially become hypervisible to whites, which leads whites to the conclusion that blacks have "made it." When presented with data that show the existence of persistent racial inequality, many whites become confused because of an unwillingness to accept the facts. Instead of exploring the data further, far too many simply ignore the issue and hide "behind their walls of whiteness."[1]

The success of the highest-earning black professional athletes masks the ongoing problems facing blacks as a whole. The high visibility of professional black athletes who make more per game than most blacks and whites earn in a year provides a convenient cover for the true nature of racial inequality in America. Outside the world of sports there are few instances where blacks earn more than their white counterparts. Far too many blacks are living in what is called *asset poverty*.

Asset poverty occurs when an individual or household lacks assets that could be easily converted to sustain the individual or group for a specified time period (usually at least three months) due to an economic or unexpected health crisis.[2] Owing to historic and contemporary discrimination, blacks as a group are less likely than whites to own assets. The existence of multimillion-dollar black athletes, however, perpetuates what scholars refer to as blaming the victim. The message that millions of black and white Americans receive—directly or indirectly—is that blacks as a whole would do better if they simply put forth more effort. If blacks worked harder, they would be rewarded handsomely. We know that this is simply not the case. Blacks who are asset owners tend to own assets at levels that are significantly lower than their white counterparts. Additionally, blacks are more likely than whites to have a zero or negative net worth.

Explanations for the lack of involvement in social justice issues on the part of contemporary black athletes may be found in ongoing discussions about the disuniting of black America. There was a time when there was a consensus among blacks about the group's goals, objectives, and needs. Blacks did not always agree regarding the means, but they agreed on the ends. However, setting a one-size-fits-all agenda for black America may no longer necessary. "Not after decades of desegregation, affirmative action, urban decay; not after globalization decimated the working class and trickle-down economics sorted the nation into winners and losers; not after the biggest wave of black immigration from Africa and the Caribbean since slavery; not after most people ceased to notice—much less care—when a black man and a white woman walked down the street hand in hand. These are among the forces and trends that have had the unintended consequence of tearing black America into pieces."[3]

Robinson claims that there is no need for a "black agenda" or for black athletes to use, or risk, their status and prospective economic future, because there are many black Americas. There are the black middle class, the black elite, the black underclass, black immigrants, and mixed-raced blacks, and no single black professional athlete—or group of black professional athletes—can speak on behalf of all these distinctive groups.

Although the black population is economically, ethnically, and politically diverse, this does not mean that there is no longer a need for a black agenda. It does not mean that there is no longer a need for a discussion about the state of black America, or a need for black professional athletes to use their status to draw attention to important issues facing the black community. The problem lies in the fact that the characterizations of black Americans are oversimplified.

Black athletes are not that far removed from the majority of black Americans who are neither middle class nor poor. For centuries blacks have been more likely to be working class than any other social class. Indeed, many black athletes still come from largely working-class backgrounds and can identify with the struggles this group faces.

Professional black athletes therefore tend to come from a tradition of activism. Researchers have shown that the group is significant not only because of its relative population size, but because the black working class played in important role in one of the most significant periods of social change in American history. While much of the leadership of the civil rights movement came from the middle class, it was the black working class that served as the "foot soldiers," and black professional athletes were among them.[4]

As professional athletes with relatively short careers, black athletes should identify even with the black middle class, whose socioeconomic status is quite fragile. The work of the Institute on Assets and Social Policy at Brandeis University on the black middle class highlights its fragile status. Wheary et al. created a middle-class security index to measure the extent to which various racial and ethnic groups enter and stay in the historic middle class. The middle class, according to the report, emerged after World War II and was the result of a number of broadly based public investments. Unfortunately, many of these public investments benefited some groups more than others, and the racial and ethnic disparities that resulted are still evident today, even among those with membership in the middle class.

The index includes indicators of education, assets, housing, budgeting, and health care. Households with at least three of the indicators are said to be secure in their middle-class status, while households lacking three or more indicators are said to be at high risk of losing their middle-class status. The report showed not only that it is more difficult to enter the middle class for blacks, but that blacks are less secure and at higher risk than others, especially whites, of losing their middle-class status. Upon closer examination, the researchers find that while 31 percent of Americans, regardless of race and ethnicity, are secure in their middle-class status, only 26 percent of blacks can say the same. One in three blacks in the middle class is at high risk, compared to about one in five of all middle-class Americans.

Asset poverty is greater among blacks in the middle class than among their white counterparts. While 13 percent of Americans in the middle class can meet 75 percent of their essential expenses for a nine-month period, were they to lose their income source, only 2 percent of blacks are equipped to do so. Even when the researchers considered the number of middle-class Americans with the resources to meet three-quarters of their essential living expenses for a period of just three months, racial differences were evident. Ninety-five percent of blacks lacked the net assets needed, compared with 78 percent of the middle-class, nationally. In fact, 68 percent of blacks had no assets at all and reported living check to check. Inequalities between the races are still evident when blacks with college degrees are compared with whites with similar levels of education. These findings should be cause for alarm—especially to professional black athletes, since most of them do not come from "old money" and know firsthand what is like to live in economic insecurity.

Black athletes who maintain the status quo by not challenging the system may be rewarded and considered model minorities. Model minorities allegedly earn the title by overcoming discrimination and diversity with little or no resistance. The term is often used to describe Asian Americans. However, the same fallacies that have been noted in the application of the model minority label to Asian Americans can be applied to the mislabeling of conforming black athletes.

The stereotypical model minority is hardworking, college educated, and law abiding. Professional black athletes who earned a college degree, work hard on the field or hardwood, and avoid police and legal problems are viewed more favorably than black athletes who never spend a day in college, miss games or practices, do not perform well, or get in trouble with the law. The myth, Park (2008) adds, portrays the group "as exemplary models for other minorities based (usually) upon measures of income, education, and public benefit utilization rates." Individuals within a so-called model minority are often placed on a pedestal and "mistakenly regarded as normative representatives" of the group.[5]

The model minority myth, even when applied to professional black athletes, hides the discrimination faced by other black athletes and blacks in the broader society. The idea of the model minority simultaneously perpetuates the American Dream and the idea that less successful black athletes and blacks are responsible for their failure to succeed. Viewing selected black athletes as model minorities divides those athletes from other black athletes and from the larger black community. The idea that some black athletes represent a model minority not only masks the discrimination that other black athletes and nonathletes face, it also contributes to stereotypes of blacks more generally, and creates tensions that may negatively impact collaborative efforts to bring about positive social changes inside and outside the sports world.

Pitting black athletes and the black community against one another causes individuals with membership in the same racial group to see those of different athletic abilities through the lens of otherness. This can have a negative impact on the efforts to work collaboratively to bring about change that benefits the group as a whole.

Clearly, the shortcomings associated with the application of the term *model minority* to people of Asian ancestry can also be observed in its use relating to black athletes who meet certain criteria. The experiences of many blacks reveal the continuing significance and complexity of race in America. The myth of the black athlete as evidence that society is indeed a meritocracy "alters one's sense of reality to justify the unequal social order."[6]

Sports are places of white space. The walls of whiteness include spatial walls, curricular walls, and ideological walls. Within the institution of sports, there are sports that are considered decidedly black or white. Despite efforts to officially desegregate sports, athletes are resegregated into particular sports and into particular positions within a given sport. Some observers would say that blacks and whites "naturally" gravitate toward particular sports.

The process of racial socialization for whites "conditions and creates whites' racial tastes, perceptions, feelings, emotions, and their views on racial matters so they seem natural."[7] Such socialization creates a sense of group consciousness, solidarity, and a prejudicial view of blacks and other nonwhites. These patterns, what Brunsma et al. call *white habitus*, inculcate sports.

One of the most important walls of whiteness is white privilege. White athletes, owners, spectators, and fans are the recipients of privileges bestowed upon them because of their race. Whites can enjoy the benefits of their race-based privileges without ever having to think about how such privileges were gained, and without considering the impact of the privileges on disadvantaged groups. In sports, whites often use the "special provisions, maps, passports, codebooks, visas, clothes, tools, and blank checks" to make and shape the world of sports at will.[8]

Reactions to black athletes today are reflective of what Eduardo Bonilla-Silva identifies as the four frames of color-blind racism. These frames are: abstract liberalism, naturalization, cultural racism, and minimization of racism.[9]

Abstract liberalism involves the use of terms associated with equality, justice, and fairness to justify the ill-treatment of black athletes and the black population as a whole. In explaining why locker rooms at all levels of competition look very much like a school cafeteria where people of similar racial groups engage one another and avoid others, we say that athletes have a right to choose who they befriend and that all that matters is that the team wins. However, this viewpoint ignores the practices and policies that have perpetuated stereotypes, myths, and misconceptions about blackness that have contributed to the preeminence of intragroup relationships over time.

The *naturalization* frame of white racism contends that whites attempt to dismiss manifestations of racism by saying they are natural occurrences. *Cultural racism* depends upon culturally based explanations. A number of black athletes come from poor backgrounds, so they have a different set of norms and values than white or black athletes from more affluent backgrounds. This explains differences in how blacks and whites are portrayed in the media, or even whether they get the votes of the largely white men who decide whether an athlete will get the distinction of being added to the Hall of the Fame for his or her respective sport.

There is a tendency to *minimize the significance of racism*. This frame suggests that opportunities for black athletes, and the black community as a whole, are determined by a host of factors and that race is no longer central. When black athletes complain of unequal treatment because of their race and physical appearance, many, especially some whites, note that the treatment of black athletes today is better than in the past. Again, the continuing significance of race is ignored or minimized.

Despite claims to the contrary—including viewpoints held by some black athletes—black athletes continue to have much in common with the larger black community. The process of racial socialization simultaneously reminds society of these similarities but is mindful to point out the differences, especially when doing so supports the larger goal of maintaining the web of ideas associated with the view that whites are superior to blacks. For instance, race has not declined in significance, and this is an experience that blacks share—athlete or not. In fact, black athletes may experience more manifestations of racism than less high-profile blacks, because black athletes possesses greater access to white space and are under much greater scrutiny than average black Americans.

It is clear that American sports reflect the values, beliefs, language, symbols, and traditions of the nation. Sports serve to perpetuate enduring ideologies, including racial ideologies. Perhaps the most enduring racial ideology in America is the belief of white superiority and black inferiority. Throughout this book, it has been shown that efforts to further this ideology have historically involved the forced separation of racial groups, including in sports. Even after the integration of sports, it remains clear that race still matters in sports.

The significance of race in the many sports discussed here became more salient in times of population and structural changes. Population changes included, for example, large shifts in the black population from the rural South to urban areas in the North. Structural changes in society, such as economic downturns, might also lead to greater manifestations of overt racism. The case of hard economic times in the Michigan town surrounding Howell High School (see chapter 8) is an example of that dynamic. Racial ideologies rooted in the superiority of lighter-skinned individuals and the inferiority of darker-skinned individuals have led to restrictions on sports participation, and they continue to play a key role in determining sports participation by race.

The overrepresentation of blacks in certain sports, such as basketball and football, and the underrepresentation of blacks in other sports, such as tennis and golf, are evidence of the existence and persistence of racial ideologies in sports. Early on one of the greatest challenges in understanding the continuing significance of race in sports was identified, namely the absence of a unifying theoretical framework. Another challenge was in understanding and drawing attention to the gap between society as it is and society as it ought to be.

Few social institutions highlight the inherent contradictions and tensions between American idealism and the reality in which we all live as well as sports. Examples were provided throughout the book. The historic and contemporary limitations placed on access to participation in selected sports based upon race were reviewed. Restrictions on freedom of sports participation both past and present were analyzed. In earlier decades, restrictive membership agreements banning the membership of certain nonwhites limited the freedom of some to participate in sports, but in more recent times the freedom to participate has been limited by the disappearance of youth sports in some communities and the costs associated with sports participation in other communities. In underresourced public school districts, sports programs are extinct or on the verge of becoming extinct. School-sponsored sports teams represent one of the few opportunities some individuals have to play competitive sports. This disparity in the availability of resources also places limitations on individual freedom when it comes to participation in sports. While some public schools offer access to a wide range of athletic options, others offer relatively few choices.

Sports—as we have seen throughout the book—also provide evidence of the gap between American idealism and American realism where the ideas of prosperity, fairness, and democracy are concerned. Sports associations at all levels have rules and guidelines that limit the ability of athletes to prosper.

Throughout the book, it was also demonstrated how sports mirror society. It was shown that sports not only are a reflection of society but are sites of political contests and are socially constructed.

It was also shown how sports can be understood as concrete representations of abstract concepts and ideas about race. The idea of white supremacy and black inferiority was foundational to the development of sports and society, and at the same time the success or failure of athletes by race either supported or disputed the dominant racial ideology. The ideas and beliefs that whites were superior to blacks in all areas of life led to the exclusion of blacks from professional sports.

The manifestations of these ideas and beliefs around race changed in form, but not function. Overt examples of racial discrimination were replaced—with the exception of incidents such as the remarks by Donald Sterling of the Los Angeles Clippers—with more subtle examples. Incidents of racial discrimination became harder to identify, as in the case involving Richie Incognito and Jonathan Martin of the Miami Dolphins. However, the presence of a race-based hierarchical social system remained clear. While more and more black players can be found in some sports, they remained underrepresented in other sports.

It was also shown how athletic associations moved from the explicit exclusion of blacks from sports to the inclusion of black athletes—but with restrictions on their behavior to conform to seemingly race-neutral policies aimed at controlling the actions of black players. We also examined how rule changes, codes of conduct aimed at improving safety or avoiding delays in the game, and efforts to enhance sportsmanship were actually intended to satisfy whites who control the associations, individual teams, and shell out money for tickets to the games.

We also offered discussions of the new racism and the myth of the color-blind era. Evidence of the continued significance of race, which is all around us, including in the world of sports, was cited. It was made clear that there are few social settings that illustrate how easy it is to be lulled into a sense of believing that race no longer matters in sports.

Throughout the book, the role of sports as an agent of socialization was introduced and expanded. It was also shown that sports play an important role in shaping racial identity and in determining sports participation. The processes that help shape sports, racial identity, and participation by race include racial socialization and variations in opportunity structures for blacks both within and outside of the sports. The process of racial socialization in sports is evident at the youth, collegiate, and professional levels.

This book should raise awareness of race-conscious messages that are communicated during the process of racial socialization. It is through the process of socialization that certain sports are considered black and others are considered white. Focusing specifically on racial socialization in the media and the racial socialization of minority athletes in youth sports, we also introduced a new framework for understanding the roles of race and racism in sports while also taking into account the roles of population and structural changes. Readers were encouraged to make connections between sports and society as a whole.

Considering certain sports as either black or white and then attaching meaning and policies to individuals in those categories, whether they are direct participants or not, is an important issue that was previously largely underdeveloped. It is hoped that this book will serve as a catalyst for other scholars to further explore the complex relationship between sports and other social and demographic factors such as social class and gender.

White Sports/Black Sports is different from other books about race and sports because it covers an array of sports, including sports in which racial minorities are in the numerical minority in terms of participation. The book also weaved the literature on race and sports with population studies, which should become common practice.

White Sports/Black Sports focused simultaneously on the professional, college, and community levels. Going forward greater scholarly attention should be devoted to community-based sports, as they are ideal places for examining racial socialization. Community-based sports, as we have seen, feed the pipeline for college and professional athletics.

Now that our understanding of the significance of racial socialization is enhanced, and we have seen more clearly how sports and society are mutually influential, we can begin to think about ways to bring about positive changes. While we may not be able to tackle large-scale institutional matters immediately, or even in our lifetime, there are a number of things that can be done.

Each of us can work to change the representations of black athletes in the media by letting advertisers know of our displeasure. Creating and expanding mentoring programs, particularly for black boys and girls, will develop awareness of the array of legitimate career options, beyond sports, than can also provide the means to maintain one's social position or experience upward social mobility.

Support for organizations that aim to increase sports participation by blacks in sports in which they are underrepresented is imperative. For example, there is a movement under way to increase the number of black participants in running. The National Black Marathoners Association and Black Girls Run! are two organizations that support this initiative.

The National Black Marathoners Association, established in 2001, is "the largest and oldest, national, not-for-profit organization that supports Black American distance runners." Historically, blacks in America have not routinely participated in distance running. Founder Tony Reed and other black distance runners began meeting regularly and taking part in distance races in numbers seldom seen. These black distance runners decided to "gather at a different marathon annually. This later became one of the missions for the NBMA."[10] The organization also awards scholarships to college-bound high school seniors.

Black Girls Run! began in 2009. Toni Carey and Ashley Hicks created the organization "to tackle the growing obesity epidemic in the African-American community and provide encouragement and resources to both new and veteran runners." Black Girls Run!'s mission includes the encouragement of African-American women "to make fitness and healthy living a priority." Carey and Hicks were moved by statistics showing that as many as "80 percent of African-American women are overweight. BGR!" Through their efforts, the group hopes "to create a movement to lower that percentage and subsequently, lower the number of women with chronic diseases associated with an unhealthy diet and sedentary lifestyle."[11]

The expansion of job opportunities for historically disadvantaged minorities such as blacks is also important. Even when the unemployment rate for the nation reaches record highs, it often pales in comparison to the unemployment rates for the black population. Shoring up the economy for all Americans is what is best for the nation, but special attention should be devoted to populations that are hardest hit by economic downturns and among the first to be scapegoated.

Armed with a greater knowledge of the roles of population and structural changes in sports participation by race, readers should have arrived at the realization that race and sports are social constructions and as a result sports can be both a liberating and an oppressive force.

The underrepresentation of blacks in some sports and the hypervisibility of blacks in others present some of the most convincing evidence of the enduring racial divide in America. It is clear that racism is not dead; it is not even dying. Integrating sports and ensuring that individuals can participate regardless of race is a start, but such solutions are shortsighted and will not have the desired long-term effect of bringing about true equality in sports and the broader society. Fundamental and transformative changes that grant equal access to wealth, status, and power for all racial groups is required. The aforementioned goals cannot be realized by merely changing the policies of professional sports associations.

It is not a coincidence that the fascination of black youth with sports is connected to the belief that his or her chance of playing professional sports is greater than the chance of securing a job or career that pays a living wage or leads to the increasingly elusive American Dream.

The ability to attain and accumulate wealth is an important benefit of white privilege. In order to narrow the racial income and wealth gaps and to lower black asset poverty rates—and provide realistic options to black youth—our society must undergo a fundamental transformation. We need to address the issue of racial wealth inequality and black asset poverty in fundamentally different ways than in the past, so that black youth will not only not view some sports as white, or wealth as white, but also will view asset ownership as an attainable rite of passage to adulthood.

To make sure that all Americans—including blacks and other people of color—enjoy America's promises of fairness, justice, and equality, we must address the structural barriers that perpetuate inequality in all areas of social life, including sports. We must become more keenly aware of the role of race and of racism, and work to rid our society of structural racism. Earlier efforts have failed because they were symbolic attempts, at best, to address a legacy of racial inequalities and were not designed to bring about long-term substantive change.

Fundamental societal change requires an understanding that the effects of racial prejudice and racial discrimination exist at all levels of society and that racial socialization is the process by which they are communicated to society. Investment in improving the overall economic well-being of all Americans, including the asset accumulation of historically disadvantaged groups, is an act of social justice toward achieving a civil right all Americans should enjoy.

Blacks should be encouraged to own homes, sports franchises, and so on, with assurances that individuals in positions of authority will make truly good faith efforts to root out policies and practices that discriminate on the basis of race.

We should seek an infusion of funds from governmental and private sources to restore or create access to sports in economically disadvantaged and working-class communities. Government and/or private funds could provide seed money for neighborhood-based cooperative sports programs that provide opportunities for interaction between young athletes from different racial and economic backgrounds.

Administrators of such programs should come from within the community when possible, and they should approach their mission with patience as well as passion. Bringing about social change is a *process*. It is very seldom an *event*. Therefore debunking myths about race and sports participation will take time and patience, but the benefits can be witnessed in improved race relations while progressing toward the economic security and autonomy of future generations.

We must work to erase an emergent epidemic I call "sports deserts." Modeled after the U.S. Department of Agriculture's definition of food deserts, I define sports deserts as urban neighborhoods and rural towns without ready access to a full array of sports and leisure activities. Instead of recreational facilities and community-based sports programs, these communities have no access or are served only by entities that provide very limited options. The lack of access contributes to an overrepresentation of residents in a few sports and an underrepresentation of residents in the remaining sports. The lack of access also contributes to poor health outcomes such as obesity and diet-related diseases. Low-access communities are based on the determination that at least 500 persons and/or at least 33 percent of the census tract's population live more than 1 mile from a facility that offers an area for sports and leisure activities (or 10 miles, in the case of nonmetropolitan census tracts).

Sports deserts are created, at least in part, because those with power and privilege, an overwhelming majority of whom are white, continue to have access to what most would consider to be good schools. Good schools often provide a number of sports and leisure activities for youth and for the community. Economically disadvantaged children, and children of color, remain trapped in bad schools with limited access to sports and leisure activities. In contemporary times, these children, who are overwhelmingly black and brown, watch as more affluent students, often white, have unencumbered access to schools, sports, and leisure activities that prepare them for a lifelong love of learning as well as for success in college. These opportunities also translate into social ties and jobs in what social scientists call the primary sector, and social ties that facilitate the identification of primary-sector jobs.

Jobs in the primary sector of a split labor force provide security, opportunities for advancement, and benefits. People of color are often relegated to the secondary sector, which is characterized by low wages, the absence of benefits, and very little job security. It is no wonder that people of color are disproportionately employed in the secondary sector, if they are employed at all, when one examines the inequalities in education that continue to set individuals on separate paths based upon the social groups to which they belong.

Far too many children of color find themselves in schools that, thanks to the new educational reform movement, are slapped with the label *failing*—so recess is cut and sports and leisure activities are eliminated. Students, parents, and teachers are made out to be scapegoats in many of these districts, in part to call attention away from decades of misguided educational policies. Contemporary educational policies that appear race-neutral yield outcomes that are similar to, if not worse than, the race-specific policies of the past.

Black and brown children, as a result, are disproportionately forced to learn in educational environments unimaginable decades ago. An increasingly popular mark on the relatively new educational landscape is a phenomenon I call "pop-up schools." Much like popular children's pop-up books, pop-up schools may be aesthetically pleasing and attractive at first glance, but in the wrong hands are easily destroyed.

More specifically, pop-up schools are schools that were designated as failing and closed down to prevent state takeovers. They were then given new life, if not a new name, while retaining many of their problems, and are devoid of sports programs and leisure activities, which are deemed as less important than test scores. Students in these pop-up schools (e.g., charter schools, magnet schools, gifted and talented programs) still lack access to the levels and types of resources readily available to more affluent and predominantly white schools, including access to sports and leisure activities.

School administrators at these pop-up schools are forced to take on the role of used-car salesmen. They are expected to sell students, parents, teachers, and the community a bill of goods. They promise higher test scores, a new approach to instruction, and so on. The frequent result, in reality, are new schools that have been hastily put together. The consequences are varied and quite severe.

Pop-up schools, particularly during the first few years of their existence, may lack the basic infrastructure to handle critical activities, such as schedule changes, leaving many bright students in courses that lack the academic rigor advertised, and with limited or no access to sports or leisure activities.

Estimated initial enrollment at pop-up schools may be inflated to show school boards and state education departments that they are viable. Such inflation can lead to the transfer of seasoned teachers within weeks of the start of the school year. A consequence of this "overstaffing" is the severing of the teacher-student relationship at one of its most critical moments. This may also result in the transfer of highly qualified teachers who are passionate about what they do, only to be replaced by inadequately trained teachers who lack the passion but possess requisite certifications to teach multiple subjects. This new breed of teachers can be shuffled from one grade or subject matter to another, which results in a staff that could best be described as "jacks of all trades and masters of none." It also results in lower budgets per pupil, making sports and leisure programs unaffordable.

Trends such as these have been reported throughout the country. This issue is not affecting only children of color and low-income children in America's inner cities. It is a cancer that is eating away at educational systems in America's midsection and in the Deep South.

Those with the means, most of whom are white, along with many public officials whose concern is the way the political wind is blowing, have in far too many cases abandoned, wholeheartedly, the public educational system. They have done so in at least one of the following ways:

1. They leave the central city and create their own public school districts, which are predominantly affluent and white as a result of residential segregation (as distinct from self-segregation).
2. They take their students out of public schools and place them in private and parochial schools with tuition rates that often exceed the tuition at state universities.
3. They create an illusion of inclusion by offering a relatively small portion of economically disadvantaged students, and students of color, the opportunity to attend private and parochial schools, and at the same time divest from the public school system, where hundreds of thousands of children must remain.
4. They create public schools that are seemingly open to the general public but charge tuition.
5. They create pop-up programs within abandoned schools where the savage inequalities Jonathan Kozol wrote about in his book by that name are highly visible.
6. They resort to blaming the victim instead of addressing the structural inequalities underpinning the entire educational system in America.[12]

Paying for facilities that would eliminate sports deserts would not only require public and private partnerships, it may also require the creation of cooperative recreational associations modeled after other common forms of collective assets such as credit unions and co-ops. Joint ownership is a pathway to asset ownership for individuals and communities and a way to get around the politics that often lead to delays to funding projects that benefit the common good. An added benefit is that the cooperative sports programs would be indigenous to the community and community controlled. Additionally, user fees would remain and be used in the community in which they originate.

The importance of addressing inequalities throughout society, including in sports, cannot be emphasized enough. There is the need to explore creative strategies that eliminate sports deserts and the process of racial socialization in sports, and there is an equally critical need to transform the opportunity structure in America, which is organized around issues of race. This will require willingness to talk openly and honestly about race. It requires the realization on the part of members in the dominant racial group that blacks and other nonwhites are not culturally deficient but are living proof of the historic legacy of institutionalized racism, as well as structural and economic changes that have historically disadvantaged blacks and forced them to compete in sports and in the broader society with competitors who were given an unfair start.

We must come to the realization that, despite the election of the country's first black president, we are not yet living in a postracial era. Racial equality in America, including in sports, will not be secured in one or two terms of a presidency, no matter the race of the person sitting in the Oval Office. It will take time to achieve the radical reconstruction that is long overdue.

It is imperative that we understand race not as a problem but as an organizing principle of American society. When we understand race as foundational to our society, the "processes by which racial categories are created, inhabited, transformed, and destroyed" may be understood, including the processes whereby the ways of society for blacks and whites in general and in sports in particular are understood and result in the association of certain sports as black sports and others as white.[13]

Notes

Chapter 1

1. "Race and Its Continuing Significance on Our Campuses: An Interview with Dr. Joe R. Feagin." (2003). *Black Issues in Higher Education*, 19(24), 24–27; Bonilla-Silva, E. (2004). "From Bi-racial to Tri-racial: Towards a New System of Racial Stratification in the USA." *Ethnic and Racial Studies*, 27(6), 931–50; Fryer, R. G., Jr., and Levitt, S. D. (2004). "The Causes and Consequences of Distinctively Black Names." *Quarterly Journal of Economics*, 119(3), 767–805.

2. Williamson, Joel. (1968). *The Origins of Segregation.* Boston: Heath; Hine, D., Hine, W., and Harrold, S. (2010). *The African-American Odyssey.* Upper Saddle River, NJ: Pearson.

3. Ross, C. (1999). *Outside the Lines: African Americans and the Integration of the National Football League.* New York: New York University Press.

4. Grasso, J. (2011). *Historical Dictionary of Tennis.* New York: Scarecrow Press, 8.

5. Lomax, M. E. (2008). *Sports and the Racial Divide: African American and Latino Experience in an Era of Change.* Jackson: University of Mississippi Press; Grasso, *Historical Dictionary of Tennis.*

6. Wettenstein, B. (August 30, 2007). "Let Us Remember Alice Marble, the Catalyst for Althea Gibson to Break the Color Barrier." *Huffington Post,* http://www.huffingtonpost.com/beverly-wettenstein/let-us-remember-alice-mar_b_62571.html (accessed June 22, 2014).

7. Government Press Releases (USA). (July 12, 2013). "Kirk, Durbin, Quigley Honor 1963 Loyola Men's Basketball Team; Celebrate 50th Anniversary of Only Illinois Division I Team to Win NCAA Championship, First to Start Four African-American Players."

8. Neumann, T. (March 11, 2011). "Michigan's Fab Five in Their Own Words." ESPN Page 2. http://sports.espn.go.com/espn/page2/story?page=neumann/110311_fab_five_documentary&sportCat=ncb (accessed June 22, 2014).

9. Ibid.

10. Eligon, J. (October 27, 2005). "Dressing Up Basketball? Been There, Done That." *New York Times,* G7.

11. Leonard, D. (2012). *After Artest: The NBA and the Assault on Blackness.* Albany: State University of New York Press, 166.

12. Ibid.

13. Ibid.

14. Weinberg, R. (1993). "Jordan, Age 30, Retires for the First Time." http://sports.espn.go.com/espn/espn25/story?page=moments/91 (accessed June 22, 2014)

15. Yep, K. (2012). "Peddling Sport: Liberal Multiculturalism and the Racial Triangulation of Blackness, Chineseness and Native American-ness in Professional Basketball." *Ethnic and Racial Studies*, 35(6), 971–87.

16. Maconis, J. (2011). *Sociology.* Upper Saddle River, NJ: Pearson, 310.

17. Yep, "Peddling Sport."

18. Ibid.

19. Hill, S. A. (2006). "Racial Socialization." In G. Handel, ed., *Childhood Socialization.* 2nd ed.. New Brunswick, NJ: Aldine Transaction, 89–112.

20. Joseph, N., and Hunter, C. D. (2011). "Ethnic-Racial Socialization Messages in the Identity Development of Second-Generation Haitians." *Journal of Adolescent Research*, 26(3), 344–80.

21. Coakley, Jay. (2008). *Sports and Society: Issues and Controversies.* New York: McGraw-Hill.

22. Martin, L. L., and Horton, H. D. (2014). "Racism Front and Center." In Martin, L. L., ed. *Out of Bounds: Racism and the Black Athlete.* Santa Barbara, CA: Praeger, 105–132.

23. Bell, D. A. (1995). "Who's Afraid of Critical Race Theory?" *University of Illinois Law Review*, 893–910.

24. Burton, L. M., Bonilla-Silva, E., Ray, V., Buckelew, R., and Freeman, E. (2010). "Critical Race Theories, Colorism, and the Decade's Research on Families of Color." *Journal of Marriage and Family*, 72(3), 440–59.

25. Bell, "Who's Afraid of Critical Race Theory?"

26. Onwuachi-Willig, A. (2009). "Celebrating Critical Race Theory at 20." *Iowa Law Review*, 94, 1502.

27. Hylton, K. (2008). *Race and Sport.* New York: Routledge; http://www.bl.uk/sportandsociety/exploresocsci/sportsoc/sociology/articles/hylton.pdf (accessed June 22, 2014).

28. Louis, B. (2004). "Sport and Common-Sense Racial Science." *Leisure Studies*, 23(1), 31–46.

29. Hylton, *Race and Sport*; http://www.bl.uk/sportandsociety/exploresocsci/sportsoc/sociology/articles/hylton.pdf (accessed June 2, 2014).

30. Treviño, A., Harris, M. A., and Wallace, D. (2008). "What's So Critical about Critical Race Theory?" *Contemporary Justice Review*, 11(1), 7–10.

31. Herring, C. (2004). "Skin Deep: Race and Complexion in the 'Color-Blind' Era." In C. Herring, V. M. Keith, and H. D. Horton, eds. *Skin Deep: How Race*

and Complexion Matter in the "Color-Blind" Era. Champaign: University of Illinois Press, 3.

32. See, for example, Edwards, K., Carter-Tellison, K. M., and Herring, C. (2004). "For Richer, for Poorer, Whether Dark or Light: Skin Tone, Marital Status, and Spouse's Earnings."; Herring, C. (2004). "Skin Deep: Race and Complexion in the 'Color-Blind' Era; and Thompson, M. S., and Keith, V. M. (2004). "Copper Brown and Blue Black: Colorism and Self Evaluation. All in Herring, Keith, and Horton, *Skin Deep*, 65–81, 1–21, and 45–64, respectively.

33. Harris, A. P. (2008). "From Color Line to Color Chart?: Racism and Colorism in the New Century." *Berkeley Journal of African-American Law and Policy*, 10 (1), 52–69.

34. Keith, V. M. (2009). "A Colorstruck World: Skin Tone, Achievement, and Self-Esteem among African American Women." In Glenn, Evelyn Nakano, ed. *Shades of Difference: Why Skin Color Matters*. Los Altos, CA: Stanford University Press, 25–39.

35. Robst, J., VanGilder, J., Coates, C. E., and Berri, D. J. (2011). "Skin Tone and Wages: Evidence from NBA Free Agents." *Journal of Sports Economics*, 12 (2), 143–56.

36. Hersch, J. (2008). "Skin Color Discrimination and Immigrant Pay." *Emory Law Journal*, 58(2), 357–77; Hunter, M. (2008). "Teaching and Learning Guide for: The Persistent Problem of Colorism: Skin Tone, Status, and Inequality." *Sociology Compass*, 2(1), 366; Keith, V. M., and Herring, C. (1991). "Skin Color and Stratification in the Black Community." *American Journal of Sociology*, 97, 760–78.

37. Robst, VanGilder, Coates, and Berri, "Skin Tone and Wages"; Akee, R., and Yuksel, M. (2012). "The Decreasing Effect of Skin Tone on Women's Full-Time Employment." *Industrial and Labor Relations Review*, 65(2), 398–426.

38. Horton, H., and Allen, B. (1998). "Race, Family Structure and Rural Poverty: An Assessment of Population and Structural Change." *Journal of Comparative Family Studies*, 29(2), 398.

39. Horton, H. (1999). "Critical Demography: The Paradigm of the Future?" *Sociological Forum*, 14(3), 363.

40. Lapchick, R., Hippert, A., Rivera, S., and Robinson, J. (2013). *The 2013 Race and Gender Report Card: National Basketball Association*. See http://www .tidesport.org/RGRC/2013/2013_NBA_RGRC.pdf (accessed June 22, 2014).

Chapter 2

1. Boustan, L. P. (2011). Racial Residential Segregation in American Cities. In Brooks, N., Donaghy, K., and Knaap G.-J., eds. *The Oxford Handbook of Urban Economics and Planning*. Oxford: Oxford University Press, 318–39.

2. Martin, L. L. (2013). *Black Asset Poverty and the Enduring Racial Divide.* Boulder, CO: First Forum Press.

3. Bonilla-Silva, E. (2014). *Racism without Racists: Color-Blind Racism and the Persistence of Racial Inequality in America.* 4th ed. Lanham, MD: Rowman and Littlefield.

4. Charles, C. (2000). "Neighborhood Racial-Composition Preferences: Evidence from a Multiethnic Metropolis." *Social Problems,* 47(3), 379–407.

5. Denton, N. A. (2006). "Segregation and Discrimination in Housing." In Bratt, R. G., Stone, M. E., and Hartman, C., eds. *A Right to Housing: Foundation of a New Social Agenda.* Philadelphia: Temple University Press, 61.

6. Ibid.

7. Mackin, Robert Sean, and Walther, Carol S. (2012). "Race, Sport and Social Mobility: Horatio Alger in Short Pants? *International Review for the Sociology of Sport,* 47(6), 670–89.

8. Gimino, A. (March 27, 2013). "Arizona Basketball: All about Mark Lyons." *Tucson Citizen.* http://tucsoncitizen.com/wildcatreport/2013/03/27/arizona-basket ball-all-about-mark-lyons/ (accessed June 24, 2014).

9. Joravsky, B. (1996). *Hoop Dreams: A True Story of Hardship and Triumph.* New York: HarperCollins.

10. Jones, A. C., and Naison, M. (2011). *The Rat That Got Away.* New York: Fordham University Press.

11. Mallozzi, V. M. (November 11, 1990). "Basketball: Legend of the Playground." *New York Times.* http://www.nytimes.com/1990/11/11/sports/basketball-legend-of-the-playground.html?pagewanted=all&src=pm (accessed June 24, 2014).

12. Coakley, J. (2008). *Sports and Society.* New York: McGraw-Hill, 286.

13. Lapchick, R., Lecky, A., and Trigg, A. (2012). *The 2012 Racial and Gender Report Card: National Basketball Association.* http://www.tidesport.org/RGRC/2012/2012_NBA_RGRC[1].pdf (accessed June 24, 2014).

14. Lapchick, R., Milkovich, M., and O'Keefe, S. (2012). *The 2012 Women's National Basketball Association Racial and Gender Report Card.* http://www.tidesport.org/RGRC/2012/2012_WNBA_RGRC.pdf (accessed June 24, 2014).

15. Lapchick, R., Costa, P., Sherod, T., and Anjorin, R. (2012). *The 2012 Racial and Gender Report Card: National Football League.* http://www.tidesport.org/RGRC/2012/2012_NFL_RGRC.pdf (accessed June 24, 2014); Lapchick, R., Costa, P., Nickerson, B., and Rodriguez, B. (2012). *The 2012 Racial and Gender Report Card: Major League Baseball.* http://www.tidesport.org/RGRC/2012/2012_MLB _RGRC.pdf (accessed June 24, 2014); Lapchick, R., Gunn, O., and Trigg, A. (2012). *The 2012 Racial and Gender Report Card: Major League Soccer.* http://www.tidesport.org/RGRC/2012/2012_MLS_RGRC.pdf (accessed June 24, 2014).

16. Lapchick, R. (2011). *The 2011 Racial and Gender Report Card: College Sport.* http://www.tidesport.org/RGRC/2011/2011_College_RGRC.pdf (accessed June 24, 2014).

17. Edwards, H. (1979). "Sports within the Veil: The Triumphs, Tragedies, and Challenges of African American Involvement." *Annals of the American Academy of Political and Social Science,* 445, 116–27.

18. Lapchick, *The 2011 Racial and Gender Report Card: College Sport,* 5.

Chapter 3

1. *The Oxford English Dictionary Online,* quoted in Newman, L. (n.d.), "Mass Media." The Chicago School of Media Theory. http://lucian.uchicago.edu/blogs/mediatheory/keywords/mass-media/ (accessed June 27, 2014).

2. McChesney, R. (n.d.) "Media Made Sport: A History of Sports Coverage in the U.S." http://www.ux1.eiu.edu/~jjgisondi/MediaMade.pdf (accessed June 27, 2014).

3. Ibid.

4. Ibid.

5. Boyle, R. (2006). *Sports Journalism.* New York: Sage.

6. Morgan, D. C. (1999). "Jack Johnson: Reluctant Hero of the Black Community." *Akron Law Review,* 32(3), 529–56.

7. Public Broadcasting System (n.d.). Timeline of the Black Press. http://www.pbs.org/blackpress/timeline/contenttimeline.html (accessed June 29, 2014).

8. University of Illinois at Chicago, University Library. (n.d.). Associated Negro Press Collection: An Inventory of the Collection at the University of Illinois at Chicago. http://www.uic.edu/depts/lib/specialcoll/services/rjd/findingaids/NegroPressf.html (accessed June 27, 14).

9. Perloff, R. (2000). "The Press and Lynchings of African Americans." *Journal of Black Studies,* 30(3), 315–30.

10. Brooke-Ball, P., Snelling, O. F., and O'Dell, D. (1995). *The Boxing Album: An Illustrated History.* New York: Smithmark.

11. African American Registry. (n.d.). World Heavyweight Champ and Legend, Jack Johnson. http://www.aaregistry.org/historic_events/view/world-heavyweight-champ-and-legend-jack-johnson (accessed June 27, 2014).

12. Morgan, "Jack Johnson."

13. Washington, B. T. (1895). "Booker T. Washington Delivers the 1895 Atlanta Compromise Speech." http://historymatters.gmu.edu/d/39/ (accessed June 29, 2014).

14. Du Bois, W. E. B. (1903). *The Souls of Black Folk.* Chicago: A. C. McClurg and Co.

15. Griffith, Clark C. (2003). "Sports Licensing." *Licensing Journal,* 23(9), 20–21.

16. McChesney, "Media Made Sport."

17. Pilgrim, D. (2012). "The Brute Caricature." http://www.ferris.edu/htmls/news/jimcrow/brute (accessed June 29, 2014).

18. Pilgrim, D. (2012). "The Sapphire Caricature." http://www.ferris.edu/htmls/news/jimcrow/sapphire (accessed June 29, 2014).

19. Chase, C. (June 19, 2013). "Williams Still Doesn't Know How to Apologize." http://ftw.usatoday.com/2013/06/serena-williams-apology-steubenville/ (accessed June 29, 2014).

20. Goldberg, A. (2011). "Serena Williams Fined $2,000 by U.S. Open for Berating Chair Umpire." *Huffington Post.* http://www.huffingtonpost.com/2011/09/12/serena-williams-fined-us-open_n_958862.html (accessed June 30, 2014).

21. Killion, A. (2009). "Serena's Outburst Common among Athletes—but Not Women." *Sports Illustrated.* http://www.si.com/more-sports/2009/09/15/serena (accessed June 29, 2014).

22. Tarrant, S. (March 31, 2010). "Wheaties Fuels a Breakfast of Stereotypes." http://msmagazine.com/blog/2010/03/31/wheaties-fuels-a-breakfast-of-stereotypes/ (accessed June 29, 2014).

23. The Root Staff. (2012). "Tennis Player Mocks Serena's Body?" http://www.theroot.com/articles/culture/2012/12/tennis_player_mocks_serenas_body.html (accessed June 30, 2014).

24. Pilgrim, D. (2012). "Jezebel Stereotype." http://www.ferris.edu/jimcrow/jezebel.htm.

Chapter 4

1. Schilken, C. (February 4, 2013). "Ravens' 2013 Super Bowl Victory Sets TV Ratings Record." *Los Angeles Times.* http://articles.latimes.com/2013/feb/04/sports/la-sp-sn-super-bowl-ratings-20130204 (accessed July 1 2014).

2. Waller, M. (April 18, 2013). "Super Bowl 2013 Drove $480 Million in Spending in New Orleans, Beating Expectations, Economic Study Shows." *Times-Picayune.* http://www.nola.com/business/index.ssf/2013/04/super_bowl_2013_drove_480_mill.html (accessed July 1, 2014).

3. Wiggins, D. K., and Miller, P. B. (2005). *The Unlevel Playing Field.* Champaign: University of Illinois Press.

4. Bowen, R. T. (1982). "Race, Home Town and Experience as Factors in Deep South Major College Football." *International Review of Sport Sociology*, 17(2), 41–51.

5. Rhoden, W. (2006). *Forty Million Dollar Slaves.* New York: Crown.

6. Jones, Gregg A., Leonard, Wilbert M. II, Schmitt, Raymond L., Smith, D. Randall, and Tolone, William L. (1987). "Racial Discrimination in College Football." *Social Science Quarterly*, 68(1), 70–83.

7. Murrell, A. J., and Curtis, E. M. (1994). "Causal Attributions of Performance for Black and White Quarterbacks in the NFL." *Journal of Sport and Social Issues,* 18(3), 224–33.

8. Ferguson, T. (2009). "Combating Unseen Struggles: The African American Male Football Player." *Journal of Indiana University Student Personnel Association,* 52–64.

9. Lapchick, R. (2012). *Keeping Score When It Counts: Assessing the 2012–2013 Bowl-Bound College Football Teams' Graduation Rates.* http://www.tidesport.org/Grad%20Rates/2012_FBS_Bowl_Study.pdf (accessed July 1, 2014).

10. Ibid.

11. Harper, S. R., Williams, C. D., and Blackman, H. W. (2013). *Black Male Student-Athletes and Racial Inequities in NCAA Division I College Sports.* Philadelphia: University of Pennsylvania, Center for the Study of Race and Equity in Education.

12. Ferguson, "Combating Unseen Struggles."

13. Agyemang, K., Singer, J., and DeLorme, J. (2010). "An Exploratory Study of Black Male College Athletes' Perceptions on Race and Athlete Activism." *International Review for the Sociology of Sport,* 45(4), 419–35.

14. Edwards, H. (1979). "Sport within the Veil: The Triumphs, Tragedies and Challenges of Afro-American Involvement." *Annals of the AAPSS,* 445, 116–27.

15. Day, J. C., and McDonald, S. (2010). "Not So Fast, My Friend: Social Capital and the Race Disparity in Promotions among College Football Coaches." *Sociological Spectrum,* 30(2), 138–58.

16. Leonard, D. J. (2012). "Joe Paterno, White Patriarchy and Privilege." *Cultural Studies Critical Methodologies,* 12(4), 373–76.

17. Foley, D. (1990). "The Great American Football Ritual: Reproducing Race, Class, and Gender Inequality." http://www.qcc.cuny.edu/pv_obj_cache/pv_obj_id_EB4CBD6288BD55F5E595F9D8C099751EA0D80200/ (accessed July 1, 2014).

18. Kooistra, P., Mahoney, J., and Bridges, L. (1993). "The Unequal Opportunity for Equal Ability Hypothesis: Racism in the National Football League." *Sociology of Sport Journal* [serial online], 10(3), 242.

19. Ibid., 243.

20. Lapchick, R., Costa, P., Sherod, T.. and Anjorin, R. (2012). *The 2012 Racial and Gender Report Card: National Football League.* http://www.tidesport.org/RGRC/2012/2012_NFL_RGRC.pdf (accessed June 24, 2014).

21. Day and McDonald, "Not So Fast, My Friend," 154.

22. Braddock, J. H., E Smith, E., and Dawkins, M. P. (2012). "Race and Pathways to Power in the National Football League." *American Behavioral Scientist,* 56(5), 711–27.

23. Lapchick, Costa, Sherod, and Anjorin, *The 2012 Racial and Gender Report Card.*

Chapter 5

1. "Abner Doubleday." http://www.tulane.edu/~latner/Doubleday.html (accessed July 3, 2014).

2. Nucciarone, M. (2009). *Alexander Cartwright: The Life behind the Baseball Legend.* Lincoln: University of Nebraska Press.

3. National Baseball Hall of Fame. (n.d.). "Cartwright, Alexander." http://baseballhall.org/hof/cartwright-alexander (accessed July 3, 2014).

4. Gendin, S. (1998). "Moses Fleetwood Walker : Jackie Robinson's Accidental Predecessor." In Dorison, J., and Warmund, J., eds. *Jackie Robinson: Race, Sports and the American Dream.* Armonk, NY: M. E. Sharpe, 22–29.

5. Zang, D. (1995). *Fleet Walker's Divided Heart: The Life of Baseball's First Black Major Leaguer.* Lincoln: University of Nebraska Press.

6. Abrams, D. (2007). *Ty Cobb.* New York: Chelsea House; Jaffe, C. (2012). "Centennial Anniversary: Ty Cobb Beats Up a Cripple." *Hardball Times.* http://www.hardballtimes.com/tht-live/centennial-anniversary-ty-cobb-beats-up-a-cripple/ (accessed July 10, 2014).

7. Olbermann, K. (June 1, 1998). "Remembering a Pioneer: Some 30 Years before Jackie Robinson, There Was Jimmy Claxton." *Sports Illustrated.* http://sportsillustrated.cnn.com/vault/1998/06/01/243922/remembering-a-pioneer-some-30-years-before-jackie-robinson-there-was-jimmy-claxton (accessed July 3, 2014).

8. Heaphy, L. (2011). "Baseball and the Color Line: From Negro Leagues to the Major Leagues." In Cassuto, L., and Partridge, S., eds. *The Cambridge Companion to Baseball.* Cambridge, England: Cambridge University Press, 61–74.

9. Martin, L. L., and Horton, H. D. (2014). "Racism Front and Center: Introducing the Critical Demography of Athletic Destinations." In Martin, L. L., ed. *Out of Bounds: Racism and the Black Athlete.* Santa Barbara, CA: Praeger, 105–132.

10. "Negro Leagues Baseball: A Brief History." Negro Leagues Baseball eMuseum. http://www.coe.ksu.edu/annex/nlbemuseum/history/overview.html (accessed July3, 2014).

11. Negro Leagues Baseball Museum home page. http://www.nlbm.com (accessed July 3, 2014).

12. Gardner, R., and Shortelle, D. (1993). *The Forgotten Players: The Story of Black Baseball in America.* New York: Walker and Co., 45.

13. Hill, J. B. (n.d.). "Traveling Show: Barnstorming Was Common Place in the Negro Leagues." MLB.com. http://mlb.mlb.com/mlb/history/mlb_negro_leagues_story.jsp?story=barnstorming (accessed July 3, 2014).

14. Overbea, L. (July 8, 1949). " 'Without Proper Support Negro Baseball Simply Cannot Survive' says R.S. Simmons of Chicago." *Plaindealer.*

15. Kahn, R. (1996–97). "The Jackie Robinson I Remember." *Journal of Blacks in Higher Education,* 14, 88–93.

16. Ibid.

17. Lapchick, R., Costa, P., Nickerson, B., and Rodriguez, B. (2012). *The 2012 Racial and Gender Report Card: Major League Baseball.* http://www.tidesport.org/RGRC/2012/2012_MLB_RGRC.pdf (accessed July 4, 2014).

18. Ibid.

19. Ruck, R. (2011). *Raceball: How the Major Leagues Colonized the Black and Latin Game.* Boston: Beacon Press.

20. Ogden, D. G., and Rose, R. A. (2005). "Using Gidden's Structuration Theory to Examine the Waning Participation of African Americans in Baseball." *Journal of Black Studies*, 35, 225–45.

Chapter 6

1. Lapchick, R., Hippert, A., Rivera, S., and Robinson, J. (2013). *The 2013 Racial and Gender Report Card: National Basketball Association.* http://www.tidesport.org/RGRC/2013/2013_NBA_RGRC.pdf (accessed July 7, 2014).

2. Lapchick, R. (2011). *The 2011 Racial and Gender Report Card: College Sport.* http://www.tidesport.org/RGRC/2011/2011_College_RGRC.pdf (accessed June 24, 2014).

3. Lapchick, R., Milkovich, M., and O'Keefe, S. (2012). *The 2012 Women's National Basketball Association Racial and Gender Report Card.* http://www.tidesport.org/RGRC/2012/2012_WNBA_RGRC.pdf (accessed June 24, 2014).

4. "True Reformer's Hall." George Washington University website. http://www.gwu.edu/~jazz/venuest.html (accessed July 7, 2014).

5. Coffey, W. (February 2, 2013). "The First Kings of Brooklyn." *New York Daily News.* http://www.nydailynews.com/sports/basketball/zone-lost-era-black-basketball-history-brought-life-article-1.1253875 (accessed July 7, 2014).

6. "Timeline." Black Fives Foundation. http://www.blackfives.org/timeline/page/2/ (accessed July 9, 2014).

7. Nelson, M. R. (2009). *The National Basketball League.* Jefferson, NC: McFarland.

8. Peterson, R. W. (November 11, 1991). "When the Court Was a Cage." Sports Illustrated Vault. http://sportsillustrated.cnn.com/vault/1991/11/11/125381/when-the-court-was-a-cage-in-the-early-days-of-pro-basketball-the-players-were-segregated-from-the-fans (accessed July 7, 2014).

9. Ibid.

10. Fry, S. (October 10, 2009). " '49 Basketball Teams Segregated." *Topeka Capital-Journal.* http://cjonline.com/news/local/2009-10-10/49_basketball_teams_segregated (accessed July 7, 2014).

11. Ibid.

12. Loyola (Ill.) Athletics. (July 16, 2012). " 'Game of Change' to Be Remembered." NCAA.com. http://www.ncaa.com/news/basketball-men/article/2012-07-24/game-change-be-remembered (accessed July 8, 2014).

13. Corley, C. (March 15, 2013). "Game of Change: Pivotal Matchup Helped End Segregated Hoops." National Public Radio. http://wap.npr.org/news/U.S./174304630 (accessed July 8, 2014).

14. Kimmel, M. S., and Aronson, A., eds. (2004). *Men and Masculinities : A Social, Cultural, and Historical Encyclopedia.* Santa Barbara, CA: ABC-CLIO.

15. "American Basketball Association Debuts." History.com. http://www.history.com/this-day-in-history/american-basketball-association-debuts (accessed July 8, 2014).

16. George, N. (1999). *Elevating the Game.* New York: HarperCollins.

17. Ibid.

18. Dyson, Michael Eric. (1993). *Reflecting Black: African-American Cultural Criticism.* Minneapolis: University of Minnesota Press.

19. "Lebron James Biography." NBA website. http://www.nba.com/playerfile/lebron_james/bio/ (accessed July 10, 2014).

20. Schoenberger, R. (June 28, 2010). "How Much Is LeBron James Worth to Northeast Ohio?" *Cleveland Plain Dealer.* http://www.cleveland.com/business/index.ssf/2010/06/how_much_is_lebron_james_worth.html (accessed July 8, 2014).

21. Guarini, D. (June 8, 2012). "Life After LeBron." *Huffington Post.* http://www.huffingtonpost.com/2012/06/08/life-after-lebron-how-clevelands-economy-is-faring_n_1582328.html (accessed July 9, 2014).

22. Prada, M. (July 7, 2014). "Cavs Explain Why They Took Down Dan Gilbert's Letter to LeBron James." SB Nation. http://www.sbnation.com/lookit/2014/7/7/5877047/dan-gilbert-letter-lebron-james-preserved-cavaliers (accessed July 8, 2014).

23. Pilgrim, D. (2012). "The Coon Caricature." http://www.ferris.edu/htmls/news/jimcrow/coon/ (accessed July 9, 2014).

24. Adande, J. A. (October 1, 2010). "LeBron James, Race and the NBA." ESPN. http://sports.espn.go.com/nba/trainingcamp10/columns/story?columnist=adande_ja&page=LeBronRace-101001 (accessed July 9, 2014).

25. Leonard, D. J. (n.d.). "Not a Question of Courage: Anti-black Racism and the Politics of the NBA Lockout." http://newblackman.blogspot.com/2011/10/not-question-of-courage-anti-black.html (accessed July 9, 2014).

26. Wilson, G. (October 19, 2011). "Bryant Gumbel Calls NBA Commish 'Plantation Overseer.'" NBC Bay Area. http://www.nbcbayarea.com/entertainment/television/Bryant-Gumbel-Calls-NBA-Commish-Plantation-Overseer-132129268.html (accessed July 9, 2014).

27. Bolch, B. (September 10, 2013). "Linsanity Documentary Is a Spine-Tingling Homage to Jeremy Lin." *Los Angeles Times.* http://www.latimes.com/sports/sportsnow/la-sp-sn-linsanity-documentary-jeremy-lin-20130909,0,3116852.story#axzz2gJIxFUpu (accessed July 9, 2014).

28. Hill, M. L. (November 28, 2012). "The Linsanity Sham: Why Jeremy Lin Can't Really Play." *Huffington Post.* http://www.huffingtonpost.com/marc-lamont-hill/linsanity-jeremy-lin_b_2199606.html (accessed July 9, 2014).

29. Park, L. S.-H. (2008). "Continuing Significance of the Model Minority Myth: The Second Generation." *Social Justice*, 35(2), 135.

30. Lindgren, J., and McGowan, M. (2006). "Testing the 'Model Minority Myth.'" *Northwestern University Law Review*, 100, 331–78.

31. Martin, L. L. (2013). *Black Asset Poverty and the Enduring Racial Divide*. Boulder, CO: First Forum Press.

32. Mazzeo, M. (2013). "Jeremy Lin Cites College Race Barrier." ESPN. http://espn.go.com/nba/story/_/id/9141475/jeremy-lin-houston-rockets-race-was-barrier-college (accessed July 10, 2014).

33. Simmons, R. (2013). "The Insanity of Linsanity, 1 Year Later." SFGate. http://www.sfgate.com/warriors/article/The-insanity-of-Linsanity-1-year-later-4254389.php (accessed July 10, 2014).

34. Hartmann, D. (2012). "Beyond the Sporting Boundary." *Ethnic and Racial Studies*, 35(6), 1007–22.

Chapter 7

1. Coakley, J. (2008). *Sports and Society*. New York: McGraw-Hill, 293.

2. Ibid., 294.

3. "African Americans and Golf, a Brief History." African American Registry. http://aaregistry.org/historic_events/view/african-americans-and-golf-brief-history (accessed July 13, 2014).

4. Burton, L. (January 4, 2003). "Despite No Local Course, Polk Players Made Black Golf Hall of Fame." *Ledger*. http://www.theledger.com/article/20030104/COLUMNISTS0303/301040443 (accessed July 13, 2014).

5. Tramel, J. (July 29, 2007). "The Little Known Story of Oklahoma Native and Golfing Pioneer Bill Spiller." http://www.baystate-banner.com/issues/2007/08/16/news/natl08160720.htm (accessed July 13, 2014).

6. McDaniel, P. (2000). *Uneven Lies: The Heroic Story of African-Americans in Golf*. Greenwich, CT: American Golfer.

7. Glenn, R. (February 6, 2007). "Paving the Rhodes for African American Golfers." USGA. http://www.usga.org/news/2007/February/Paving-The-Rhodes-For-Other-African-American-Golfers—USGA/ (accessed July 13, 2014).

8. Wiggins, D., and Miller, P. B. (2005). *The Unlevel Playing Field*. Champaign: University of Illinois Press, 241.

9. Wang, J. (2013). "Tiger Woods." *People*. http://www.people.com/people/tiger_woods/ (accessed July 13, 2014).

10. Nishime, L. (2012). "The Case for Cablinasian: Multiracial Naming from Plessy to Tiger Woods." *Communication Theory*, 22(1), 92–111.

11. Cashmore, E. (2008). "Tiger Woods and the New Racial Order." *Current Sociology*, 56(4), 621–34.

12. Gittings, P. (April 14. 2010). "A Short History of Tennis: Henry VIII to Federer." CNN. http://www.cnn.com/2010/SPORT/tennis/04/14/history.of.tennis .federer.henryIII/index.html (accessed July 13, 2014).

13. Botsch, C. S. (2004). "Althea Gibson." USC Aiken. http://www.usca.edu/ aasc/AltheaGibson.htm (accessed July 13, 2014).

14. Shapiro, R. (1970). "Interview with Arthur Ashe." *Africa Today*, 17(6), 6–7.

15. Dell, D. (February 5, 2013). "Remembering a Pioneer in Fields Far Beyond the Sport." *New York Times*. http://straightsets.blogs.nytimes.com/2013/02/05/ remembering-a-pioneer-far-beyond-his-sport/?_r=0 (accessed July 13, 2014).

16. Ashe, A. (2000). *A Hard Road to Glory*. New York: Amistad.

17. Douglas, D. D. (2002). "To Be Young, Gifted, Black and Female: A Meditation on the Cultural Politics at Play in Representations of Venus and Serena Williams." *SOSOL: Sociology of Sport Online*, 5(2), 1.

18. Douglas, D. D. (2005). "Venus, Serena, and the Women's Tennis Association (WTA): When and Where 'Race' Enters." *Sociology of Sport Journal*, 22(3), 256.

19. Sullivan, J. J. (August 23, 2012). "Venus and Serena against the World." *New York Times*. http://www.nytimes.com/2012/08/26/magazine/venus-and -serena-against-the-world.html?pagewanted=all (accessed July 13, 2014).

20. Douglas, Delia D. (2005). "Venus, Serena, and the Women's Tennis Association (WTA): When and Where 'Race' Enters." *Sociology of Sport Journal*, 22(3), 256.

21. Sullivan, "Venus and Serena against the World."

22. Schultz, J. (2005). "Reading the Catsuit: Serena Williams and the Production of Blackness at the 2002 U.S. Open." *Journal of Sport and Social Issues*, 29(3), 338–57.

23. Ibid., 351.

Chapter 8

1. Stefancic, J., Delgado, R., and Bell, D. A. (2005). *The Derrick Bell Reader*. New York: New York University Press.

2. Dreier, P. (2013). "The Real Story of Baseball's Integration That You Won't See in 42." *The Atlantic*. http://www.theatlantic.com/entertainment/archive/2013/ 04/the-real-story-of-baseballs-integration-that-you-wont-see-in-i-42-i/274886/ (accessed July 27, 2014).

3. Lacy, S., and Newson, M. (1998). *Fighting for Fairness: The Life Story of Hall of Fame Sportswriter Sam Lacy*. Centreville, MD: Tidewater.

4. Wilson, J. (1987). *The Truly Disadvantaged*. Chicago: University of Chicago Press.

5. Collins, P. H. (2006). *From Black Power to Hip Hop: Racism, Nationalism, and Feminism*. Philadelphia: Temple University Press, 3.

6. Hubbard, D. (2007). *The Souls of Black Folk: One Hundred Years Later*. Columbia: University of Missouri Press, 8.

7. Brinson, W. (January 19, 2014). "Richard Sherman Calls Michael Crabtree a Sorry Receiver in Wild Rant." CBSSports.com. http://www.cbssports.com/nfl/eye -on-football/24414525/richard-sherman-calls-michael-crabtree-sorry-receiver-in -postgame-rant (accessed 0July 18, 2014).

8. Lopez, I. H. (2014). *Dog Whistle Politics*. New York: Oxford University Press.

9. Martin, L. L. (December 16, 2011). "The New War on Poverty." *Amsterdam News*. http://amsterdamnews.com/news/2011/dec/16/the-new-war-on-poverty/ (accessed July 18, 2014).

10. Augustine, B. (January 21, 2014). "Richard Sherman Responds to Racist Remarks about Him on Twitter Following Interview with Erin Andrews." *New York Daily News*. http://www.nydailynews.com/sports/football/sherman -responds-racist-twitter-toughguys-article-1.1585571 (accessed July 18, 2014).

11. Gleeson, S. (September 11, 2012). "Durant Says Skip Bayless Brainwashing with Comments." *USA Today*. http://content.usatoday.com/communities/ gameon/post/2012/09/Durant-says-Skip-Bayless-brainwashing-with-comments -70000140/kevin-durant-skip-bayless-twitter-feud/70000140/1#.U8ldjo1dXlQ (accessed July 18, 2014).

12. Ellman, S. (March 4, 2014). "Is the NFL Ready for Michael Sam?" *Huffington Post*. http://www.huffingtonpost.com/scott-ellman/is-the-nfl-ready-for-mich _b_4895585.html (accessed July 18, 2014).

13. National Football League. (2013). "The NFL's Ongoing Commitment to Excellence in Workplace Conduct: Sexual Orientation." http://nfllabor.files .wordpress.com/2014/02/nfl-ewc-sexual-orientation.pdf (accessed July 27, 2014).

14. Paul, Weiss, Rifkind, Wharton and Garrison LLP. (February 14, 2014). "Report to the National Football League Concerning Issues of Workplace Conduct at the Miami Dolphins." http://63bba9dfdf9675bf3f10-68be460ce43dd2a60dd64 ca5eca4ae1d.r37.cf1.rackcdn.com/PaulWeissReport.pdf (accessed July 18, 2014).

15. Wallace, M. (March 1, 2014). "LeBron James Ditches Black Mask." ESPN. http://espn.go.com/nba/truehoop/miamiheat/story/_/id/10536938/lebron-james -miami-heat-ditch-black-mask-vs-orlando-magic (accessed July 18, 2014).

16. Young, M. (March 15, 2014). "Shocking Racist Tweets Follow High School Basketball Win by All-White Team." MLive. http://www.mlive.com/news/flint/ index.ssf/2014/03/members_of_howell_high_school.html. (accessed July 18, 2014).

Chapter 9

1. Brunsma, D. L., Brown, E. S., and Placier, P. (2013). "Teaching Race at Historically White Colleges and Universities: Identifying and Dismantling the Walls of Whiteness." *Critical Sociology*, 39(5), 717–38.

2. Martin, L. L. (2013). *Black Asset Poverty and the Enduring Racial Divide*. Boulder, CO: First Forum Press.

3. Robinson, E. (2010). *Disintegration: The Splintering of Black America*. New York: Anchor, 4.

4. Horton, H. D., Allen, B. L., Herring, C., and Thomas, M. E. (2000). "Lost in the Storm: The Sociology of the Black Working Class, 1850 to 1990." *American Sociological Review*, 1, 128; Martin, L. L. and Horton, H. D. (forthcoming). *Lost in the Storm: America's Black Working Class in the Age of Obama*. Boulder, CO: Lynne Rienner.

5. Wheary, J., Shapiro, T., Draut, T., and Meschede, T. (2008). "Economic (In) Security: The Experience of the African American and Latino Middle Classes." Brandeis University. http://iasp.brandeis.edu/pdfs/2008/Economic_Insecurity _AA_Latinos.pdf (accessed July 18, 2014); Park, L. (2008). "Continuing Significance of the Model Minority Myth: The Second Generation." *Social Justice*, 35(2), 134–44.

6. Canales, M. (2000). "Othering: Toward an Understanding of Difference." *Advances in Nursing Science*, 22, 16–31.

7. Park, "Continuing Significance of the Model Minority Myth," 136.

8. Brunsma, Brown, and Placier, "Teaching Race at Historically White Colleges and Universities," 721; McIntosh, P. (1990). "White Privilege: Unpacking the Invisible Knapsack." *Independent School*, 49(2), 31.

9. Bonilla-Silva, E. (2014). *Racism without Racists*. Lanham, MD: Rowman and Littlefield.

10. National Black Marathoners Association. Home page. http://www .blackmarathoners.org/ (accessed July 18, 2014).

11. Black Girls Run! Home page. http://www.blackgirlsrun.com/ (accessed July 18, 2014).

12. Kozol, J. (1992). *Savage Inequalities*. New York: Harper.

13. Omi, M., and Winant, H. (1994). *Racial Formation in the United States*. New York: Routledge.

Bibliography

Chapter 1: Toward a Unifying Perspective of Race, Racism, and Sports

Akee, R., and Yuksel, M. (2012). "The Decreasing Effect of Skin Tone on Women's Full-Time Employment." *Industrial and Labor Relations Review*, 65(2), 398–426.

Arai, S., and Kivel, B. D. (2009). "Critical Race Theory and Social Justice Perspectives on Whiteness, Difference(s), and (Anti)racism: A Fourth Wave of Race Research." *Journal of Leisure Research*, 41(4), 459–70.

Baumgardner, N. (February 8, 2013). "Jalen Rose: Michigan Basketball Needs to Repair Its Fractured Past, and Dave Brandon Is the Man to Do It." http://www.mlive.com/wolverines/index.ssf/2013/02/jalen_rose_michigan_basket ball.html (accessed June 23, 2014).

Bejan, A., Jones, E. C., and Charles, J. (2010). "The Evolution of Speed in Athletics: Why the Fastest Runners Are Black and Swimmers White." *International Journal of Design and Nature*, 5(3), 199–211.

Bell, D. A. (1995). "Who's Afraid of Critical Race Theory?" *University of Illinois Law Review*, 893–910.

Bonilla-Silva, E. (2004). "From Bi-racial to Tri-racial: Towards a New System of Racial Stratification in the USA." *Ethnic and Racial Studies*, 27(6), 931–50.

Brewster, Z. W., and Rusche, S. N. (2012). "Quantitative Evidence of the Continuing Significance of Race: Tableside Racism in Full-Service Restaurants." *Journal of Black Studies*, 43(5), 359–84.

Burton, L. M., Bonilla-Silva, E., Ray, V., Buckelew, R., and Freeman, E. (2010). "Critical Race Theories, Colorism, and the Decade's Research on Families of Color." *Journal of Marriage and Family*, 72(3), 440–59.

Carrington, B. (2013). "The Critical Sociology of Race and Sport: The First Fifty Years." *Annual Review of Sociology*, 39(1), 379–98.

Carter, R. (November 17, 2005). "NBA's New Dress Code: Racist or Just Smart Business?" *Amsterdam News*, 10–41.

Cashmore, E., and Cleland, J. (2011). "Why Aren't There More Black Football Managers?" *Ethnic and Racial Studies*, 34(9), 1594–1607.

Closson, R. (2010). "Critical Race Theory and Adult Education." *Adult Education Quarterly*, 60(3), 261–83.

Coakley, Jay. (2008). *Sports and Society: Issues and Controversies*. New York: McGraw-Hill.

Eligon, J. (October 27, 2005). "Dressing Up Basketball? Been There, Done That." *New York Times*, G7.

Fasching-Varner, K. J. (2009). "No! The Team Ain't Alright! The Institutional and Individual Problematics of Race." *Social Identities: Journal for the Study of Race, Nation and Culture*, 15(6), 811–29.

Feagin, J. R. (1991). "The Continuing Significance of Race: Antiblack Discrimination in Public Places." *American Sociological Review*, 56(1), 101–16.

Fogarty, D. (February 21, 2011). "Are White People Losing Interest in the NBA Because None of Its Superstars Look Like Them?" http://www.sportsgrid.com/nba/nba-white-people-interest/ (accessed June 22, 2014).

Ford, C. L., and Airhihenbuwa, C. O. (2010). "Critical Race Theory, Race Equity, and Public Health: Toward Antiracism Praxis." *American Journal of Public Health*, 100(S1), S30–S35.

Forster-Scott, L. (2011). "Understanding Colorism and How It Relates to Sport and Physical Education." *The Journal of Physical Education, Recreation and Dance*, 82(2), 48–52.

Fryer, R. G., Jr., and Levitt, S. D. (2004). "The Causes and Consequences of Distinctively Black Names." *Quarterly Journal of Economics*, 119(3), 767–805.

Government Press Releases (USA). (July 12, 2013). "Kirk, Durbin, Quigley Honor 1963 Loyola Men's Basketball Team; Celebrate 50th Anniversary of Only Illinois Division I Team to Win NCAA Championship, First to Start Four African-American Players."

Graham, L., Brown-Jeffy, S., Aronson, R., and Stephens, C. (2011). "Critical Race Theory as Theoretical Framework and Analysis Tool for Population Health Research." *Critical Public Health*, 21(1), 81–93.

Grasso, J. (2011). *Historical Dictionary of Tennis*. New York: Scarecrow Press, 8.

Hallman, C. (June 27, 2012). "Colorblind Racism: Language of Sports Filled with Barely Disguised Bigotry." *Minnesota-Spokesman Reporter*.

Harris, A. P. (2008). "From Color Line to Color Chart?: Racism and Colorism in the New Century." *Berkeley Journal of African-American Law and Policy*, 10 (1), 52–69.

Herman, R. (2010). "An Oral History of the Integration of College Sports." *Vital Speeches of the Day*, 76(1), 6–10.

Herring, C., Keith, V., and Horton, H. D., eds. (2004). *Skin Deep: How Race and Complexion Matter in the "Color-Blind" Era*. Chicago: University of Illinois Press.

Hersch, J. (2008). "Skin Color Discrimination and Immigrant Pay." *Emory Law Journal*, 58(2), 357–77.

Hill, S. A. (2006). "Racial Socialization." In G. Handel, ed., *Childhood Socialization.* 2nd ed. New Brunswick, NJ: Aldine Transaction.

Hine, D., Hine, W., and Harrold, S. (2010). *The African-American Odyssey.* Upper Saddle River, NJ: Pearson.

Horton, H. (1999). "Critical Demography: The Paradigm of the Future?" *Sociological Forum,* 14(3), 363.

Horton, H. D. (2002). "Rethinking American Diversity: Conceptual and Theoretical Challenges for Racial and Ethnic Demography." In Tolnay, Stewart, and Denton, Nancy, eds. *American Diversity: A Demographic Challenge for the Twenty-First Century.* Albany: State University of New York Press.

Horton, H., and Allen, B. (1998). "Race, Family Structure and Rural Poverty: An Assessment of Population and Structural Change." *Journal of Comparative Family Studies,* 29(2), 397–406.

Horton, H. D., and Sykes, L. L. (2008). "Critical Demography and the Measurement of Racism: A Reproduction of Wealth, Status, and Power." In Zuberi, T., and Bonilla-Silva, E., eds. *White Logic, White Methods: Racism and Methodology.* Lanham, MD: Rowman and Littlefield.

Hunter, M. (2008). "Teaching and Learning Guide for: The Persistent Problem of Colorism: Skin Tone, Status, and Inequality." *Sociology Compass,* 2(1), 366.

Hylton, K. 2008. *Race and Sport.* New York: Routledge. http://www.bl.uk/ sportandsociety/exploresocsci/sportsoc/sociology/articles/hylton.pdf (accessed June 22, 2014).

Hylton, K. (2010). "How a Turn to Critical Race Theory Can Contribute to Our Understanding of 'Race,' Racism and Anti-racism in Sport." *International Review for the Sociology of Sport,* 45(3), 335–54.

Isola, Frank. (February 8, 2010). "Chris Kaman, the Great White Hope." *New York Daily News* blog. http://www.nydailynews.com/blogs/knicks/chris-kaman -great-white-hope-blog-entry-1.1641439 (accessed June 23, 2014).

Joseph, N., and Hunter, C. D. (2011). "Ethnic-Racial Socialization Messages in the Identity Development of Second-Generation Haitians." *Journal of Adolescent Research,* 26(3), 344–80.

Keith, V. M. (2009). "A Colorstruck World: Skin Tone, Achievement, and Self-Esteem among African American Women." In Evelyn Nakano Glenn, ed. *Shades of Difference: Why Skin Color Matters.* Los Altos, CA: Stanford University Press, 25–39.

Keith, V. M., and Herring, C. (1991). "Skin Color and Stratification in the Black Community." *American Journal of Sociology,* 97, 760–78.

Lapchick, R., Hippert, A., Rivera, S., and Robinson, J. (2013). *The 2013 Race and Gender Report Card: National Basketball Association.* http://www.tidesport .org/RGRC/2013/2013_NBA_RGRC.pdf (accessed June 22, 2014).

Leonard, D. (2012). *After Artest: The NBA and the Assault on Blackness.* Albany: State University of New York Press, 166.

Lomax, M. E. (2008). *Sports and the Racial Divide: African American and Latino Experience in an Era of Change.* Jackson: University of Mississippi Press.

Louis, B. (2004). "Sport and Common Sense Racial Science." *Leisure Studies,* 23(1), 31–46.

Maconis, J. (2011). *Sociology.* Upper Saddle River, NJ: Pearson, 310.

Martin, L. (2009). "Black Asset Ownership: Does Ethnicity Matter?" *Social Science Research,* 38(2), 312–23.

Martin, L. L. (2013). *Black Asset Poverty and the Enduring Racial Divide.* Boulder, CO: First Forum Press.

Martin, L. L., and Horton, H. D. (2014). "Racism Front and Center: Introducing the Critical Demography of Athletic Destinations." In Martin, L. L., ed. *Out of Bounds: Racism and the Black Athlete.* Santa Barbara, CA: Praeger, 105–132.

Massey, D. S. (1999). "What Critical Demography Means to Me." *Sociological Forum,* 14(3), 525.

Neumann, T. (March 11, 2011). "Michigan's Fab Five in Their Own Words." ESPN Page 2. http://sports.espn.go.com/espn/page2/story?page=neumann/110311_fab_five_documentary&sportCat=ncb (accessed June 22, 2014).

Onwuachi-Willig, A. (2009). "Celebrating Critical Race Theory at 20." *Iowa Law Review,* 94, 1497–1504.

"Race and Its Continuing Significance on Our Campuses: An Interview with Dr. Joe R. Feagin." (2003). *Black Issues in Higher Education,* 19(24), 24–27.

Robst, J., VanGilder, J., Coates, C. E., and Berri, D. J. (2011). "Skin Tone and Wages: Evidence from NBA Free Agents." *Journal of Sports Economics,* 12 (2), 143–56.

Romero, M. (2008). "Crossing the Immigration and Race Border: A Critical Race Theory Approach to Immigration Studies." *Contemporary Justice Review,* 11 (1), 23–37.

Ross, C. (1999). *Outside the Lines: African Americans and the Integration of the National Football League.* New York: New York University Press.

Sack, A. L., Singh, P., and Thiel, R. (2005). "Occupational Segregation on the Playing Field: The Case of Major League Baseball." *Journal of Sport Management,* 19(3), 300–318.

Sailes, G. A. (1991). "The Myth of Black Sports Supremacy." *Journal of Black Studies,* (4), 480.

Schneider-Mayerson, M. (2010). "Too Black: Race in the Dark Ages of the National Basketball Association." *International Journal of Sport and Society,* 1(1), 223–33.

Treviño, A., Harris, M. A., and Wallace, D. (2008). "What's So Critical about Critical Race Theory?" *Contemporary Justice Review,* 11(1), 7–10.

Warren, P. Y. (2010). "The Continuing Significance of Race: An Analysis Across Two Levels of Policing." *Social Science Quarterly,* 91(4), 1025–42.

Weinberg, R. (1993). "Jordan, Age 30, Retires for the First Time." http://sports
.espn.go.com/espn/espn25/story?page=moments/91 (accessed June 22, 2014)

Wettenstein, B. (August 30, 2007). "Let Us Remember Alice Marble, the Catalyst
for Althea Gibson to Break the Color Barrier." *Huffington Post*. http://www
.huffingtonpost.com/beverly-wettenstein/let-us-remember-alice-mar_b_62571
.html (accessed June 22, 2014).

Wilbon, M. (June 25, 2011). "The Foreign Flavor of This NBA Draft." ESPN.
http://sports.espn.go.com/espn/commentary/news/story?page=wilbon-110624
(accessed June 22, 2014).

Williamson, Joel. (1968). *The Origins of Segregation*. Boston: Heath.

Yep, K. (2012). "Peddling Sport: Liberal Multiculturalism and the Racial Triangulation of Blackness, Chineseness and Native American-ness in Professional
Basketball." *Ethnic and Racial Studies*, 35(6), 971–87.

Zuberi, T. (2011). "Critical Race Theory of Society." *Connecticut Law Review*, 43
(5), 1573–91.

Chapter 2: Race, Place, and Sports

Bonilla-Silva, E. (2014). *Racism without Racists: Color-Blind Racism and the
Persistence of Racial Inequality in America*. 4th ed. Lanham, MD: Rowman
and Littlefield.

Boustan, L. P. (2011). "Racial Residential Segregation in American Cities."
In Brooks, N., and Knaap, G.-J., *Oxford Handbook of Urban Economics and
Planning*. Oxford, UK: Oxford University Press, 318–39.

Charles, C. (2000). "Neighborhood Racial-Composition Preferences: Evidence
from a Multiethnic Metropolis." *Social Problems*, 47(3), 379–407.

Coakley, J. (2008*). Sports and Society*. New York: McGraw-Hill, 286.

Darden, J. T., and Kamel, S. M. (2000). "Black Residential Segregation in the City
and Suburbs of Detroit: Does Socioeconomic Status Matter?" *Journal of
Urban Affairs*, 22(1), 1.

Dawkins, C. J. (2004). "Recent Evidence on the Continuing Causes of Black-White
Residential Segregation." *Journal of Urban Affairs*, 26(3), 379–400.

Denton, N. A. (2006). "Segregation and Discrimination in Housing." In Bratt, R. G.,
Stone, M. E., and Hartman, C., eds. *A Right to Housing: Foundation of a New
Social Agenda*. Philadelphia: Temple University Press, 61–81.

Edwards, H. (1979). "Sports within the Veil: The Triumphs, Tragedies, and
Challenges of African American Involvement." *Annals of the American
Academy of Political and Social Science*, 445, 116–27.

Gimino, A. (March 27, 2013). "Arizona Basketball: All about Mark Lyons." *Tucson
Citizen*. http://tucsoncitizen.com/wildcatreport/2013/03/27/arizona-basket
ball-all-about-mark-lyons/ (accessed June 24, 2014).

Jones, A. C., and Naison, M. (2011). *The Rat That Got Away*. New York: Fordham University Press.

Joravsky, B. (1996). *Hoop Dreams: A True Story of Hardship and Triumph*. New York: HarperCollins.

Lapchick, R. (2011). *The 2011 Racial and Gender Report Card: College Sport*. http://www.tidesport.org/RGRC/2011/2011_College_RGRC.pdf (accessed June 24, 2014).

Lapchick, R., Costa, P., Nickerson, B., and Rodriguez, B. (2012). *The 2012 Racial and Gender Report Card: Major League Baseball*. http://www.tidesport.org/RGRC/2012/2012_MLB_RGRC.pdf (accessed June 24, 2014).

Lapchick, R., Costa, P., Sherod, T. and Anjorin, R. (2012). *The 2012 Racial and Gender Report Card: National Football League*. http://www.tidesport.org/RGRC/2012/2012_NFL_RGRC.pdf (accessed June 24, 2014).

Lapchick, R., Gunn, O., and Trigg, A. (2012). *The 2012 Racial and Gender Report Card: Major League Soccer*. http://www.tidesport.org/RGRC/2012/2012_MLS_RGRC.pdf (accessed June 24, 2014).

Lapchick, R., Lecky, A., and Trigg, A. (2012). *The 2012 Racial and Gender Report Card: National Basketball Association*. http://www.tidesport.org/RGRC/2012/2012_NBA_RGRC[1].pdf (accessed June 24, 2014).

Lapchick, R., Milkovich, M., and O'Keefe, S. (2012). *The 2012 Women's National Basketball Association Racial and Gender Report Card*. http://www.tidesport.org/RGRC/2012/2012_WNBA_RGRC.pdf (accessed June 24, 2014).

Mackin, Robert Sean, and Walther, Carol S. (2012). "Race, Sport and Social Mobility: Horatio Alger in Short Pants?" *International Review for the Sociology of Sport*, 47(6), 670–89.

Mallozzi, V. M. (November 11, 1990). "Basketball: Legend of the Playground." *New York Times*. http://www.nytimes.com/1990/11/11/sports/basketball-legend-of-the-playground.html?pagewanted=all&src=pm (accessed June 24, 2014).

Martin, L. L. (2013). *Black Asset Poverty and the Enduring Racial Divide*. Boulder, CO: First Forum Press.

Massey, D. S., Denton, N. A. (1993). *American Apartheid: Segregation and the Making of the Underclass*. Cambridge, MA: Harvard University Press.

South, S., Crowder, K., and Pais, J. (2011). "Metropolitan Structure and Neighborhood Attainment: Exploring Intermetropolitan Variation in Racial Residential Segregation." *Demography*, 48(4), 1263–92.

Chapter 3: A Perfect Combination: The Mass Media and Representations of Race in Sports

African American Registry. (n.d.). "World Heavyweight Champ and Legend, Jack Johnson." http://www.aaregistry.org/historic_events/view/world-heavyweight-champ-and-legend-jack-johnson (accessed June 27, 2014).

Andrews, K. T., and Briggs, M. (2006). "The Dynamics of Protest Diffusion: Movement Organizations, Social Networks, and News Media in the 1960 Sit-Ins." *American Sociological Review*, 71(5), 752–77.

Bailey, B. (1993). :The Double-V Campaign in World War II Hawaii: African Americans, Racial Ideology, and Federal Power." *Journal of Social History*, 26(4), 817–43.

Bohn, Michael K. (2009). *Heroes and Ballyhoo: How the Golden Age of the 1920s Transformed American Sports*. Washington, DC: Potomac Books, 2009.

Bonilla-Silva, E. (2014). *Racism without Racists*. Lanham, MD: Rowman and Littlefield.

Boyle, R. (2006). *Sports Journalism*. New York: Sage.

Brooke-Ball, P., Snelling, O. F., and O'Dell, D. (1995). *The Boxing Album: An Illustrated History*. New York: Smithmark.

Brown, E. (April 6, 2013). "New Push to Pardon Boxing Legend Jack Johnson." *Salon*. http://www.salon.com/2013/04/06/new_push_to_pardon_boxing_legend_jack_johnson_partner/ (accessed June 27, 2014).

Brown, J. (2007). *Freedom's Journal: The First African American Newspaper*. Lanham, MD: Lexington Books.

Byfield, N. (2009.) "Modern Newspapers and the Formation of White Racial Group Consciousness." *Conference Papers—American Sociological Association*, 1.

Chase, C. (June 19, 2013). "Williams Still Doesn't Know How to Apologize." http://ftw.usatoday.com/2013/06/serena-williams-apology-steubenville/ (accessed June 29, 2014).

City of Alexandria, Virginia. (n.d.) "Civil War Baseball—Battling on the Diamond." http://alexandriava.gov/historic/fortward/default.aspx?id=40132 (accessed June 27, 2014).

Du Bois, W. E. B. (1903). *The Souls of Black Folk*. Chicago: A. C. McClurg and Co.

Goldberg, A. (2011). "Serena Williams Fined $2,000 by U.S. Open for Berating Chair Umpire." *Huffington Post*, http://www.huffingtonpost.com/2011/09/12/serena-williams-fined-us-open_n_958862.html (accessed June 30, 2014).

Greer, J. D. (2004.) "Advertising on Traditional Media Sites: Can the Traditional Business Model be Translated to the Web?" *Social Science Journal*, 41(1), 107.

Griffith, Clark C. (2003). "Sports Licensing." *Licensing Journal*, 23(9), 20–21.

Hietala, T. (2002). *The Fight of the Century: Jack Johnson, Joe Louis, and the Struggle for Racial Equality*. New York: M. E. Sharpe.

Higginbotham, A. L. (1980). *In the Matter of Color: Race and the American Legal Process: The Colonial Period*. New York: Oxford University Press.

Hine, D., Hine, W., and Harrold, S. (2010). *The African-American Odyssey*. Upper Saddle River, NJ: Pearson.

Jim Crow Museum of Racist Memorabilia. http://www.ferris.edu/htmls/news/jimcrow/index.htm (accessed June 29, 2014).

Jordan, W. G. (2001). *Black Newspapers and America's War for Democracy, 1914–1920*. Chapel Hill: University of North Carolina Press.

Kennedy, R. (1998). *Race, Crime and the Law*. New York: Vintage.

Killion, A. (2009). "Serena's Outburst Common among Athletes—but Not Women." *Sports Illustrated*. http://www.si.com/more-sports/2009/09/15/serena (accessed June 29, 2014).

Kinshasa, K. M. (1988). *Emigration vs. Assimilation: The Debate in the African-American Press*. Jefferson, NC: McFarland.

Kinshasa, K. (2006). "An Appraisal of *Brown v. Board of Education*, Topeka, KS (1954) and the Montgomery Bus Boycott." *Journal of Black Studies*, 30(4), 16–23.

Latty, Y. (2005). *We Were There: Voices of African American Veterans from World War II to the War in Iraq*. New York: Amistad.

Linder, D. O. (2012). "The Emmett Till Murder Trial: An Account." http://law2.umkc.edu/faculty/projects/ftrials/till/tillhome.html (accessed June 29, 2014).

McChesney, R. (n.d.). "Media Made Sport: A History of Sports Coverage in the U.S." http://www.ux1.eiu.edu/~jjgisondi/MediaMade.pdf (accessed June 27, 2014).

Morgan, D. C. (1999). "Jack Johnson: Reluctant Hero of the Black Community." *Akron Law Review*, 32(3), 529–56.

Morris, A. D. (1984). *The Origins of the Civil Rights Movement: Black Communities Organizing for Change*. New York: Free Press.

Niedner, F. (January 25, 2013). "When Athletes Became Heroes, Plot Lines Changed." *Post-Tribune* (IN).

O'Connor, L. A., Brooks-Gunn, J., and Graber, J. (2000). "Black and White Girls' Racial Preferences in Media and Peer Choices and the Role of Socialization for Black Girls." *Journal of Family Psychology*, 14(3), 510–21.

Oxford English Dictionary Online, quoted in Newman, L. (n.d.). "Mass Media." The Chicago School of Media Theory. http://lucian.uchicago.edu/blogs/mediatheory/keywords/mass-media/ (accessed June 27, 2014).

Perloff, R. (2000). "The Press and Lynchings of African Americans. *Journal of Black Studies*, 30(3), 315–30.

Pilgrim, D. (2012). "Jezebel Stereotype." http://www.ferris.edu/jimcrow/jezebel.htm.

Pilgrim, D. (2012). "The Sapphire Caricature." http://www.ferris.edu/htmls/news/jimcrow/sapphire (accessed June 29, 2014).

Public Broadcasting System. (n.d.). Timeline of the Black Press. http://www.pbs.org/blackpress/timeline/contenttimeline.html (accessed June 29, 2014).

Public Broadcasting System, American Experience web page. (n.d.). "People and Events: The Negro World." http://www.pbs.org/wgbh/amex/garvey/peopleevents/e_negroworld.html (accessed June 27, 2014).

Raney, A. A., and Bryant J. (2006). *Handbook of Sports and Media*. Mahwah, NJ: Lawrence Erlbaum Associates.

Roberts, D. (1998). *Killing the Black Body*. New York: Vintage.

Root Staff. (2012). "Tennis Player Mocks Serena's Body?" http://www.theroot. com/articles/culture/2012/12/tennis_player_mocks_serenas_body.html (accessed June 30, 2014)

Smart, B. (2007). "Not Playing Around: Global Capitalism, Modern Sport and Consumer Culture." *Global Networks*, 7(2), 113–34.

Smith, P. (1970). "Men Who Think Black." *Personnel and Guidance Journal*, 48(9), 763–66.

Smith, R. A. (2001). *Play-by-Play: Radio, Television, and Big-Time College Sport*. Baltimore: John Hopkins University Press.

Tarrant, S. (March 31, 2010). "Wheaties Fuels a Breakfast of Stereotypes." http:// msmagazine.com/blog/2010/03/31/wheaties-fuels-a-breakfast-of-stereotypes/ (accessed June 29, 2014).

Ward, G. C. (2004). *Unforgivable Blackness : The Rise and Fall of Jack Johnson*. New York: Knopf.

Washington, B. T. (1895). "Booker T. Washington Delivers the 1895 Atlanta Compromise Speech." http://historymatters.gmu.edu/d/39/ (accessed June 29, 2014).

Wilson, S. K. (2000). *The Messenger Reader*. New York: Modern Library.

Wintz, C. D., and Finkelman, P. (2004). *Encyclopedia of the Harlem Renaissance*. New York: Routledge.

Yuen, N. (2010). "Playing 'Ghetto': Black Actors, Stereotypes, and Authenticity." *Conference Papers—American Sociological Association*.

Chapter 4: Race Thinking and Minority Athletes in Football

Agyemang, K., Singer, J., and DeLorme, J. (2010). "An Exploratory Study of Black Male College Athletes' Perceptions on Race and Athlete Activism." *International Review for the Sociology of Sport*, 45(4), 419–35.

"American Football and Its Heritage." http://www.acsu.buffalo.edu/~samuelpe/ history-american-football.html (accessed July 1, 2014).

Ball, D. W. (1973). "Ascription and Position: A Comparative Analysis of 'Stacking' in Professional Football." *Canadian Review of Sociology and Anthropology*, 10 (2), 97.

Bentley, L. (December 2, 2010). "Racism Alive and Swell in NFL." *SFGate*, http:// www.sfgate.com/sports/article/Racism-Alive-and-Swell-in-NFL-2387503.php (accessed July 1, 2014).

Bowen, R. T. (1982). "Race, Home Town and Experience as Factors in Deep South Major College Football." *International Review of Sport Sociology*, 17(2), 41–51.

Braddock, J. H., Smith, E., and Dawkins, M. P. (2012). "Race and Pathways to Power in the National Football League." *American Behavioral Scientist*, 56 (5), 711–27.

Buffington, D. (2005). "Contesting Race on Sundays: Making Meaning out of the Rise in the Number of Black Quarterbacks." *Sociology of Sport Journal*, 22 (1), 12.

Day, Jacob C., and McDonald, Steve. (2010). "Not So Fast, My Friend: Social Capital and the Race Disparity in Promotions among College Football Coaches." *Sociological Spectrum*, 30(2), 138–58.

Edwards, H. (September 1979). "Sport within the Veil: The Triumphs, Tragedies and Challenges of Afro-American Involvement." *Annals of the AAPSS*, 445, 116–27.

Ferguson, T. (2009). "Combating Unseen Struggles: The African American Male Football Player." *Journal of Indiana University Student Personnel Association*, 52–64.

Foley, D. (1990). "The Great American Football Ritual: Reproducing Race, Class, and Gender Inequality." http://www.qcc.cuny.edu/pv_obj_cache/pv_obj_id _EB4CBD6288BD55F5E595F9D8C099751EA0D80200/ (accessed July 1, 2014).

Football History. Professor Stelzer's Site, PhD. http://coefaculty.valdosta.edu/jiri/ the_history_of_american_football.htm (accessed July 1, 2014).

"Four Stories of NFL Desegregation." Shmoop. http://www.shmoop.com/ nfl-history/race.html (accessed July 1, 2014).

Harper, S. R., Williams, C. D., and Blackman, H. W. (2013). *Black Male Student-Athletes and Racial Inequities in NCAA Division I College Sports*. Philadelphia: University of Pennsylvania, Center for the Study of Race and Equity in Education.

Hysell, P. (October 19, 2009). "On This Day: Football Rules Were First Set Down." *Examiner*. http://www.examiner.com/article/on-this-day-football-rules-were -first-set-down (accessed July 1, 2014).

Jones, Gregg A., Leonard, Wilbert M. II, Schmitt, Raymond L., Smith, D. Randall, and Tolone, William L. (1987). "Racial Discrimination in College Football." *Social Science Quarterly*, 68(1), 70–83.

Kooistra, P., Mahoney, J., and Bridges, L. (1993). "The Unequal Opportunity for Equal Ability Hypothesis: Racism in the National Football League." *Sociology of Sport Journal* [serial online], 10(3), 241–55.

Lapchick, R. (2012). *Keeping Score When It Counts: Assessing the 2012–2013 Bowl-Bound College Football Teams' Graduation Rates*. http://www.tidesport.org/ Grad%20Rates/2012_FBS_Bowl_Study.pdf (accessed July 1, 2014).

Lapchick, R., Costa, P., Sherod, T. and Anjorin, R. (2012). *The 2012 Racial and Gender Report Card: National Football League*. http://www.tidesport.org/ RGRC/2012/2012_NFL_RGRC.pdf (accessed June 24, 2014).

Leonard, D. J. (2012). "Joe Paterno, White Patriarchy and Privilege." *Cultural Studies Critical Methodologies*, 12(4), 373–76.

Linkings, J. (June 13, 2013). "Roger Goodell, in Defending 'Redskins' Name, Must Think People Are Stupid." *Huffington Post.* http://www.huffingtonpost .com/2013/06/13/roger-goodell-redskins_n_3436917.html (accessed July 1, 2014).

Martin, Charles H. (1996). "Racial Change and 'Big-Time' College Football in Georgia: The Age of Segregation, 1892–1957." *The Georgia Historical Quarterly,* 3, 532.

"Minority Players and the American Football League." AFL Internet Network. http://www.remembertheafl.com/MinorityPlayers.htm (accessed July 1, 2014).

Murrell, A. J., and Curtis, E. M. (1994). "Causal Attributions of Performance for Black and White Quarterbacks in the NFL." *Journal of Sport and Social Issues,* 18(3), 224–33.

Nestor. (October 15, 2009). "Remembering Bruin Legends Kenny Washington/ Woody Strode: Jackie Robinson(s) of Pro Football." *Bruins Nation.* http:// www.bruinsnation.com/2009/10/10/1079303/honoring-bruin-legends-kenny (accessed July 1, 2014).

Rhoden, W. (2006). *Forty Million Dollar Slaves.* New York: Crown.

Schilken, C. (February 4, 2013). "Ravens' 2013 Super Bowl Victory Sets TV Ratings Record." *Los Angeles Times,* http://articles.latimes.com/2013/feb/04/sports/la -sp-sn-super-bowl-ratings-20130204 (accessed July 1, 2014).

Waller, A. (April 18, 2013). "Super Bowl 2013 Drove $480 Million in Spending in New Orleans, Beating Expectations, Economic Study Shows." *Times- Picayune.* http://www.nola.com/business/index.ssf/2013/04/super_bowl _2013_drove_480_mill.html (accessed July 1, 2014).

Wiggins, D. K., and Miller, P. B. (2005). *Unlevel Playing Field.* Champaign: University of Illinois Press.

Chapter 5: America's Other Favorite Pastime: Baseball

"Abner Doubleday." http://www.tulane.edu/~latner/Doubleday.html (accessed July 3, 2014).

Abrams, D. (2007). *Ty Cobb.* New York: Chelsea House.

Alexander, C. C. (1984). *Ty Cobb.* New York: Oxford University Press.

Babwin, D. (n.d.). "Did Black Sox Get Idea to Throw 1919 World Series from Cubs?" *Chicago Sun-Times.* http://www.suntimes.com/news/metro/4938714 -418/did-black-sox-get-idea-to-throw-1919-world-series-from-cubs.html# .U7W7-kDyRmg (accessed July 3, 2014).

Blackburn, B. T. (2007). "Racial Stacking in the National Football League: Reality or Relic of the Past?" Dissertation, University of Missouri, Kansas City.

Burgos, A., Jr. (October 25, 2012). "Best Way to Honor Robinson: Hire Black Managers in Baseball." *Lexington Herald-Leader* (KY). http://www.kentucky

.com/2012/10/25/2384020/best-way-to-honor-robinson-hire.html (accessed July 3, 2014).

Chen, A. S. (2009). *The Fifth Freedom: Jobs, Politics, and Civil Rights in the United States, 1941–1972.* Princeton, NJ: Princeton University Press.

Crawford, A. (n.d.). "The First Lady of Black Baseball: Manley Was an Innovator in the Negro Leagues." MLB.com. http://mlb.mlb.com/mlb/history/mlb _negro_leagues_story.jsp?story=effa_manley (accessed July 3, 2014).

Donahue, W. (January 23, 2005). "The Other White-Collar Sport." *Chicago Tribune.* http://articles.chicagotribune.com/2005-01-23/features/0501230407_1 _squash-racquets-association-racquet-sports-industry-tennis-industry-magazine (accessed July 3, 2014).

Edes, G. (May 31, 1992). "Blacks Still Perceive Baseball as the White Sport." *Sun Sentinel.*

Elias, R. (2001). *Baseball and the American Dream: Race, Class, Gender, and the National Pastime.* Armonk, NY: M. E. Sharpe.

Engstrom, D. F. (2011). "The Lost Origins of American Fair Employment Law: Regulatory Choice and the Making of the Modern Civil Rights, 1943–1972." *Stanford Law Review*, 3(5), 1071–1143.

Feinsand, M. (August 11, 2007). "Lofton: Torre No Racist." *New York Daily News.* http://www.nydailynews.com/sports/baseball/yankees/lofton-torre-racist -article-1.238606 (accessed July 3, 2014).

Fiebernitz, C. (April 19, 2012). "Moses Fleetwood Walker: The Forgotten Man Who Actually Integrated Baseball." *The Mountaineer* (Waynesville, NC).

Finding Dulcinea Staff. (September 23, 2011). "On This Day: Knickerbocker Club Establishes Rules of Modern Baseball." Finding Dulcinea. http://www .findingdulcinea.com/news/on-this-day/September-October-08/On-This-Day —First-Organized-Baseball-Team-Founded.html (accessed July 3, 2014).

Fresh Air. (March 16, 2011). "The 'Secret History' of Baseball's Early Days." http:// www.npr.org/2011/03/16/134570236/the-secret-history-of-baseballs-earliest -days (accessed July 3, 2014).

Gardner, R., and Shortelle, D. (1993). *The Forgotten Players: The Story of Black Baseball in America.* New York: Walker and Co., 45.

Gendin, S. (1998). "Moses Fleetwood Walker : Jackie Robinson's Accidental Predecessor." In Dorison, J., and Warmund, J., eds. *Jackie Robinson: Race, Sports and the American Dream.* Armonk, NY: M. E. Sharpe, 22–29.

Gibbons, L. (August 18, 2013). "Former Owner of Negro League Baseball Team Honored by President Obama at White House." Mlive. http://www.mlive .com/news/grand-rapids/index.ssf/2013/08/former_owner_of_negro_league _b.html (accessed July 3, 2014).

Guarini, D. (June 8, 2012). "Life after LeBron." *Huffington Post.* http://www .huffingtonpost.com/2012/06/08/life-after-lebron-how-clevelands-economy-is -faring_n_1582328.html (accessed July 9, 2014).

Harris, M. (1995). "Blacks and Baseball: Where've You Gone, Jackie Robinson?" *Nation*, 260(19), 674–76.

Hay, C. (July 30, 2013). " '42' is No. 1 in Movies on Demand; 'Evil Dead' No. 2; 'Bullet to the Head' No. 4." *Entertainment Examiner*.

Heaphy, L. (2011). "Baseball and the Color Line: From Negro Leagues to the Major Leagues." In Cassuto, L., and Partridge, S., eds. *The Cambridge Companion to Baseball*. Cambridge, England: Cambridge University Press.

Hill, J. B. (n.d.). "Traveling Show: Barnstorming Was Common Place in the Negro Leagues." MLB.com. http://mlb.mlb.com/mlb/history/mlb_negro_leagues _story.jsp?story=barnstorming (accessed July 3, 2014).

Holway, John B. (2001). *The Complete Book of Baseball's Negro Leagues: The Other Half of Baseball History*. Fern Park, FL: Hastings House, 61–74.

Jaffe, C. (2012). "Centennial Anniversary: Ty Cobb Beats Up a Cripple." *Hardball Times*. http://www.hardballtimes.com/tht-live/centennial-anniversary-ty -cobb-beats-up-a-cripple/ (accessed July 10, 2014).

Johnston, A. (January 29, 2013). "Ty Cobb Elected to Hall in 1936." *Atlanta Journal-Constitution*.

Kahn, R. (1996–97). "The Jackie Robinson I Remember." *Journal of Blacks in Higher Education*, 14, 88–93.

Knee, S. (2003). "Jim Crow Strikes Out: Branch Rickey and the Struggle for Integration in American Baseball." *Culture, Sport, Society*, 6(2/3), 71–87.

"Knickerbocker Baseball Club of New York." BaseballReference.com. http:// www.baseball-reference.com/bullpen/Knickerbocker_Base_Ball_Club_of _New_York (accessed July 3, 2014).

Lanctot, N. (2004). *Negro League Baseball: The Rise and Ruin of a Black Institution*. Philadelphia: University of Pennsylvania Press.

Lapchick, R., Costa, P., Nickerson, B., and Rodriguez, B. (2012). *The 2012 Racial and Gender Report Card: Major League Baseball*. http://www.tidesport.org/ RGRC/2012/2012_MLB_RGRC.pdf (accessed July 4, 2014).

Lavoie, M., and Leonard, W. M. II. (1994). "In Search of an Alternative Explanation of Stacking in Baseball: The Uncertainty Hypothesis." *Sociology of Sport Journal* 11(2), 140–54.

Lowrey, A. (April 28, 2013). "Wealth Gap among Races Has Widened since Recession." *New York Times*.

Lumpkin, A. (2011). "Negro Leagues: Black Diamonds." *Phi Kappa Phi Forum*, 91(2), 22.

Margolis, B., and Piliavin, J. A. (1999). "Stacking in Major League Baseball: A Multivariate Analysis." *Sociology of Sport Journal*, 16(1), 16–34.

Martin, L. L., and Horton, H. D. (2014). "Racism Front and Center: Introducing the Critical Demography of Athletic Destinations." In Martin, L. L., ed. *Out of Bounds: Racism and the Black Athlete*. Santa Barbara, CA: Praeger, 105–132.

Massie, J. (July 3, 2007). "Hallowed Be His Record; Hank Aaron Endured Segregation and Death Threats on His Way to 755 Career Home Runs, Revered as One of Baseball's Sacred Milestones." *Columbus Dispatch* (OH).

Mathewson, A. (1998). "Major League Baseball's Monopoly Power and the Negro Leagues." *American Business Law Journal*, 35(2), 291.

McCarron, J. (October 21, 2013). "The History of Women's Baseball Leagues in 1943–1954." Livestrong.com. http://www.livestrong.com/article/352490-the-history-of-the-women-baseball-league/ (accessed July 3, 2014).

National Baseball Hall of Fame. (n.d.). "Cartwright, Alexander." http://baseballhall.org/hof/cartwright-alexander (accessed July 2014).

"National League of Baseball Is Founded." History Channel. http://www.history.com/this-day-in-history/national-league-of-baseball-is-founded (accessed July 3, 2014).

"Negro Leagues Baseball: A Brief History." Negro Leagues Baseball eMuseum. http://www.coe.ksu.edu/annex/nlbemuseum/history/overview.html (accessed July 3, 2014).

Nucciarone, M. (2009). *Alexander Cartwright: The Life behind the Baseball Legend.* Lincoln: University of Nebraska Press.

Ogden, D. G., and Rose, R. A. (2005). "Using Gidden's Structuration Theory to Examine the Waning Participation of African Americans in Baseball." *Journal of Black Studies*, 35, 225–45.

Olbermann, K. (June 1, 1998). "Remembering a Pioneer: Some 30 Years before Jackie Robinson, There Was Jimmy Claxton." *Sports Illustrated.* http://sportsillustrated.cnn.com/vault/1998/06/01/243922/remembering-a-pioneer-some-30-years-before-jackie-robinson-there-was-jimmy-claxton (accessed July 3, 2014).

Overbea, Luix. (July 8, 1949). " 'Without Proper Support Negro Baseball Simply Cannot Survive' Says R.S. Simmons of Chicago." *Plaindealer.*

Pilgrim, D. (2012). "The Coon Caricature." http://www.ferris.edu/htmls/news/jimcrow/coon/ (accessed July 9, 2014).

Prada, M. (July 7, 2014). "Cavs Explain Why They Took Down Dan Gilbert's Letter to LeBron James." SB Nation. http://www.sbnation.com/lookit/2014/7/7/5877047/dan-gilbert-letter-lebron-james-preserved-cavaliers (accessed July 8, 2014).

Primm, E., Piquero, N. L., Piquero, A. R., and Regoli, R. M. (2011). "Investigating Customer Racial Discrimination in the Secondary Baseball Card Market." *Sociological Inquiry*, 81(1), 110–32.

Ruck, R. (2011). *Raceball: How the Major Leagues Colonized the Black and Latin Game.* Boston: Beacon Press.

Ruck, R. (March 5, 2011). "Where Have African-American Baseball Players Gone?" *Salon.* http://www.salon.com/2011/03/05/race_in_baseball/ (accessed July 3, 2014).

Vecsey, G. (2006). *Baseball: A History of America's Favorite Game*. New York: Modern Library.

Zang, D. (1995). *Fleet Walker's Divided Heart: The Life of Baseball's First Black Major Leaguer*. Lincoln: University of Nebraska Press.

Chapter 6: The New Plantation?: Racism on the Hardwood

Abdul-Jabbar, K. (2010). *On the Shoulders of Giants*. New York: Simon and Schuster.

Adande, J. A. (October 1, 2010). "LeBron James, Race and the NBA." ESPN. http://sports.espn.go.com/nba/trainingcamp10/columns/story?columnist=adande_ja&page=LeBronRace-101001 (accessed July 9, 2014).

"American Basketball Association Debuts." History.com. http://www.history.com/this-day-in-history/american-basketball-association-debuts (accessed July 8, 2014).

Bird: "A Black Man's Game". ESPN.com. http://sports.espn.go.com/nba/news/story?id=1818396 (accessed July 7, 2014).

Bolch, B. (September 10, 2013). "Linsanity Documentary Is a Spine-Tingling Homage to Jeremy Lin." *Los Angeles Times*. http://www.latimes.com/sports/sportsnow/la-sp-sn-linsanity-documentary-jeremy-lin-20130909,0,3116852.story#axzz2gJIxFUpu (accessed July 9, 2014).

Coffey, W. (February 2, 2013). "The First Kings of Brooklyn." *New York Daily News*. http://www.nydailynews.com/sports/basketball/zone-lost-era-black-basketball-history-brought-life-article-1.1253875 (accessed July 7, 2014).

Colored World's Basketball Championship, 1907–1925. Black Fives Foundation. http://www.blackfives.org/champions/ (accessed July 9, 2014).

Corley, C. (March 15, 2013). "Game of Change: Pivotal Matchup Helped End Segregated Hoops." National Public Radio. http://wap.npr.org/news/U.S./174304630 (accessed July 8, 2014).

Dyson, Michael Eric. (1993). *Reflecting Black: African-American Cultural Criticism*. Minneapolis: University of Minnesota Press.

"Edwin Bancroft Henderson." Naismith Memorial Basketball Hall of Fame. http://www.hoophall.com/hall-of-famers/tag/eb-henderson (accessed July 10, 2014).

Fry, S. (October 10, 2009). " '49 Basketball Teams Segregated." *Topeka Capital-Journal*. http://cjonline.com/news/local/2009-10-10/49_basketball_teams_segregated (accessed July 7, 2014).

George, N. (1999). *Elevating the Game*. New York: Harper Collins.

Hartmann, D. (2012). "Beyond the Sporting Boundary." *Ethnic and Racial Studies*, 35(6), 1007–22.

"Henderson, Edwin." Black Fives Foundation. http://www.blackfives.org/players/edwin-henderson/ (accessed July 9, 2014).

Herring, C., Keith, V., and Horton, H. D., eds. *Skin Deep: How Race and Complexion Matter in the "Color-Blind" Era*. Urbana : University of Illinois Press.

Hill, M. L. (November 28, 2012). "The Linsanity Sham: Why Jeremy Lin Can't Really Play." *Huffington Post.* http://www.huffingtonpost.com/marc-lamont -hill/linsanity-jeremy-lin_b_2199606.html (accessed July 9, 2014).

Horton, H. D., and Sykes, L. (2004). "Toward a Critical Demography of Neo-mulattos: Structural Change and Diversity within the Black Population." In Herring, C., Keith, V., and Kimmel, M. S., and Aronson, A., eds. *Men and Masculinities: A Social, Cultural, and Historical Encyclopedia.* Santa Barbara, CA: ABC-CLIO.

Lapchick, R. (2011). *The 2011 Racial and Gender Report Card: College Sport.* http:// www.tidesport.org/RGRC/2011/2011_College_RGRC.pdf (accessed July 24, 2014).

Lapchick, R., Hippert, A., Rivera, S., and Robinson, J. (2013). *The 2013 Racial and Gender Report Card: National Basketball Association.* http://www.tidesport .org/RGRC/2013/2013_NBA_RGRC.pdf (accessed July 7, 2014).

Lapchick, R., Milkovich, M., and O'Keefe, S. *The 2012 Women's National Basket- ball Association Racial and Gender Report Card.* http://www.tidesport.org/ RGRC/2012/2012_WNBA_RGRC.pdf (accessed June 24, 2014).

"Lebron James Biography." NBA website. http://www.nba.com/playerfile/lebron _james/bio/ (accessed July 10, 2014).

Leonard, D. J. (n.d.). "Not a Question of Courage: Anti-black Racism and the Politics of the NBA Lockout." http://newblackman.blogspot.com/2011/10/ not-question-of-courage-anti-black.html (accessed July 9, 2014).

Lindgren, J., and McGowan, M. (2006). "Testing the 'Model Minority Myth.'" *Northwestern University Law Review,* 100, 331–78.

Loyola (Ill.) Athletics. (July 16, 2012). "'Game of Change' to Be Remembered." NCAA.com. http://www.ncaa.com/news/basketball-men/article/2012-07-24/ game-change-be-remembered (accessed July 8, 2014).

Lynch, R. (July 5, 2012). "Michael Johnson Says Slave Descendants Make Better Athletes." *Los Angeles Times.* http://articles.latimes.com/2012/jul/05/nation/ la-na-nn-michael-johnson-slave-descendants-make-better-athletes-20120705 (accessed July 7, 2014).

Martin, L. L. (2013). *Black Asset Poverty and the Enduring Racial Divide.* Boulder, CO: First Forum Press.

Mazzeo, M. (2013). "Jeremy Lin Cites College Race Barrier." ESPN. http://espn.go .com/nba/story/_/id/9141475/jeremy-lin-houston-rockets-race-was-barrier -college (accessed July 10, 2014).

Murray, J. A. (March 19, 2010). "The Spiritual Pathway to March Madness." *Wall Street Journal.*

Nelson, M. R. (2009). *The National Basketball League.* Jefferson, NC: McFarland.

"Obama Makes Stop Near Historic Black Basketball Venue." (January 12, 2009). http://www.blackfives.org/obama-stop-historic-black-basketball-venue/ (accessed July 9, 2014).

Park, L. S.-H. (2008). "Continuing Significance of the Model Minority Myth: The Second Generation." *Social Justice*, 35(2), 135.

Peterson, R. W. (November 11, 1991). "When the Court Was a Cage." Sports Illustrated Vault. http://sportsillustrated.cnn.com/vault/1991/11/11/125381/when-the-court-was-a-cage-in-the-early-days-of-pro-basketball-the-players-were-segregated-from-the-fans (accessed July 7, 2014).

Pluto, T. (2007). *Loose Balls: The Short, Wild Life of the American Basketball Association*. New York: Simon and Schuster.

Sailes, G. (1991). "The Myth of Black Sports Supremacy." *Journal of Black Studies*, 21(4), 480–87.

Schoenberger, R. (June 28, 2010). "How Much Is LeBron James Worth to Northeast Ohio?" *Cleveland Plain Dealer*. http://www.cleveland.com/business/index.ssf/2010/06/how_much_is_lebron_james_worth.html (accessed July 8, 2014).

Simmons, R. (2013). "The Insanity of Linsanity, 1 Year Later." SFGate. http://www.sfgate.com/warriors/article/The-insanity-of-Linsanity-1-year-later-4254389.php (accessed July 10, 2014).

"Springfield College: The Birthplace of Basketball." http://www.spfldcol.edu/welcome/birthplace-of-basketball/index (accessed July 7, 2014).

"St. Christopher Club." Black Fives Foundation. http://www.blackfives.org/st-christopher/ (accessed July 9, 2014).

"True Reformer Building, African American Heritage Trail." Cultural Tourism DC. http://www.culturaltourismdc.org/portal/true-reformer-building-african-american-heritage-trail#.U77yB41dXlQ (accessed July 10, 2014).

"True Reformer's Hall." George Washington University website. http://www.gwu.edu/~jazz/venuest.html (accessed July 7, 2014).

Webb, B. L. (1973/1994). *The Basketball Man—James Naismith*. Lawrence, KS: Kappelman's Historic Collections.

Wilson, G. (October 19, 2011). "Bryant Gumbel Calls NBA Commish 'Plantation Overseer.'" NBC Bay Area. http://www.nbcbayarea.com/entertainment/television/Bryant-Gumbel-Calls-NBA-Commish-Plantation-Overseer-132129268.html (accessed July 9, 2014).

Chapter 7: Black-Free Zones: Black Athletes on the Course and on the Court

"African Americans and Golf, a Brief History." African American Registry. http://aaregistry.org/historic_events/view/african-americans-and-golf-brief-history (accessed July 13, 2014).

Ashe, A. (2000). *A Hard Road to Glory*. New York: Amistad.

Botsch, C. S. (2004). "Althea Gibson." USC Aiken. http://www.usca.edu/aasc/AltheaGibson.htm (accessed July 13, 2014).

Burton, L. (January 4, 2003). "Despite No Local Course, Polk Players Made Black Golf Hall of Fame." http://www.theledger.com/article/20030104/COLUMNIS TS0303/301040443 (accessed July 13, 2014).

Cashmore, E. (2008). "Tiger Woods and the New Racial Order." *Current Sociology*, 56(4), 621–34.

Coakley, J. (2008). *Sports and Society*. New York: McGraw-Hill.

Dell, D. (February 5, 2013). "Remembering a Pioneer in Fields Far beyond the Sport. *New York Times*. http://straightsets.blogs.nytimes.com/2013/02/05/ remembering-a-pioneer-far-beyond-his-sport/?_r=0 (accessed July 13, 2014).

"Despite No Local Course, Polk Players Made Black Golf Hall of Fame." http:// www.theledger.com/article/20030104/COLUMNISTS0303/301040443 (accessed July 13, 2014).

Douglas, D. D. (2002). "To Be Young, Gifted, Black and Female: A Meditation on the Cultural Politics at Play in Representations of Venus and Serena Williams." *SOSOL: Sociology of Sport Online*, 5(2), 1.

Douglas, D. D. (2005). "Venus, Serena, and the Women's Tennis Association (WTA): When and Where 'Race' Enters." *Sociology of Sport Journal*, 22(3), 256.

Gittings, P. (April 14, 2010). "A Short History of Tennis: Henry VIII to Federer." CNN. http://www.cnn.com/2010/SPORT/tennis/04/14/history.of.tennis .federer.henryIII/index.html (accessed July 13, 2014).

Glenn, R. (February 6, 2007). "Paving the Rhodes for African American Golfers." USGA. http://www.usga.org/news/2007/February/Paving-The-Rhodes-For -Other-African-American-Golfers—USGA/ (accessed July 13, 2014).

"Golf Tee Patented." African American Registry. http://www.aaregistry.org/ historic_events/view/golf-tee-patented (accessed July 12, 2014).

"John M. Shippen, Jr., Golf's First Black Professional." African American Registry. http://www.aaregistry.org/historic_events/view/john-m-shippen-jr-golfs-first -black-professional (accessed July 12, 2014).

Kennedy, J. (2005). *A Course of Their Own: A History of African American Golfers*. Lincoln, NE: Bison Books.

McDaniel, P. (2000). *Uneven Lies: The Heroic Story of African-Americans in Golf*. Greenwich, CT: American Golfer.

Nishime, L. (2012). "The Case for Cablinasian: Multiracial Naming from Plessy to Tiger Woods." *Communication Theory*, 22(1), 92–111.

"PGA of America History." http://www.pga.com/pga-america/pga-information/ pga-america-history (accessed July 12, 2014).

"Playing Tennis on the ATA Tour." (September 1997). *Black Enterprise*, 28(2), 144.

Robson, D. (August 27, 2012). "Serena Williams Serves Up the Best Weapon in Tennis." *USA Today*. http://usatoday30.usatoday.com/sports/tennis/story/

2012-08-27/us-open-serena-williams-serve-is-best-shot-in-tennis/57336298/1 (accessed July 13, 2014).

Schultz, J. (2005). "Reading the Catsuit: Serena Williams and the Production of Blackness at the 2002 U.S. Open." *Journal of Sport and Social Issues*, 29(3), 338–57.

Shapiro, R. (1970). "Interview with Arthur Ashe." *Africa Today*, 17(6), 6–7.

Sherwell, P. (June 16, 2013). "Venus and Serena Williams: Hard-Wired for Glory the Moment They Were Born." *Telegraph*. http://www.telegraph.co.uk/culture/10122371/Venus-and-Serena-Williams-hard-wired-for-glory-the-moment-they-were-born.html (accessed July 13, 2014).

Smith, J. C. (2009). "American Tennis Association (est. 1916)." In *Freedom Facts and Firsts: 400 Years of the African American Civil Rights Experience*. Canton, MI: Visible Ink Press, 342–43.

Sullivan, J. J. (August 23, 2012). "Venus and Serena against the World." *New York Times*. http://www.nytimes.com/2012/08/26/magazine/venus-and-serena-against-the-world.html?pagewanted=all (accessed July 13, 2014).

Tramel, J. (July 29, 2007). "The Little Known Story of Oklahoma Native and Golfing Pioneer Bill Spiller." http://www.baystate-banner.com/issues/2007/08/16/news/natl08160720.htm (accessed July 13, 2014).

Wang, J. (2013). "Tiger Woods." *People*. http://www.people.com/people/tiger_woods/ (accessed July 13, 2014).

Wiggins, D., and Miller, P. B. (2005). *The Unlevel Playing Field*. Champaign: University of Illinois Press.

Yocom, Guy. (2006). "Dr. Charlie Sifford." *Golf Digest*, 57(12), 144. http://connection.ebscohost.com/c/interviews/22834341/dr-charlie-sifford (accessed September 29, 2013).

Chapter 8: Sports and the Myth of a Color-Blind Society

Armstrong, K. (January 25, 2014). "Richard Sherman." *New York Daily News*. http://www.nydailynews.com/sports/football/straight-compton-started-sherman-article-1.1591123, (accessed July 18, 2014).

Associated Press. (May 23, 2013). "Zoeller: Sergio Mess Will Blow Over." ESPN. http://espn.go.com/golf/story/_/id/9306204/fuzzy-zoeller-talks-sergio-garcia-tiger-woods-fried-chicken-feud (accessed July 18, 2014).

Augustine, B. (January 21, 2014). "Richard Sherman Responds to Racist Remarks about Him on Twitter Following Interview with Erin Andrews." *New York Daily News*. http://www.nydailynews.com/sports/football/sherman-responds-racist-twitter-toughguys-article-1.1585571 (accessed July 18, 2014).

Bianchi, M. (August 8, 2013). "Racists Still Taunting Jackie Robinson after All These Years." *Orlando Sentinel*. http://articles.orlandosentinel.com/2013-08

-08/sports/os-mike-bianchi-racism-riley-cooper-0809-20130808_1_stan-van
-gundy-lapchick-race-relations (accessed July 18, 2014).

Bigler, M., and Jefferies, J. (2008). " 'An Amazing Specimen': NFL Draft Experts'
Evaluations of Black Quarterbacks." *Journal of African American Studies*, 12
(2), 120–41.

Bonilla-Silva, E. (2001). *White Supremacy and Racism in the Post–Civil Rights Era.*
Boulder, CO: Lynne Rienner.

Branch, J. (February 9, 2014). "N.F.L. Prospect Michael Sam Proudly Says What
Teammates Knew: He's Gay." *New York Times.* http://www.nytimes.com/
2014/02/10/sports/michael-sam-college-football-star-says-he-is-gay-ahead
-of-nfl-draft.html (accessed July 18, 2014).

"Breaking the Color Line: 1940–1946." The Library of Congress. Memory.loc.gov/
ammem/collections/robinson/jr1940.html (accessed July 27, 2014).

Bretz, B. (2010). "The Poor People's Campaign: An Evolution of the Civil Rights
Movement." *Sociological Viewpoints*, 18–25.

Brinson, W. (January 19, 2014). "Richard Sherman Calls Michael Crabtree a Sorry
Receiver in Wild Rant." CBSSports.com. http://www.cbssports.com/nfl/eye
-on-football/24414525/richard-sherman-calls-michael-crabtree-sorry-receiver
-in-postgame-rant (accessed July 18, 2014).

Brown, T. (2005). "Allen Iverson as America's Most Wanted: Black Masculinity as
a Cultural Site of Struggle." *Journal of Intercultural Communication Research*,
34(1), 65–87.

Buffington, D. (2005). "Contesting Race on Sundays: Making Meaning Out of the
Rise in the Number of Black Quarterbacks." *Sociology of Sport Journal*, 22(1), 12.

Cacciola, S., and Witz, B. (April 26, 2014). "N.B.A. Investigating Racial Remarks
Tied to Clippers Owner." *New York Times.* http://www.nytimes.com/2014/
04/27/sports/basketball/nba-clippers-owner-donald-sterling.html?_r=0
(accessed July 18, 2014).

Carson, D. (2009). "Reflections on Message from the Grassroots: Participatory
Democracy, Community Empowerment and the Reconstruction of Urban
America." *Berkeley Journal of African American Law and Policy*, 11(1),19.

Carter, C., and Ellis, R. (May 11, 2014). "Obama Congratulates Michael Sam, First
Openly Gay Player Drafted by NFL." CNN. http://www.cnn.com/2014/05/10/
us/football-michael-sam/ (accessed July 18, 2014).

Cashmore, E. (2008). "Tiger Woods and the New Racial Order." *Current Sociology*,
56(4), 621–34.

Collins, P. H. (2006). *From Black Power to Hip Hop: Racism, Nationalism, and
Feminism.* Philadelphia: Temple University Press, 3.

Connolly, M. (April 25, 2014). "Northwestern's Team Just Voted on Unionization.
Here's What Happened Next." *Mother Jones.* http://www.motherjones.com/
mojo/2014/04/northwestern-football-unionization-vote (accessed July 18,
2014).

Conway, T. (February 24, 2014). "Michael Sam: Combine Results and Instant Reaction." *Bleacher Report*. http://bleacherreport.com/articles/1971528 -michael-sam-combine-results-and-instant-reaction (accessed July 18, 2014).

Crowley, M. (1999). "Muhammad Ali Was a Rebel. Michael Jordan Is a Brand Name." *Nieman Reports*. http://www.nieman.harvard.edu/reports/article/ 102181/Muhammad-Ali-Was-a-Rebel-Michael-Jordan-Is-a-Brand-Name.aspx (accessed July 18, 2014).

Dreier, P. (2013). "The Real Story of Baseball's Integration That You Won't See in 42." *The Atlantic*. http://www.theatlantic.com/entertainment/archive/2013/ 04/the-real-story-of-baseballs-integration-that-you-wont-see-in-i-42-i/ 274886/ (accessed July 27, 2014).

Dunbar, P. (1896). "We Wear the Mask." http://www.poetryfoundation.org/poem/ 173467. (accessed July 18, 2014).

Ellman, S. (March 4, 2014). "Is the NFL Ready for Michael Sam?" *Huffington Post*. http://www.huffingtonpost.com/scott-ellman/is-the-nfl-ready-for-mich_b_489 5585.html (accessed July 18, 2014).

Feagin, J. (2009). *White Racial Frame: Centuries of Racial Framing and Counter-Framing*. New York: Taylor and Francis.

Feinsand, M. (August 23, 2012). "Yankees Captain Derek Jeter Suggests Skip Bayless Should Check Himself for HGH Usage." *New York Daily News*. http://www.nydailynews.com/sports/baseball/yankees/yankees-captain-derek -jeter-suggests-skip-bayless-check-hgh-usage-article-1.1142392 (accessed July 18, 2014).

Florio, M. (March 7, 2013). "Richard Sherman Takes Swings at Skip Bayless." NBC Sports. http://profootballtalk.nbcsports.com/2013/03/07/richard-sherman -takes-his-swings-at-skip-bayless/ (accessed July 18, 2014).

Foster, F. (2012). "The Forgotten League: A History of Negro League Baseball." *Book Caps Study Guides*.

Franklin, J. H. (2013). *Reconstruction after the Civil War*. Chicago: University of Chicago Press.

Gleeson, S. (September 11, 2012). "Durant Says Skip Bayless Brainwashing with Comments." *USA Today*. http://content.usatoday.com/communities/gameon/ post/2012/09/Durant-says-Skip-Bayless-brainwashing-with-comments-70000140/ kevin-durant-skip-bayless-twitter-feud/70000140/1#.U8ldjo1dXlQ (accessed July 18, 2014).

Goldman, L., and Giang, V. (June 28, 2011). "The 25 Most Famous Stanford Students of All-Time." *Business Insider*. http://www.businessinsider.com/ famous-stanford-students-2011-6?op=1 (accessed July 18, 2014).

Granderson, L. Z. (January 15, 2010). "Black Athletes Must Repair Image." ESPN. http://sports.espn.go.com/espn/commentary/news/story?id=4829046 (acc-essed July 18, 2014).

Hall, B. (July 15, 2014). "Kluwe to Sue Vikings, Says Investigation on Homophobic Remarks Not Released." Fox Sports. http://www.foxsports.com/north/story/ kluwe-vikings-reneged-on-releasing-investigation-071514 (accessed July 18, 2014).

Harris, C. (1993). "Whiteness as Property." *Harvard Law Review*, 106(8), 1707.

Henry, P. (1997). "Jackie Robinson: Athlete and American Par Excellence." *Virginia Quarterly Review*, 73(2), 189–204.

Henslin, J. (2010). *Essentials of Sociology*. Upper Saddle River, NJ: Pearson.

Herman, R. (2010). "An Oral History of the Integration of College Sports." *Vital Speeches of the Day*, 76(1), 6–10.

Hine, D., Hine, W. C., and Harrold, S. (2010). *The African American Odyssey*. Upper Saddle River, NJ: Pearson.

"Howell Students to Take Corrective Action Following Racist Tweets by Students." ABC News. (March 17, 2014). http://www.abc12.com/story/24998450/ howells-schools-to-take-corrective-action-following-racist-tweets-by-students (accessed July 18, 2014).

Hubbard, D. (2007). *The Souls of Black Folk*. Columbia: University of Missouri Press.

"Incognito, Others Tormented Martin." ESPN. (February 15, 2014). http://espn.go .com/nfl/story/_/id/10455447/miami-dolphins-bullying-report-released-richie -incognito-others-responsible-harassment (accessed July 18, 2014).

James, S., dir. (1994). *Hoop Dreams*. Fine Line Features.

King, P. (n.d.). "The NFL's Big Test." *Sports Illustrated*. http://mmqb.si.com/2014/ 02/09/michael-sam-monday-morning-quarterback/ (accessed July 18, 2014).

Lacy, S., and Newson, M. (1998). *Fighting for Fairness: The Life Story of Hall of Fame Sportswriter Sam Lacy*. Centreville, MD: Tidewater.

Lopez, I. H. (2014). *Dog Whistle Politics*. New York: Oxford University Press.

Loy, J., and McElvogue, J. (1971). "Racial Segregation in American Sport." *International Review of Sport Sociology*, 5, 5–24.

Manfred, T. (February 28, 2014). "LeBron Wears Black Mask, Terrifies NBA." *Business Insider*. http://www.businessinsider.com/lebron-mask-2014-2 (accessed July 18, 2014).

Manweller, M. (2005). *The People vs. the Courts*. Salt Lake City, UT: Academia Press.

Martin, L. L. (December 16, 2011). "The New War on Poverty." *Amsterdam News*. http://amsterdamnews.com/news/2011/dec/16/the-new-war-on-poverty/ (accessed July 18, 2014).

Martin, L. L. (2014). *Out of Bounds: Racism and the Black Athlete*. Santa Barbara, CA: Praeger.

Miller, P., and K. Wiggins, D. K. (2004). *Sport and the Color Line: Black Athletes and Race Relations in Twentieth-Century America*. New York: Routledge.

Morris, A. (1984). *The Origins of the Civil Rights Movement*. New York: Free Press.

National Football League. (2013). "The NFL's Ongoing Commitment to Excellence in Workplace Conduct: Sexual Orientation." http://nfllabor.files .wordpress.com/2014/02/nfl-ewc-sexual-orientation.pdf (accessed July 27, 2014).

NewsOne Staff. (January 27, 2014). "Former Cop Indicted in Fatal Shooting of Unarmed Jonathan Ferrell." NewsOne. http://newsone.com/2853047/former -cop-randall-kerrick-indicted-in-fatal-shooting-of-unarmed-jonathan-ferrell/ (accessed July 18, 2014).

Olin, E., and Rogers, J. (2010). *American Society: How It Really Works*. New York: Norton.

Paul, Weiss, Rifkind, Wharton and Garrison LLP. (February 14, 2014). "Report to the National Football League Concerning Issues of Workplace Conduct at the Miami Dolphins." http://63bba9dfdf9675bf3f10-68be460ce43dd2a60dd6 4ca5eca4ae1d.r37.cf1.rackcdn.com/PaulWeissReport.pdf (accessed July 18, 2014).

Pierce, J. L. (2013). "White Racism, Social Class, and the Backlash against Affirmative Action." *Sociology Compass*, 7(11), 914.

Portillo, E., and Wootson, C. (September 18, 2013). "CMPD Chief Contradicts Lawyer's Account of Ferrell Shooting." WCNC. http://www.wcnc.com/news/ local/CMPD-chief-contradicts-lawyers-account-of-Ferrell-shooting-224322871 .html (accessed July 18, 2014).

Posnanski, J. (February 10, 2014). "Robinson, Sam Blazing Trails Seven Decades Apart." NBC Sports. http://www.nbcsports.com/joe-posnanski/robinson -sam-blazing-trails-seven-decades-apart (accessed July 18, 2014).

Powell, S. (2008). *Souled Out*. New York: Human Kinetics.

Rang, R. (February 10, 2014). "Examining Why Michael Sam's NFL Draft Stock Is Falling." CBS Sports. http://www.cbssports.com/nfl/draft/nfl-draft-scout/ 24438468/examining-why-michael-sams-nfl-draft-stock-is-falling (accessed July 18, 2014).

Rhoden, W. (2006). *Forty Million Dollar Slaves*. New York: Crown.

"Richard Sherman to Skip Bayless: I Am Better at Life Than You." (March 7, 2013). *Huffington Post*. http://www.huffingtonpost.com/2013/03/07/richard -sherman-skip-bayless-first-take-life-video_n_2832163.html (accessed July 18, 2014).

Scott, N. (January 22, 2014). "Richard Sherman Equates Being Called a Thug to a Racial Slur." *USA Today*. http://ftw.usatoday.com/2014/01/richard-sherman -compares-thug-racial-slur (accessed July 18, 2014).

Siddiqui, S. (March 20, 2014). "Paul Ryan Confronted at Town Hall Inner-City Poverty, Obama Care Video." *Huffington Post*. http://www.huffingtonpost .com/2014/03/20/paul-ryan-confronted_n_5000952.html (accessed July 18, 2014).

Stefancic, J., Delgado, R., and Bell, D. A. (2005). *The Derrick Bell Reader.* New York: New York University Press.

Tygiel, J. (1997). *Baseball's Great Experiment: Jackie Robinson and His Legacy.* New York: Oxford University Press.

Wallace, M. (March 1, 2014). "LeBron James Ditches Black Mask." ESPN. http://espn.go.com/nba/truehoop/miamiheat/story/_/id/10536938/lebron-james-miami-heat-ditch-black-mask-vs-orlando-magic (accessed July 18, 2014).

Washington, J. R. (1990). *Critical Civil Conflict of Interest of Class and Caste Calvinists and Competing Religious and Secular Puritans Patriot Lemuel Haynes Portrayed as the Initial Colored Congregational Clergyman.* Lewiston, NY: Edwin Mellen Press.

Wiggins, D. (2006). *Out of the Shadows: A Biographical History of African American Athletes.* Akron, OH: University of Akron Press.

Wiggins, D., and Miller, P. (2005). *Unlevel Playing Field.* Champaign: University of Illinois Press.

Wilson, J. (1987). *The Truly Disadvantaged.* Chicago: University of Chicago Press.

Wright, B. M. (1987). *Black Robes, White Justice.* Secaucus, NJ: Lyle Stuart.

Young, M. (March 15, 2014). "Shocking Racist Tweets Follow High School Basketball Win by All-White Team." MLive. http://www.mlive.com/news/flint/index.ssf/2014/03/members_of_howell_high_school.html. (accessed July 18, 2014).

Chapter 9: Conclusion

Black Girls Run! Home page. http://www.blackgirlsrun.com/ (accessed July 18, 2014).

Bonilla-Silva, E. (2014). *Racism without Racists.* Lanham, MD: Rowman and Littlefield.

Brunsma, D. L., Brown, E. S., and Placier, P. (2013). "Teaching Race at Historically White Colleges and Universities: Identifying and Dismantling the Walls of Whiteness." *Critical Sociology*, 39(5), 717–38.

Canales, M. (2000). "Othering: Toward an Understanding of Difference." *Advances in Nursing Science*, 22, 16–31.

Horton, H. D., Allen, B. L., Herring, C., and Thomas, M. E. (2000). "Lost in the Storm: The Sociology of the Black Working Class, 1850 to 1990." *American Sociological Review*, 1, 128.

Kozol, J. (1992). *Savage Inequalities.* New York: Harper.

Martin, L. L. (2013). *Black Asset Poverty and the Enduring Racial Divide.* Boulder, CO: First Forum Press.

Martin, L. L., and Horton, H. D. (forthcoming). *Lost in the Storm: America's Black Working Class in the Age of Obama.* Boulder, CO: Lynne Rienner.

McIntosh, P. (1990). "White Privilege: Unpacking the Invisible Knapsack." *Independent School*, 49(2), 31.

National Black Marathoners Association. Home page. http://www.black marathoners.org/ (accessed July 18, 2014).

Omi, M., and Winant, H. (1994). *Racial Formation in the United States*. New York: Routledge.

Park, L. (2008). "Continuing Significance of the Model Minority Myth: The Second Generation." *Social Justice*, 35(2), 134–44.

Robinson, E. (2010). *Disintegration: The Splintering of Black America*. New York: Anchor, 4.

Wheary, J., Shapiro, T., Draut, T., and Meschede, T. (2008). "Economic (In) Security: The Experience of the African American and Latino Middle Classes." Brandeis University. http://iasp.brandeis.edu/pdfs/2008/Economic _Insecurity_AA_Latinos.pdf (accessed July 18, 2014).

Index

About the Author

Lori Latrice Martin, PhD, is associate professor of sociology and African and African American studies at Louisiana State University. Her previously published works include Praeger's *Out of Bounds: Racism and the Black Athlete*. Martin holds a doctorate in sociology from University at Albany, State University of New York.